Barbara Dunn and Archie Dunlop are both graduates of the London School of Economics. They have extensive experience in the teaching, practice and lecturing of astrology. They are directors of the London School of Traditional Astrology.

They each hold a diploma from the Faculty of Astrological Studies and the Olivia Barclay School of Horary Astrology. Their experience in this field has afforded them membership of the Association of Professional Astrologers. They are also delegates on the Advisory Panel for Astrological Education.

Barbara Dunn is a hugely successful media astrologer. She was the astrologer for *Cosmopolitan* and *Best* magazine for a number of years. She has made frequent appearances on radio and television shows in the United Kingdom.

LIFE, LOVE AND DESTINY

A Step by Step Guide to Reading the Stars

by Barbara Dunn and Archie Dunlop

A SIGNET BOOK

SIGNET BOOKS

Published by the Penguin Group
Penguin Books Ltd, 27 Wrights Lane, London W8 5TZ, England
Penguin Books USA Inc., 375 Hudson Street, New York, New York 10014, USA
Penguin Books Australia Ltd, Ringwood, Victoria, Australia
Penguin Books Canada Ltd, 10 Alcorn Avenue, Toronto, Ontario, Canada M4V 3B2
Penguin Books (NZ) Ltd, 182–190 Wairau Road, Auckland 10, New Zealand

Penguin Books Ltd, Registered Offices: Harmondsworth, Middlesex, England

First published 1994
10 9 8 7 6 5 4 3 2 1

Typeset by Datix International Ltd, Bungay, Suffolk

Filmset in 10/12½pt Monophoto Plantin

Printed in England by Clays Ltd, St Ives plc

Dedicated to our friend and teacher Olivia Barclay

CONTENTS

This chapter introduces the planets and the signs of the
zodiac. Readers are shown how to find out their Sun sign.
A brief description of the planets follows.

This chapter gives detailed descriptions of each Sun sign,
together with a list of safe predictions that can be given to
each sign. While this chapter is informative, it also seeks
to provide a humorous slant to the study of astrology.

Romance and love are always close to everyone's heart,
and this chapter details the love lives of the various signs.
Readers who want to find out more about existing or
potential partners will find a list of their pros and cons.

Section Three
....

THE ELEMENTS

Section Four
....

YOUR ASCENDANT SIGN

to find out what your Ascendant is, using our special Ascendant tables. A working example using Madonna takes readers through the various stages step by step.

between planets. They show how planets affect each other. This chapter describes the aspects and how important they are. Three big diagrams explain the conjunction, opposition and trine.

Now that the planets, houses and aspects have been covered, readers are shown how to put it all together into an easy-to-understand interpretation of people's personality and destiny, using examples of Madonna and Princess Diana.

Section Seven

WHAT IT ALL MEANS: FIRST STEPS TO BECOMING AN ASTROLOGER

These chapters focus on special areas of life which people find of particular importance such as children, love, home life, money, career etc.

Section Eight

FINAL STEPS TO BECOMING AN ASTROLOGER

Section Nine

ACKNOWLEDGEMENTS

We would like to acknowledge the following:
Robert Dunlop for the illustrations.
Victor Downer for creative input.
Alasdair Campbell and Martin Davis for technical assistance.
Simon Trewin for his support and encouragement.
Pat Richardson and *Best* magazine for their co-operation with
the GMT conversion diagram on page 208.
Mark Plummer for his portraits of the authors.
And finally Tremayne Bidgood for being so patient while his
mother was deluged with work.

SIGN ABBREVIATION TABLE

Ari	Aries	**Lib**	Libra
Tau	Taurus	**Sco**	Scorpio
Gem	Gemini	**Sag**	Sagittarius
Can	Cancer	**Cap**	Capricorn
Leo	Leo	**Aqu**	Aquarius
Vir	Virgo	**Pis**	Pisces

INTRODUCTION

Buying this book was an absolutely brilliant decision which you will never regret. After all, you have discovered no less than the secret key to your life, your love and your destiny.

As you read the pages in front of you, you will discover amazing facts about yourself which will give you the opportunity to be happier, richer and more successful. Not only that, but you will gain powerful insights into the desires and motivations of your family, your loved ones, your friends and your work-mates. You can use these insights both to solve their problems and to beat them in arguments.

You may be wondering how a single book can offer so much. Well, this book is no ordinary astrology book. It is a complete guide to the subject, telling you everything you need to know. You will find out about the planets and the signs, and you will learn how to draw up your own horoscope. As you do this, you'll build up a picture of your personality, with special emphasis on your love life, your family and your career. By the end of the book, you will be able to make predictions about your future using methods that have been tried and tested by countless generations of astrologers.

This book has been written by two of Britain's most experienced astrologers. We have been practising astrology full-time for many years and have an understanding of our subject which is very difficult to match. Every day we deal with clients who come to us, looking for help and advice. We tell them about their lives and their destinies. Time and time again, our predictions prove to be devastatingly accurate. We both have a Diploma from the Faculty of Astrological Studies and are also graduates of the élite Qualifying Horary Diploma course. The latter was pioneered by Olivia Barclay, and is perhaps the most difficult astrological qualification in the world.

Both of us teach astrology, and it is through our experience of teaching that we are able to provide you with a super-simple method of learning astrology. As you read through this book, you will find that our step by step format is user-friendly and incredibly easy to follow. We do all the hard work for you, which means that you don't have to do any calculations – not even adding or subtracting.

While astrology is an important part of our lives, we don't believe that it should be taken too seriously. This is reflected in our light-hearted approach. We often use cartoons to illustrate our text and we are not afraid of making wild exaggerations in order to drive a point home. To us, astrology is not just a profession, but also a form of entertainment which can raise a laugh and a smile. So, as we learn astrology together, let's make sure that we have a lot of fun.

A Note on Accuracy

The tables in this book are user-friendly. They require no mathematical skills whatsoever. In the majority of cases, these tables will provide accurate sign positions for the Sun, the Moon, the planets and the Ascendant. However, we cannot guarantee their total accuracy.

YOUR SUN SIGN

1. HOW TO DISCOVER YOUR SUN SIGN

Astrology has never been so popular. Most newspapers and magazines have a Sun sign column, and every good bookshop has shelves stacked with books on astrology. You can find books describing your year ahead, your perfect astrological diet and even the character of your Cancerian goldfish! An increasing amount of people are now taking notice not only of their own Sun signs, but those of their loved ones. If you read a lonely hearts column, you will often read entries like 'Attractive, single Taurus, 34, looking for a Virgo or a Capricorn with a good sense of humour and loads of money.'

This kind of astrology, which is gripping the public's imagination, is of course based on Sun signs. This is because Sun signs are dead easy to work out. If you know what day you were born, you immediately know what your Sun sign is. You don't have to ask an astrologer or consult complicated tables. You just look at a very simple list, like the one below:

Aries	21 March – 19 April
Taurus	20 April – 20 May
Gemini	21 May – 20 June
Cancer	21 June – 22 July
Leo	23 July – 22 August

Attractive single Taurus, 34, looking for Virgo or Capricorn with a good sense of humour and loads of money.

Virgo	23 August – 22 September
Libra	23 September – 22 October
Scorpio	23 October – 21 November
Sagittarius	22 November – 21 December
Capricorn	22 December – 19 January
Aquarius	20 January – 18 February
Pisces	19 February – 20 March

Well done! You have just learned how to find someone's Sun sign. Keep this list to hand and you'll be able to tell anyone's Sun sign.

SUN SIGNS AND STAR SIGNS

Anyone that reads astrological columns in the press will notice that Sun signs are sometimes called 'star signs'. Sun signs are exactly the same as star signs. When magazines talk about 'Your Stars for the Year Ahead', this does not mean that the magazine's astrologer will be looking at the positions of all the stars in the sky. Instead, he or she will be describing the fortunes of the twelve Sun signs. The reason the media uses the term 'star sign' is probably because it sounds more glamorous than 'Sun sign'. However, there is nothing wrong with talking about star signs because, technically speaking, the Sun is a star, around which the Earth and the other planets travel.

DOES THE SUN MOVE?

Astrologers say that the Sun moves through the signs of the zodiac. We also say that the Sun stays still, while all the other planets, including the Earth, move round it. Our critics say that we don't know what we're talking about. So, before we proceed any further, it might be a good idea for us to put the record straight.

As astrologers, we are concerned about what is happening on Earth. We tell people about their characters and we predict events in their everyday lives. So, when we look up into the heavens, we are looking at things from the point of view of Earth and its inhabitants. Although scientists tell us that the Earth travels around the Sun, it appears to us, on Earth, that it is the other way round.

To illustrate this, we would like you to take an orange, an apple or a tennis ball, and place it on the floor, in the very middle of the room. Pretend that this object is the Sun. Now imagine that you are the Earth, and walk around the pretend Sun, always keeping yourself at least four feet away from it. What do you notice? Although the pretend Sun is still, it appears to move around you, as you walk around it. This is what astrologers mean, when they say that the Sun moves round the Earth.

THE PLANETS AND THE SIGNS OF THE ZODIAC

There are twelve signs of the zodiac: Aries, Taurus, Gemini, Cancer, Leo, Virgo, Libra, Scorpio, Sagittarius, Capricorn, Aquarius and Pisces. These signs of the zodiac can be joined together in a huge ring, which surrounds the Earth, the Sun and the planets. From the Earth's point of view, the Sun and the planets appear to pass through these signs of the zodiac.

You have already seen how the Sun moves through them, taking one year to travel through them all. The other planets move around at different speeds. For example, the Moon takes a month to go through all the signs, while Pluto takes 248 years.

All the planets are positioned in certain signs of the zodiac – not just the Sun. Madonna, the pop star, for example, has the Sun in Leo, the Moon in Virgo, Mercury in Virgo, Venus in Leo, Mars in Taurus, Jupiter in Libra, Saturn in Sagittarius, Uranus in Leo, Neptune in Scorpio and Pluto in Virgo.

The position of the planets in the sky at the time of a person's birth are fixed. The horoscope that is drawn up using these planets remains the same throughout their whole life.

To give an example: it is as if a roulette wheel is spinning around – all the planets are moving through the sky, and at the moment of birth the wheel stops. Where the planets stop (i.e. what sign of the zodiac they land in) is noted and the astrologer uses these positions to set up the horoscope. The roulette wheel then starts spinning once more.

If you look quickly at the position of Madonna's planets when she was born, you'll see that they fell in a variety of different positions. Later on in the book we'll take a detailed look at her horoscope, and we will tell you what these positions mean.

Although this chapter is on the Sun signs, we feel that at this stage you should have a taste of the different planets. So read through the following descriptions:

The Sun

As you know now, the Sun is technically not a planet, but a star. However, for convenience's sake, astrologers group it as a planet. The Sun describes our core personality, and has a decisive influence on all aspects of our lives.

The Moon

Like the Sun, the Moon is technically not a planet, but a satellite of Earth. This is because it goes around the Earth. It rules feelings, as well as the domestic environment. It is often associated with the family and with the mother.

Mercury

Mercury is the planet of communication. Its position in the horoscope can tell us about the way we speak. It also has a connection with our intellectual capacities.

Venus

Venus is the planet of love. It can tell us about our love lives, as well as our sense of beauty.

Mars

In ancient times, Mars was the planet of war. It can be connected with aggression, as well as passion. Sometimes it can describe our sexuality.

Jupiter

This is the planet of expansion. It usually describes areas of life where people are fortunate.

Saturn

Saturn is very different to Jupiter. It rules discipline and restraint.

Uranus, Neptune and Pluto

These planets were only discovered during the last two centuries. They cannot be seen with the naked eye and are not as important as the other planets. They can highlight events which are beyond a person's control.

THE IMPORTANCE OF THE SUN

Although there are other planets to consider, there can be no doubt that the Sun is of critical importance. This is why astrologers pay so much attention to it. Once you know a person's Sun sign, you can tell an enormous amount about his or her character, future and relationships. Sun signs are of so much value that we have devoted the next three chapters to them. Once you have read these chapters, you will be able to gain valuable insights into the lives of yourself and others.

In Chapter Two we give lengthy descriptions of all the Sun signs. These descriptions come from our long experience of astrology, and we hope that you find them both meaningful and useful. At the end of each sign description we give a couple of 'safe predictions' which you can make. We don't expect you to take these predictions too seriously, but they may help you to get a feel for the sort of events which the various signs have to face in their everyday lives. Later, we will be telling you how to make real predictions.

In Chapters Three and Four you will find out about the Sun signs and love. These are very important chapters. As an astrologer, one of the commonest questions you will have to face is how the various signs get on with each other. If you are asked, 'I'm a Leo, my boyfriend's a Virgo – how do we match up?' you will have to come up with a quick reply. So, to help you out, we firstly describe the love potential of the twelve signs and, secondly, list the compatibilities between all possible sign combinations.

One final thing you should appreciate is that there is no substitute for experience. Take careful note of how the various Sun signs behave and what you think makes each one tick. When looking at the compatibilities between the signs, look at the people around you and see how they treat each other. In this way, you will develop an instinctive understanding of the dynamics of astrology, which will enrich the lives of both yourself and those around you.

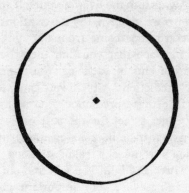

The Sun is the centre of the solar system and it is also the centre of the personality. So it is the core self, which we are always trying to express. The Sun also represents our most important goals and ambitions. By looking at the Sun sign you can quite literally tell who someone is.

Remember that the Sun moves into different signs of the zodiac at regular intervals. For instance, if you are an Aries, you'll know that this is true because you were born between 21 March and 19 April. Every year, the Sun has a regular cycle. There are minor variations to this cycle, but on the whole this is a regular and unchanging pattern. (This is why newspapers and magazines use these positions for their star sign columns.)

Career: The Sun's position in the horoscope gives important indicators about career. After all, people often express their ambitions through their work. If someone is experiencing career problems, it may mean that their responsibilities at work don't allow them to live out the full potential of their Sun sign.

Creativity: If you want to know about someone's creativity, always look at the Sun. It will tell you what someone enjoys doing and the sign placement can pin-point specific talents. The Sun is sometimes connected with children, and the Sun can tell us what people expect from their children.

Relationships: The Sun is very important in relationships, particularly in the horoscopes of women. This is because the Sun is a male energy and its sign placement may indicate the kind of man that a woman is looking for. So a woman with the Sun in Scorpio might be attracted to a man who is intense and brooding.

Now look at Chapter Two for the meaning of the Sun in each sign of the zodiac.

2. WHAT YOUR SUN SIGN MEANS: THE POSITION OF THE SUN IN EVERY SIGN

SUN IN ARIES

Aries is the first sign of the zodiac. As a result, Aries people are often described as the children of the zodiac. They want things their own way and they want results *now*. Aries doesn't like spending too long weighing up the pros and cons of a particular action; instead, Aries just does it. Given the Arien impulsiveness, you might expect Aries people to make frequent mistakes. However, luck is on their side, and if they trust their intuition they usually get away with the most outrageous risks. They only run into trouble when they think too much, because this makes them lose their spontaneity. So, if you are being driven by an Aries at 90 mph down the wrong lane of a motorway, don't say a word. Somehow they'll get you home in one piece.

On the whole, Aries people are easy to understand. They have simple likes and dislikes and, once you know where you are with them, you can't go far wrong . . . provided it's not you that Aries dislikes. Aries people certainly don't mince words, and they tell everyone exactly how they feel. This could be construed as tactlessness, although it is probably fairer to describe it as honesty. When Aries people are in a bad mood they are particularly honest about the way they feel. This is not always a good thing. The whole world has to know about their feelings, which can be a real pain. A typical situation might be that your Aries friend has a cold. Most people would ignore a cold and get on with their lives, but Aries regards it as a national disaster, which everyone around them must know about. As a result of this over-dramatization, the cold will end up dragging on for much longer than expected.

When it comes to money and personal possessions, Aries has an interesting attitude. They regard money as being there to be enjoyed. If Aries people have plenty of money at hand, they are quick to share it with friends. They won't worry too much about the fine details of who owes what, and this gives them a reputation for spontaneous generosity. However, if other people have money and Aries doesn't, they expect the same generosity in return. Aries will take without asking and, at first sight, may seem to be taking liberties. But this isn't true. If you give or lend something to Aries, you will always get it back in the end.

Aries do like to be in control, which may be why so many of them get involved in politics. They feel that they have all the answers to the world's problems and if they can cut through the red tape anything can be achieved. While Aries people certainly make good leaders, they have to be careful not to run out of steam. Once they have the responsibility of leadership, they find that the red tape doesn't go away. In fact, it can end up strangling them. As a result, Aries people in positions of power often fail to live up to their promises. At the very worst, Aries can go one step further and start causing panic. As Aries is a Fire sign, they like fire – and often like setting things on fire. So, if you are at a party and your neighbour starts smouldering, you'll know who to blame.

Since Aries is so competitive, it is usually important that they are engaged in some kind of sport. A less energetic Aries is content to watch sport on TV. However, this really isn't good enough. Aries people need to express their feelings in a direct way and if they don't take physical exercise they quickly become irritable. As a result, they either inflict their feelings on others, or start over-eating. If you know some lazy Ariens, try to get them involved in an activity like tennis, squash or the martial arts.

When it comes to their love life, Aries can be very impatient. They want everything to happen at once, and have little patience with slow romances. If Aries wants someone, they have all the subtlety of a bulldozer. So having a relationship with Aries can be an exciting and exhausting business.

Despite their apparent unsubtlety, underneath it all, they are warm and sensitive people who are able to express their feelings in an open and uncomplicated way. By the same token, Aries expect total honesty from a loved one and will not tolerate lies. However, once they are confident that they can trust their partners, Aries can turn out to be utterly loyal and faithful.

Safe Predictions for Aries Include:
* 'Today you're in a hurry.'
* 'Over the next week you're going to be in a really bad mood. Anyone that gets in your way had better watch out.'
* 'Next year you are going to begin your political career. Be realistic in your ambitions and don't expect to change the world overnight.'
* 'Don't play with matches on Wednesday.'

SUN IN TAURUS

Taurus is an Earth sign. As such, Taurus can be a very physical person. Taurus people are very interested in things like money and property, and usually have an acute sense of beauty. Taureans like to surround themselves with beautiful objects, and you will usually find that their clothes are of a very high quality. At the same time, Taurus is a very indulgent sign. All Taureans have vices, with which they occasionally go completely over the top. Possible vices include food, drink, sex, drugs or collecting expensive *objets d'art*. If you find a Taurus with no apparent vices, watch it, because you've probably discovered a psychopath, whose real vice is an obsession with power. Adolf Hitler was an example of this kind of Taurus – a vegetarian, non-smoking tee-totaller.

Given their supposed liking for beauty, it is surprising how crude Taurus can be. They often have very little subtlety, and their sense of humour is usually pretty basic. Taureans are often fairly graphic when discussing sexuality and bodily functions, and don't seem to appreciate how much offence they are causing. When discussing emotional issues they don't really understand the finer points of what is going on, as they tend to dwell on surface appearances. So if you say to a Taurus, 'I was really scarred by that experience,' he or she will look at you and say, 'whereabouts?'

There is no doubt that Taurus is the most stubborn sign of the zodiac. Once Taureans have made up their minds on something, that is it. No power on earth can shift them. This can have one of two results: if they have made an error of judgement, they are like a juggernaut out of control, which carries on moving in the same direction, until it eventually breaks up and comes to grief. However, there are some Taureans who can take advantage of this inflexibility. They have the courage of their convictions and an absolute belief that they will eventually succeed. In a quite magical way, they are able to turn inner vision into concrete reality.

As Taureans are so concerned with the physical universe, they tend to judge themselves and others on qualifications, possessions and bank balances. So it is no good telling Taureans that they are doing a good job; they will need some physical evidence of this fact. If they feel that they are not being adequately rewarded for their labours, they very quickly get a chip on their shoulders. They start feeling that the whole world is out to get them and, at this stage, start making plans to redress the balance. This is why Taurus makes such a good dictator or union leader.

You can tell when Taureans are desperate for reward and recognition, because they start making ridiculous claims, such as 'one day there will be statues of me all over the world.'

Taurus people can also be highly opinionated. They have views on practially everything and tend to have a rigid moral code. When Taureans see someone behaving in a way they find unacceptable, they will immediately start ranting about how disgusting this behaviour is. If you stick Taurus in front of a news programme on TV, you are likely to get a non-stop commentary on the rights and wrongs of government policy. Taurus will not listen to what is being said. After all, they believe they are always right, regardless of the objective facts.

When it comes to spiritual and religious matters, you would expect Taureans to be hard-nosed and to accept something only if they have tangible evidence of its existence. However, in practice, this is rarely the case. Taureans often have some very strange spiritual beliefs. They tend to believe in UFOs, auras, crystal healing, Atlantis and their own divinely inspired destiny. If you tell Taureans that the stock market went down two percentage points yesterday, they probably won't believe you, unless they have read it for themselves in the financial press. However, if you tell them that your next-door neighbours are vampires, they'll start sharpening the stakes.

Touch is very important to Taureans. When you meet them they will engage in a lot of physical contact. This is their way of relating, and you shouldn't be alarmed by it. Taurus is indeed a very sensual person and enjoys giving and receiving massage. The touch of a sensitive Taurus can be very powerful and Taureans are often able to channel healing energy through their fingertips. In their love lives, Taureans strongly emphasize the physical aspects of the relationship. They want their partner to be close to them all the time, and are far more interested in physical and sexual compatibility than intellectual compatibility. However, it is important that the partners of Taurus people are able to share their tastes and value system, because otherwise there is bound to be trouble.

Safe Predictions for Taurus Include:
* 'Tomorrow you are going make loads of money.'

* 'Over the course of the coming year you are going to realize that you were right all along.'
* 'The next decade is going to be critical for you. Your armies are going to take over half of Europe. Think twice before invading Russia, however.'
* 'Next weekend you will eat and drink far too much. As a result, you are going to have a terrible hangover on the following Monday.'

SUN IN GEMINI

Variety is very important to Geminis. They get bored even more quickly than Aries people, and are always looking for new challenges to keep them amused. Once they start something, however, they find it difficult to see it through to the end. The moment they see something more interesting, their attention starts to wander. Talking to Gemini can be an aggravating experience. They will keep changing the subject matter and if there is someone else in the room Gemini may try to hold several conversations simultaneously.

The symbol of Gemini is the twins. This suggests that Gemini can be two people at once: one moment, warm and loving, and the next, ice-cold. If you meet a Gemini friend in the street, you don't know whether he or she will embrace you or ignore you; it seems to rather depend on whether or not you're the flavour of the hour. Nevertheless, you'll be relieved to know that there are ways of dealing with Gemini. Underneath it all, Geminis are extremely arrogant and believe they know everything. They love showing off their knowledge and if you ask them a question they will wax lyrical. Once Geminis think that you appreciate their intellectual ability, you're a friend for life.

Gemini has some reputation for superficiality, and at worst can be a jack of all trades and master of none. They pick up a bit of knowledge here, a bit there, and then pretend that they are a world expert on everything. While they may be very good at talking about their talents, they are not so good when it comes to taking action. Geminis will hesitate and agonize about whether or not they are doing the right thing. If you see Gemini on the point of action, the worst thing you can possibly say is 'are you sure?' This will throw them into a fit of confusion and they'll end up doing nothing.

Geminis are excellent liars and con artists. They can lie through their teeth without batting an eyelid, particularly if they know that there is a financial reward at the end of it. Geminis make particularly good salesmen. It doesn't matter whether they are selling used cars, double-glazing, or the Eiffel Tower, they will convince you that you are getting a really good deal, and you will be only too pleased to hand them your money.

Gemini business people are certainly very versatile, and always thinking of new money-making schemes. They are very good at getting people to lend them money, and when they run into trouble, Geminis are at their very best, conjuring up all sorts of tricks and doing anything to avoid facing the music. The finest example of a Gemini businessman is the late, great Robert Maxwell.

Gemini is a highly-strung sign which is often connected with the nervous system. Geminis get tense very easily, and find it difficult to deal with excess nervous energy. One of the reasons that they talk so much is because they are desperate to find a way of expressing this energy.

Many Geminis try to deal with stress by smoking cigarettes. They shouldn't do this, because Gemini lungs are not particularly strong. However, Geminis find it difficult to listen to medical advice. In fact, if you tell an asthmatic Gemini to stop smoking, he or she will probably justify their behaviour by saying 'my lungs are 30 per cent bigger than average, so I'm 30 per cent less likely to get lung cancer. Anyway, if you smoke you're less likely to get Alzheimer's disease.' Another nervousness-connected problem that Gemini suffers from is insomnia. Geminis find it very difficult to turn their brain off, while at the same time they are hypersensitive to noise.

On the surface, Gemini people can be difficult to understand. They present so many different personalities, while at the same time they are useless at expressing their true feelings. The real reason that Geminis give this impression is that they don't really know how else to relate to the world. It is much easier to deal with thoughts and ideas than with feelings. Feelings are too complicated and they can easily get out of control; at the same time, Geminis are not convinced that anyone else is seriously interested in how they feel. However, at heart, Geminis are like everyone else and, once they trust you, they will eventually bring their hidden emotions into the open.

From a romantic point of view, Geminis are afraid of commitment. There are two reasons for this: firstly, they believe that commitments will inhibit their freedom of action; secondly, they are worried that if they embark on a relationship, they will eventually be let down. Geminis know how quickly they get bored with other people and, by the same token, they feel that those closest to them will eventually get bored too. So, if you are considering having a relationship with a Gemini, you should be patient. It may take a long time to build up their trust. Start off by getting to know them on an intellectual level, and then slowly introduce your emotions.

Safe Predictions for Gemini Include:
* 'Tomorrow's going to be a really boring day.'
* 'Next week your intellect will be on stunningly brilliant form.'
* 'Over the next month you are going to develop a new and exciting talent which you never knew existed. However, in the following month you'll get bored with it, and move on to something else.'

Cancer is a Water sign. This means that Cancer tends to be a fairly emotional person. Cancer people act on their feelings, rather than on their thoughts. When it comes to dealing with other people, Cancers don't weigh up the good and bad points. Instead, they come to an instant and intuitive decision about whether or not a person can be trusted. If you are taken into a Cancer's confidence, you will usually be a friend for life. However, once they mistrust you, it is impossible to get them to change their mind.

The home and the family are important to Cancers. They want a secure and nurturing base on which to ground their life, so a lot of energy is put into turning their homes into castles. A Cancerian's family is almost an extension of their own personality, and they will do anything to protect it. While Cancer people will very occasionally forgive someone who attacks them personally, they will never forgive a slight to members of their own family. Cancer people are, therefore, quite familiar with the word 'vendetta', and usually do very well in organizations such as the Mafia and the Triads. So, if you have a Cancer acquaintance, it is best to remember that, if you are lucky, he'll give you one warning – after that, it's concrete shoes and a visit to the nearest river!

Cancers are great traditionalists. They have an enormous sense of the past and tend to mistrust the future. Cancers believe in hallowed institutions such as the family Christmas, white weddings, the monarchy and the British Empire. They like to collect mementoes of the past and often have boxes of family photographs and heirlooms stacked away. Somehow, if they can hold on to these memories, the past will never quite die.

There is no doubt that Cancer people have vivid imaginations. Their fantasies can powerfully motivate their creativity, which is why Cancer people are such good artists and storytellers. Every Cancer has a secret ambition to drift off to fairyland, and leave their worldly worries behind for ever. However, they are far too grounded in the real world to be able to do this. They are terrified that if they spend too long in fairyland, unexpected troubles will build up. Cancer people imagine that, unless they are constantly vigilant, burglars will invade their home, they'll lose their jobs and end their lives as bankrupt destitutes. As a result of these fears, Cancers are very good at looking after number one. This doesn't mean that Cancer people are necessarily selfish. Once they have sorted themselves out, and feel genuinely secure, then they have time to concentrate on other people's needs. Cancers can be brilliant listeners and can show that they really understand your feelings. When Cancer people see a friend in trouble they will go out of the way to help and will be able to show an almost maternal concern. And, of course, when it comes to the needs of their families, Cancer will always be generous, both emotionally and financially.

However, Cancer parents may sometimes be over-protective. They will always want to know what their children are doing, and if there is the slightest hint of a problem the Cancer parent will immediately start worrying.

When it comes to romance, Cancers find casual flings difficult. They want the whole works – a steady relationship, security and a home. So Cancer people do really expect a lot from their partners. They want their partners to be there for them all the time, and when their partners aren't there, the Cancer imagination starts working overtime. Have their partners run away, are they being unfaithful, or have they been kidnapped by aliens? Cancers who are in a relationship should make some effort to control their imagination. They should trust their loved ones to be as good as their word, and on no account attempt to smother their freedom of action; because if they do, those fears may turn into self-fulfilling prophecies.

On a positive note, Cancers are considerate lovers. Once they trust their partners, there is no limit to their sympathy and warmth. Cancers will make a real effort to tune into their partner's feelings, and will go to great pains to behave in exactly the right way. When their partners are ill or down in the dumps, Cancer will always be there. So, if you are thinking of having a relationship with a Cancer, you are a very lucky person, provided that you can handle a certain amount of Cancer jealousy and over-protectiveness. If you are prepared to put everything you've got into the relationship, then you are certain to get a handsome return.

Safe Predictions for Cancer Include:
* 'Over the coming year you will have plenty of opportunities to settle old scores.'
* 'Next week you'll wonder whether or not you can trust your partner. However, there's no need to worry. The private detective agency you hired yesterday will shortly be giving him/her a clean bill of moral health.'
* 'Tomorrow you will meet a Gemini used car salesman called Arthur. Your intuition is absolutely right. He's a con man.'

SUN IN LEO

Leo is the aristocrat of the zodiac. Leos believe that they are born to rule and, as such, expect plenty of praise and attention from other people. Leos have a certain reputation for arrogance, and they certainly seem fond of mirrors and framed portraits of themselves. If you want an image of Leo, think of a lion basking in his own glory. He knows that he is king of the beasts and that no other animal can touch him. As a result, Leos can be very magnanimous. They appreciate that lesser mortals don't always know how to behave, which is why they can forgive minor slights. At the same time, they understand the responsibilities that go with royalty and are good at dispensing charity and favour.

When dealing with Leos, it is important to appreciate that

Leos believe that they are born to rule and expect plenty of praise and recognition from other people.

they are proud of who they are. While they can deal with criticism of non-essential aspects of their lifestyle, they cannot handle any attacks on their core personality or appearance. Leos have very strong beliefs, upon which they found their life. They will not, under any circumstances, tolerate attacks on this belief system. The kinds of beliefs that Leos are likely to hold dear can be religious, political or cultural. If, for example, Leo is a fanatical fisherman and you tell him that fishing is a cruel waste of time, he won't enter into a reasoned debate about the merits of fishing; after all, you are attacking a key aspect of his personality. Instead, he will bite your head off, unless you apologize and admit that you don't know what you are talking about. Leos, unlike Taureans or Scorpios, will accept apologies; after all, there is nothing a Leo ego likes better than to dispense a royal pardon.

The Leo ego is worth further discussion. Leos are fond of themselves and they like to inflate their own egos at every possibility. As such, they can be very vulnerable to flattery. If you tell Leos how wonderful they are, they'll lap it up and think the world of you. This can be a serious disadvantage for Leo politicians. They tend to appoint advisors who agree with them and, as a result, never get an objective opinion of their actions. This can be a recipe for disaster. However, the occasional Leo can turn his arrogance to his own advantage. He believes in himself so strongly that everyone else starts believing him too. Leo can then create a myth of total omnipotence, which can move nations and continents. Examples of this kind of Leo are Napoleon, Mussolini and Fidel Castro. However, it should be noted that such Leos don't last for ever. They eventually overestimate their brilliance and end up by destroying themselves and their countries.

Most Leos have an aversion to hard work, particularly if they are not getting constant praise and attention. If there is no one around to give their ego a boost, then they get withdrawn and unhappy, and their productivity starts to go down drastically. So, if you are an employer, make sure that you treat your

Leo employees in exactly the right way: give them plenty of encouragement and put them somewhere where they are surrounded by other people. Don't take them for granted, and let them know that they are playing an important part in the success of your organization. You should also understand that, to be at his best, Leo needs extended lunch breaks so that he can socialize with his admirers. At the same time, don't be afraid of giving Leo long holidays. He needs the life-giving energy of the Sun at regular intervals in order to keep his spirits up.

Leo is probably the most generous sign of the zodiac. Leos want to be liked and appreciated and will do their best to ingratiate themselves with others. Their friends are very important, and if you are lucky enough to have a Leo friend, you can expect an infinite amount of loyalty and support. Leos can be a bit too trusting, however. They assume that their friends will reciprocate their kindness. This is, of course, not always the case, and as a result Leos often have a considerable number of stabwounds on their backs. So Leos have to be on their guard. On balance, their greatest weakness is an over-vulnerability to flattery, because this is the means by which false friends get past their defences.

When it comes to matters of love, there is no doubt that Leos are extremely romantic. They are capable of wonderfully extravagant gestures, and know exactly how to make their partners feel special. No trouble or expense is too much, and the male Leo in particular is living evidence that the age of chivalry is far from dead. However, if you are in a relationship with a Leo, you must appreciate that he or she needs plenty of attention and reassurance. After all, one of your main roles is to remind your Leo partner that he or she is indeed the most wonderful and brilliant person on earth.

Safe Predictions for Leo Include:
* 'Tomorrow you'll take the day off.'
* 'Over the next week it will slowly dawn on you how completely amazing you are.'

* 'Next year, you will find yourself surrounded by admirers. You can trust most of them, but watch out for the Taurean with shifty eyes.'

* 'You are as passionate and romantic as ever and you will shortly meet your dream lover. She/he will match your new Ferrari perfectly.'

SUN IN VIRGO

Virgo has the reputation for being an organized person with a very fine sense of detail. Virgos are supposed to have an absolute obssession with tidiness, to the extent that every last speck of dust gets picked up by their ultra-sensitive scanners. While it is certainly the case that many Virgos are like this, there are a great many others who appear to thrive on mess. They live in bomb-sites and dress like extras from 'Plague of the Zombies'. At the same time, they have absolutely no sense of organization and will be late for, or miss, every appointment. So, what does this contradiction mean? Cynics might say that it proves once and for all that astrology doesn't work. However, there is an alternative explanation: Virgos, indeed, have a very fine sense of detail, which is picked up from a very early age. They would like everything to be perfect and in the first instance do their best to order their environment. Some Virgos find that their efforts are quickly rewarded and go on to lead efficient, organized lives. However, there are other Virgos who find organization impossible. No matter how hard they try, they still see nothing but chaos around them. Perhaps this is because they are over-perfectionists. If they cannot create total perfection, what's the point in trying? Anyway, for one reason or another, a substantial minority of Virgos give up the quest for perfection. They then see no point in making any effort whatsoever and, as a result, everything goes to pieces.

Virgos are very critical, both of themselves and other people. They are acutely aware of their own faults, although they find it difficult to openly admit them; they find it much easier to criticize other people. If Virgos want to attack someone, they will quickly find a weak point and throw all their resources at it. However, Virgos have to be careful. No one is perfect and everyone makes mistakes. If Virgos criticize people for no reason, then they will quickly make enemies. It is very important that Virgos are able to make constructive use of their critical abilities. After all, there is no point in being critical unless you can make constructive suggestions. So, if you are a Virgo theatre critic, don't just criticize a play for the sake of it. Ask yourself what improvements could be made.

One of the best professions for Virgos is driving instructing. Virgo driving instructors are brilliant at their jobs. Not only do they always know what is going on on the road, but they regard it as their personal mission to turn their students into perfect drivers. Often, Virgos find music to be an excellent outlet. They enjoy high-quality music which expresses technical flair, but are often themselves good musicians. When they play there's never a note out of place and their timing is excellent. Virgo has a particular affinity with stringed instruments, in particular guitars and violins. So, if you have a Virgo child, make sure that he or she has plenty of opportunity to test out his or her musical talents, because you may have a prodigy on your hands. Regardless of actual talent, Virgos need music in their lives more than most other signs, because listening helps them to relax like nothing else.

A common criticism of Virgos is that they cannot see the wood for the trees. When tackling a project they can only see its details and find it difficult to conceive of the overall plan. Virgos in business are going to be very concerned with accounting issues, so much so, that the actual substance of the business is forgotten. Therefore it might be a good idea if Virgos bring in a trusted Sagittarius or Gemini, in order to get a wider perspective on the situation.

Virgos do give their partners a hard time. They notice every fault, sometimes at the most inappropriate moments. A Virgo woman, at the height of romantic passion, might point out that her lover has a shirt button missing. Quite why she chooses to point this out is an interesting question. It might be because she is genuinely concerned about the missing button. Alternatively, Virgo may be afraid of emotional commitment and is looking for a way to diffuse the situation.

At heart, all Virgos are terrified that their partners will find a fault in them, so their attitude is criticize first, before they themselves are criticized. Under these circumstances, Virgos need to find someone who they know will accept them unquestioningly. Such a person can be found, provided that Virgos can let go of all their fears, worries and insecurities.

Safe Predictions for Virgo Include:
* ★ 'Over the next week you've got a lot of tidying up to do.'
* ★ 'Tomorrow you will think that you've found your perfect lover. However, you will be sorely disappointed when you discover how appalling his/her taste in music is.'
* ★ 'Having discussed things with your Piscean friends, you have decided not to tidy things up over the next week. You'll never shift that mountain of rubbish, and it is better to accept the reality of chaos.'

SUN IN LIBRA

People are really important to Libra. They think a lot about people, and there is very little they do which doesn't have social implications. Librans, of all the signs of the zodiac, are aware that man is not an island. His social environment is there to be understood and mastered, which is why Libra spends so much time thinking and worrying about other people. Typical Libra worries might, therefore, be: 'what will Joe say if I go to Jane's party?' or: 'what will Susan say if I don't turn up to Jane's party?' And, of course, to a Libra, other people are fascinating; they want to know what makes them tick and how they relate to each other.

The symbol of Libra is the scales; the scales balance and Libra wants balance. Usually, this means that they want to fit in, so in any group situation they will often strive not to be out of place, which means saying the right things and exercising their ample charm. This is helped by the fact that Librans are often wonderful and witty conversationalists who can say the right thing in almost any situation.

Of course, being a Libra can be a bit of a tightrope act. Librans don't want to offend anyone and often want to please everyone, which can be difficult when dealing with conflicting loyalties. A common Libran dilemma is having to deal with two people who don't get on: if they are nice to one, they'll offend the other. So Librans will have to go to massively elaborate lengths to keep their feet on the tightrope. Another Libran problem is over-commitment. Librans don't like turning things down, at least, not openly, and, therefore, make promises to do things which they can't possibly keep. A Libran's promises should perhaps be seen as an accommodation rather than a commitment. In their defence, at least they do mean well ... even if their road to hell is paved with good intentions.

Libra is an incredibly civilized sign, and one of the four signs of the zodiac, along with Gemini, Virgo and Aquarius, that does not have an animal as its symbol. And, as a result, Librans find the animal in man quite repugnant. They usually hate crudity, and often find the idea of bodily functions quite hard to handle.

At the same time, Librans are not the most emotional of people. As far as they are concerned, emotional excess is quite unneccessary, since everything can be dealt with in a manner which is both smooth and civilized. In fact, if any scene gets too emotional or too messy, Librans are likely to leave pretty quickly.

Libra is quite a complex sign and few Librans are exactly

what they seem. It is sometimes suggested that Librans are weak, because they are always trying to fit in with other people. Well, this is a bit of a simplification. Librans spend so long thinking about other people and the way they work, that they eventually learn to use their insight. In fact, Librans are good at playing people off against each other, to the extent that they might even be accused of being manipulative. Very often, Librans know the weaknesses of those around them, and with this knowledge they can play some very complex power-games.

Balance certainly is important. Librans and their environment usually have to fit in with each other. However, this doesn't necessarily mean that every Libran makes a compromise. Some Librans demand that their environment fits in with them. Their vision of the world is so important, so pressing, that they have to see it wherever they look.

And finally there are those Librans who are at war with their own sign. A small, but very significant group of people. Librans know what fits in and what is harmonious. They also know exactly what is inappropriate – the best way to upset the apple-cart. Once these Librans appreciate that every action has a social consequence, they will go all out to cause as much havoc and offence as possible. Alaister Crowley, the great magician, and a Libra, revelled in attention and delighted in the title 'The Wickedest Man on Earth'. Oscar Wilde was another Libra who liked to cause a stir. He was a man who understood social conventions very well, and knew exactly how to upset them with his outrageous appearance and razor wit.

Libra predictions: You won't go too far wrong if you predict that Librans are going to have problems with other people. Every day can be a social balancing act, and new people and new situations are always going to be cropping up. It is always a good idea to suggest that Librans use their charm. Though also try to encourage them to be gently assertive.

Safe Predictions for Libra Include:

* ★ 'Today you will feel as if you are walking a tightrope.'
* ★ 'Over the next week or so, your friends are going to be making heavy demands on your time and energy. Try not to over-commit yourself.'
* ★ 'On Thursday and Friday you are going to get sick of obeying your boss's every whim. You may feel tempted to deliberately shock him, just to remind him that you can be assertive. However, in the long run, a firm but diplomatic statement of your rights may be more productive than throwing a jug of boiling coffee in his face.'
* ★ 'During the first few months of this year you will be torn between your need to act for yourself and your feeling of responsibility for those close to you.'

SUN IN SCORPIO

Scorpios are special, because no one understands them ... except other Scorpios. Of all the signs of the zodiac, Scorpio is the one which commands the most awe and the most respect. Even people with no knowledge of astrology will visibly back off at the mere mention of this fascinating sign; the reason being that most people are afraid of what they don't know, and when they meet Scorpios they are forced to confront a total enigma.

For some reason, Scorpio has a rather bad reputation. Perhaps because Scorpio is associated with the symbol of the scorpion. The scorpion most certainly has a sting in its tail, but it would be wrong to associate it with murder, torture and death. Many Scorpios are interested in death, in the Gothic sense of the word, but few of them actually inflict it on other people. At least not in the real world. Of course, one of cinema's greatest killers, Charles Bronson, is a Scorpio. In his films he certainly acts out very Scorpionic roles. He doesn't say much, he broods, and above all he 'gets his man'. There is certainly no concept of forgiveness in the roles he plays, as exemplified in *Death Wish I, II, III,* and *IV*. Every Scorpio probably has something of the cinematic Charles Bronson in them, in the sense that they don't easily forget slights and will often pursue something to the very end.

Scorpios certainly have a reputation for being extremely emotional people. However, their feelings are not the nice, easy-going feelings of the other two Water signs, Cancer and Pisces. Scorpios like to keep their feelings to themselves and will only rarely give clues as to what they are thinking about – which is one of the main reasons why many people find Scorpios so threatening. There really is a lot of intensity and hidden passion about Scorpios, who always seem to be on the verge of boiling over but never quite do.

Sometimes Scorpios do let go of their anger. Although this happens once in a blue moon, when it does happen it is quite a terrifying sight. It is pure, devastating rage which has an unrivalled intensity and power. This rage can often be self-destructive – as the old adage goes: 'if you surround a scorpion with a ring of burning petrol, it will surely sting itself to death.'

Sex and death are two things which are very close to Scorpio hearts. Indeed, one sometimes wonders if Scorpios don't regard the two as being the same thing. Scorpios believe in the transformative power of emotion, even if this means that they experience some kind of a death. They want to immerse themselves in a passion and an ecstasy which transcends mere existence. Though this doesn't always have to be a sexual experience. It can be achieved by a religious awakening, or through drink or drugs.

As we've already said, when Scorpios really want something, they get it. This could refer to the Scorpionic killer stalking the streets of New York, looking for the gang that killed his wife and raped his daughter (see Charles Bronson in *Death Wish I* for further details), or it could be Scorpio looking for a partner. Once Scorpios have decided that they want someone, that is it. They will stalk and pursue their intended victim to the very end, and there is usually very little chance of escape.

Scorpios don't suffer fools gladly, which is probably another reason why other people find them threatening. There is something very judgemental about Scorpios, which is made worse by the fact that they never tell you what they think about you. Though be quite sure that they do have a definite opinion of you, and probably know you much better than you think they do. In fact, they will be aware of all your faults and weaknesses.

If a Scorpio likes you, you are indeed honoured, and there are none more loyal than Scorpio friends. They will stick by you through thick and thin, and will definitely be trustworthy and loyal. However, in return they will expect your utter discretion, and if you ever betray their trust or break your word, you will never be forgiven.

Scorpio parents are going to be extremely protective towards their children, and will usually go out of their way to look after their children's welfare. Indeed, blood will be a great deal thicker than water. The Scorpio family will be very tightly knit and outsiders, including relatives, are likely to be frowned on. They will be regarded as either intruders or idiots.

One final thing to remember about Scorpios is that they should never be underestimated. They have a remarkable capacity to recover from the most devastating blows and their inner strength and resilience is legendary. They come into their own during a crisis – indeed, they very often need a crisis in order to tune into their full power. So another symbol for Scorpio, apart from the scorpion, should be a phoenix rising from its own ashes.

Scorpio predictions: Whenever you are trying to make predictions for Scorpios, be sincere and never be trivial. Every passing day means something for Scorpio, at least on an emotional level, so emphasize the intensity and heaviness of the world. Scorpios are often involved in passionate relationships, and even if they are not, they like to think they are, so a reference to the passion in their life is always a good idea.

Safe Predictions for Scorpio Include:
* 'Wednesday's going to be a really heavy day.'
* 'Over the coming week it will be difficult for you to get your feelings out into the open.'
* 'Next year may see a major personal transformation.'
* 'Over the coming month you should avoid people who ask too many questions. They are not to be trusted, particularly if they're Geminis.'
* 'Over the next few days you will have to deal with someone for whom you feel real contempt.'

SUN IN SAGITTARIUS

Where are all the Sagittarians? It seems that you can go for months without meeting a single one – though, when you do finally meet the elusive Sagittarian, you immediately get some clue as to where he or she might have been. Yes, they will be in a state of absolute exhaustion, having driven themselves into the ground in a wild frenzy of socializing, fun and work . . . all at the same time. There can be little doubt that Sagittarians like to be on the move, and quickly get restless if they have to stay in one place for too long.

Action really matters to Sagittarians. They like to be in an environment which is both exciting and invigorating. They are great people to have in a party setting, as they know how to provide that certain buzz . . . although the way they provide this buzz may not be to everyone's taste. Tact has never been a strong point of this rather outrageous sign, and once they have had a couple of drinks they don't care who they offend. Sagittarians make excellent comedians, particularly of the loud kind. Richard Prior and Bette Midler, those two archetypal 'loud American comedians', are of course both Sagittarians.

Sagittarians are also good at inventing games and tricks, particularly of the uncomfortable kind. Once they decide that something is funny they will really push it, usually until no one else finds it funny. This is partly because they appreciate their own jokes, but also because they want to see how far they can push their audience. How long can they go on pretending that they are dying of cyanide poisoning? Do they wait for the ambulance, or do they wait for the coroner?

However, Sagittarians also need plenty of fuel, which often takes the form of support, encouragement and appreciation. In other words, they can't keep the party going on their own forever. Once the world dries up and stops fuelling their rapacious desire for more action, then the average Sagittarian can go into a bit of a spiral. This may take the form of simple exhaustion, but at its worst it can manifest itself as depression. And once Sagittarians get depressed, they get *really* depressed. It can go on for weeks and there will be very little that anyone can do to remedy the situation. All you can do is wait. In the end, something will always come up to rekindle the Sagittarius fire, and then it will be business and pleasure as normal.

In relationships, Sagittarians need very special partners. Someone who will support them without smothering them, who will share their highs and lows. It is not everyone that can keep up with the furious pace of the Sagittarian, and a sense of fun and adventure is a fairly essential requirement for his or her mate.

While Sagittarians may seem tolerant and easy-going on the surface, at heart they have real contempt for dimwits and dullards. If you can't sparkle like they can, or if you can't handle their pace, then it's probably not a good idea to get too close to the average Sagittarius.

Sagittarius is probably one of the more honest signs of the zodiac. They like to say what they feel, and have limited patience for people who beat around the bush. If something needs to be said, it should be said as directly and truthfully as possible, even if that does mean hurt feelings. Such an approach could be regarded as unfeeling tactlessness, but on the whole it comes out as disarming frankness. After all, the honest and direct Sagittarian didn't *mean* any harm. In fact, he or she was just trying to clear the air.

It is very often the case that Sagittarians like to believe in something. They like to have an overall structure which they can relate to, like a religion, a philisophy, or a political belief. And, as a result, some Sagittarians can be surprisingly narrow-minded. They are capable of making sweeping statements which take no account of actual facts. Such as, 'the Earth *is* flat' or, 'all homeless people *are* lazy'. After all, it makes life so much easier if everything can be fitted into one, huge, all-embracing system.

However, as with their tactlessness, Sagittarians can get away with being narrow-minded. Again, they didn't mean to make that sweeping generalization – it just came out! And when their generalizations are questioned, Sagittarians may well admit that they have gone too far. After all, they would hate to get bogged down in a petty argument. It is much better to change the subject and move on to something else. Which means that other people are always forgetting how narrow-minded their Sagittarian friends can be.

Sagittarius predictions: Be positive when making predictions for Sagittarians. Tell them how exciting the future looks. Because if you're wrong, they are sure to forgive you. However, if you're too negative and they are already in a depressed mood, then you're being a sadist. Another thing to remember about Sagittarians is that quite a few of them don't believe in astrology, so on one level you can say what you like!

Safe Predictions for Sagittarius Include:
* 'You really upset someone yesterday and today you are going to have to pay for it.'
* 'Over the coming week you are definitely going to enjoy yourself. Don't think for a moment about what you are doing.'

* 'It could be quite an accident-prone month, and you should avoid games which involve matches and petrol.'
* 'Another wonderful year is coming up.'
* 'This week you must write that letter which you have been putting off for so long.'

SUN IN CAPRICORN

Capricorn has a certain reputation for being a materialistic and calculating sign. Money and status seem to matter a great deal and, on the whole, they appear to be very hard-working. Their lives seem to have a distinct plan and they are not going to hurry to achieve their goals. Instead, they are rather like the mountain goat, slowly plodding to the top. There is nothing spectacular about their ascent, but they always get there in the end.

Typical Capricorns are Joseph Stalin, Mao Tse Tung and Richard Nixon. Comrade Stalin must surely be the very embodiment of Capricornian virtues. There was nothing spectacular about his ascent to a position as one of the most powerful, and certainly the most feared, men on earth. He was a bureaucrat who used his position as General Secretary of the Soviet Communist Party as a means to take over the apparatus of state. He would never take a position on his own, but instead would ally with the side he thought was strongest – always appearing to be the moderate, mediating between two conflicting sides. And, since he always made sure that he was on the winning side, he would slowly watch his rivals being denounced and shot, (never by him, always by someone else) until he was the undisputed king of the castle. What a Capricorn!

So Capricorns have excellent political instincts and know how to handle power. And provided they keep their nerve and only take action when they are sure that they have built up enough support, they will surely succeed.

However, they can make mistakes. The examples of

President Nixon and miners' leader Arthur Scargill are indeed cautionary tales for Capricorn. Nixon didn't need the Watergate break-in in order to win the 1972 presidential election. Similarly, if Scargill had had a ballot of the entire membership of the National Union of Mineworkers before the 1984 miners' strike, they would probably have supported his strike call. By not having a ballot, he split the miners and ensured that he lost the strike. In both cases we have Capricorns who, in their moment of victory, blew everything by being too clever by half. If they had been true to their sign, and had been patient and stuck to established procedures, they would surely have been stunningly successful.

But surely, you must be thinking, not all Capricorns are obsessed with power and success? Of course, everyone knows a Capricorn who doesn't fit into the above descriptions, and here we meet the other kind of Capricorn: the kind who is idealistic and freedom-loving, who seems to be completely uninterested in power or money. There seems to be a certain simplicity about these Capricorns – they don't want anything in their lives which is unnecessary or cumbersome, like money or power.

As a rule, Capricorns don't like show. They want to see things for what they are, and perhaps it is their ability to sweep away other people's façades and pretensions which makes them so successful. It means that they can get to the point and be very businesslike. It is a complete waste of time trying to impress Capricorns, because what matters to them is the reality, rather than the surface appearance. As Scorpio sees the world as heavy, Capricorn sees it as a struggle. Whether they are idealistic or materialistic, to Capricorns, everything is a bit of a grind. Nothing comes easily, and the best results come through patience, determination and hard work.

Although idealistic Capricorns will make an effort to pretend that life isn't that bad, and that they really can have fun, at the end of the day, typical Capricorns have a down-beat and rather negative attitude, which can be a bit depressing for the people around them. It is said that, as they grow older, Capricorns get younger. Underneath that dour professionalism there is a child trying to get out, and perhaps when they feel confident that they have achieved enough, they will start letting this child out into the open. And it is at that stage that some of more negative Capricornian traits will start to disappear.

From a physical point of view, Capricorns seem to age very well. Having grown old quickly in their teens and twenties, they don't change much after that. In addition, Capricorns are supposed to be the most beautiful sign in the zodiac. Very often, they have clear-cut features and distinguished cheek-bones. The Capricorn woman often feels that she doesn't need to wear make-up, because her beauty is already sufficiently emphasized.

Capricorns are not traditionally the warmest sign of the zodiac. On the whole, this is because they find it a little difficult to get their feelings out into the open. So, really, they need a partner who is able to get in touch with their feelings. However, the more cynical Capricorns may see a relationship as being rather functional – supporting their careers, stabilizing their feelings and providing some degree of status. Transcendental love, on the other hand, may be regarded as pie in the sky nonsense.

Capricorn predictions: You can't pull the wool over Capricorn eyes. Life is a struggle and there is no point in pretending otherwise. Capricorns always feel that there is something in their lives which needs to be better organized, so constant reminders to be better organized will be appreciated. Suggest to them that there might be some small administrative detail that might have been overlooked. Even if you are technically wrong, Capricorns will find something to check up on.

Safe Predictions for Capricorn Include:
* 'This week you must write that letter which you have been putting off for so long.'
* 'Provided you work hard, next year will yield some important long-term results.'

39

* 'Watch out for Librans wearing too much make-up. They are most certainly not to be trusted.'
* 'If you are planning on destroying someone's reputation over the next month, make sure your timing is perfect. Don't make your move until you have isolated them socially first. Even then, be sure that you can see the whites of their eyes.'

SUN IN AQUARIUS

Aquarius is a sign with an excellent reputation. After all, we think of the Age of Aquarius, of New Age Thinking, and so on. Aquarius is supposedly a sign which embodies the principles of freedom and open-mindedness, and under these circumstances it would surely be the case that Aquarians turn out as being quite amazing – the real heirs of the twenty-first century.

Well, there is no doubt that Aquarians like to think that they are open-minded. As far as they are concerned, they are not going to allow petty prejudices to get in the way of their clear judgement. And of course they are going to down-play emotional considerations, which should further improve their clarity of thought. However, Aquarians do have their own view of the world, and their ideas are deeply rooted. So, although they might be able to see your point of view, they might never quite agree with it. It is rather a question of them saying, 'having looked at all points of view, I know that I'm right.'

Aquarians often have very good minds, although they are probably not quite as original and inventive as is commonly believed. The reason that they can come up with some excellent ideas is that they don't allow themselves to be overly influenced by other people. They keep their distance, and this gives them the space to be original. The trouble with Aquarians is that they often find change difficult to handle, and as a result their ideas may be slightly out of step with the reality around them.

Which in turn means that there is a very fine line between the Aquarian genius and the Aquarian crank. On the whole, Aquarius is a rather detached sign. Aquarians don't get too close to any one person, and they usually have a clear sense of their own boundaries. So, if you are dealing with Aquarians, try to respect those boundaries. The moment you go too far, they will run a mile. This is an important point.

Aquarians are friendly people, and will talk to almost anyone. They are not snobs and will express an interest in what you have to say. Nevertheless, you should never read too much into this friendliness. It isn't a signal that they find you highly attractive and want to sleep with you – as many people find to their cost and eternal shame, when they try to force themselves across that all-important Aquarius boundary!

Aquarians will often claim that they are not interested in attention and recognition. They will do their own thing in their own way and won't care what other people think. Hence, the image of Aquarian inventors locking themselves up in garden sheds for half a lifetime, while they develop a time machine or a matter transporter. At some stage, though, these Aquarians will want to be recognized, even if they don't openly admit it. And, indeed, Aquarians do like to be told how brilliantly original they are – suggesting that, under it all, they might be vulnerable to flattery.

It is often quite easy to tell Aquarians by their appearance. They are usually not too bothered by what they look like, and there will be something quite practical about the way they dress. After all, they want their appearance to reflect what they want and what they are doing, rather than the whims of other people. Almost.

In fact, they are trying to show people that they don't care what they look like. So they might make a point of not removing their dirty overalls, or gas mask, or scuba-diving kit until they really have to. And, furthermore, they may deliberately leave the oil stain on their forehead, or the streak of white paint in their hair.

The more fashion-conscious Aquarians may cut quite a striking figure. Again, they won't admit to wanting to attract attention. Instead, they will just say that they are being 'them'. There might be something quite electric about their appearance, especially as they have a good awareness of colour. Their colours may well clash a bit, but it will be a calculated clash – enough to get a reaction, but not enough to cause offence. One final thing about their appearance: their eyes are very important. They often have a very real brilliance to them, whatever their colour, and it is through these eyes that Aquarians seem to be able to exercise a certain magnetic attraction.

In relationships, Aquarians will naturally demand a considerable amount of freedom. There are times when they are going to want to go off and do their own thing, and are not really going to tolerate interference in their private affairs. This is not to say that Aquarians should be allowed to just do what they like. While it is not a good idea to actively stop them doing something, it might be kind to help them see things from another point of view. Because, after all, they can get so into their own ideas that they lose touch with reality. The truly great Aquarius will, in the end, listen to what other people have to say, and moderate his or her genius accordingly.

Aquarian predictions: Aquarians are certainly going to be interested in your predictions. They will hear what you have to say, and may even claim that they will take your advice into account. Whether or not they believe you will depend on how they see you as a person.

Generally speaking, it is a good idea to emphasize the detachment that is so important in Aquarians' lives. There is either going to be too much or too little detachment in their lives, so you should have a 50–50 chance of being right on this score. It is also worth flattering Aquarians. They think that they are pretty unique and special, and it won't do any harm to tell them this again.

Safe Predictions for Aquarians Include:

* 'You may have been a bit cold over the last few days. Now is a good time to show that you really care.'
* 'Beware of unsolicited advances from over-sensitive Cancerians.'
* 'Your transcending genius is going to come into its own over the next month. So don't listen to anyone else and go ahead with your plan, regardless.'
* 'You haven't got enough silver clothes in your wardrobe. This is a situation which you should consider remedying over the weekend.'

SUN IN PISCES

Pisceans can be quite chaotic people. They may seem to be all over the place and, as with Sagittarians, it may be difficult for them to stay in one place for too long. They tend to drift off, or get carried away on whatever passing cloud takes their fantasy. Pisces people are often very good at moulding themselves to their environment. Somehow they manage to take on the features of whatever is going on around them, which is a useful skill, provided they don't get carried away.

Yes, it is a sad fact, but once Pisces gets into something it is difficult for them to stop. It all gets to be too much of a good thing. A common Pisces request is for more – more food, more drink, more cigarettes, more sex, and so on. As far as they are concerned, once you have surrendered yourself to something, you might as well completely surrender yourself to it. And the extraordinary thing is that the Pisces system can handle it. Whatever their indulgences are, it all goes down and Pisces remains standing. Wanting more. There are the occasional Pisceans who can't handle the pace. They know that they are excessive and that their very identity is on the line every second of the day, so they avoid anything which smacks of indulgence. Indeed, they can have a positive fear of any substance which might possibly upset their fragile balance. No heavy drinking sessions for them!

However, the curious thing is that these Pisceans are often a lot less secure than their more indulgent sign-mates, perhaps because they are terrified of the chaos that is intrinsic to their sign. Those that accept this chaos and jump into it seem to fare better.

Pisceans are very emotional people. They feel things to the very bottom of their hearts. Their emotions, rather than their rational thoughts, are usually more important when it comes to the way in which they make decisions. Very often, Pisceans are intuitive people and really seem to pick up vibes. Although sometimes it may be difficult for them to distinguish between their own and other people's feelings. So if they feel depressed, it might well be because someone else is feeling depressed instead.

Sometimes emotions can trip Pisces up. You do meet some Pisceans who respond to everything around them. There seems to be a certain problem of identity – because they can never say no, and never resist the pull of their feelings. And as a result, under the wrong circumstances, we encounter the violent Pisceans. They just get wrapped up in something and can't question how they react until it's too late. The drunken oaf who lunges at you with a broken bottle in a pub might well be a Pisces.

Pisceans can have a distinctly spiritual bent. Ideally, they would like to merge into something which is higher than themselves. Perhaps they want to be one with the universe, or with God. They may be interested in New Age artefacts, like tarot and crystal balls, and may believe, with some justification, that they have psychic powers. At best, Pisceans can be wonderfully sympathetic, because they can mould themselves into other people's feelings and show a real understanding. They might even want to sacrifice a part of their identity to help someone else.

However, it would be wrong to think that all Pisceans have their heads in the clouds. Pisceans are intuitive and have a feel for what is going on around them. This ability can turn them into excellent businessmen. Rupert Murdoch is a prime example of a Pisces who has been transcendingly successful in his business life, presumably because he has intuitively understood what is going to work. And of course a sussed-out Pisces would be very good at reading the motives of his or her business rivals. Generally speaking, the motivated Pisces will have the uncanny knack of being in the right place at the right time.

Pisceans often make talented artists and actors. They are usually very imaginative and can bring some of their imagination down to earth. So their paintings are going to catch some of that imagination, and since Pisceans are so good at fitting and moulding themselves into the environment, they can also mould themselves into different roles and almost become the person they are trying to be. So they can also be very good actors.

Overall, Pisceans are nice people and usually very good-natured. One of their worst traits can be unreliability, but this actually stems from their attempts to be nice. If someone asks them to do something, they will naturally adapt to the request. However, if something else turns up, they will likewise adapt again. So, really, they are passing from cloud to cloud and scene to scene. If Pisceans say that they will do something, you should know better than to rely on them. Something may always turn up which makes it impossible for them to fulfil this commitment. Instead, you should be happy that your Pisces friend has graced you with his company at that particular moment of time. Savour the moment. Don't spoil it by trying to force him or her into a commitment which he or she can't possibly keep.

Pisces predictions: It's always a good idea to emphasize the unpredictability of life. Don't tell Pisceans that something will happen, rather say it might, provided that something else doesn't come up. On the whole, you can be as vague as you like when you predict for Pisces. When they look at your prediction in retrospect, they will try hard to make it fit the actual events, so really you don't have to worry too much about being wrong. Just keep away from hard facts. Pisceans like to be told how romantic and spiritual the future is, so it is always a good idea to indulge their fantasies.

Safe Predictions for Pisces Include:
* 'Tomorrow's going to be complete chaos. Stay in bed.'
* 'Over the next week; the vivid dreams which you have been having should start making some sense.'
* 'You're going to get blind drunk over the weekend.'
* 'Next year is going to be one of the most spiritually meaningful periods of your life. Even more meaningful than the previous year.'

3. THE SUN SIGNS IN LOVE

ARIES

Aries people enjoy an exciting and varied love life. They want a partner who can keep up with their frantic pace, but who also respects their need for freedom. Emotionally, Aries wants things to be simple. Aries hates power-games and wants partners to be as open and honest as they are. If Ariens discover that a partner has been lying to them, they usually terminate the relationship.

The Aries Female: The Aries woman is very demanding. She is looking for a man who is not only able to take the initiative, but who also understands how important it is for her to be independent and self-sufficient. For many men this is an impossible balance. If he asserts himself, the Aries woman sees him as a chauvinist savage, and if he holds back, she sees him as a wimp.

The Aries Male: The Aries man believes that he is irresistible to women. As a result, he is quick to express his feelings. If a woman rejects his advances, Aries regards it as her loss and immediately moves on to new prey. This shows his attitude to courtship: if he chats up a hundred women, ninety-nine will tell him to drop dead. However, the hundredth always recognizes his brilliance.

Holding on to an Aries: Although Ariens have a dislike of heavy emotions, they are often very moody, one moment happy and easy-going, the next, tense and argumentative. So the key to holding on to an Aries partner is to be very sensitive to these moods, and to know when to be assertive and when to be docile.

Ideal partners: Leo and Sagittarius.
Difficult partners: Virgo and Scorpio.

Positive features: Spontaneous, exciting, honest and brave.
Negative features: Selfish, immature and argumentative.

TAURUS

Taurus is a very stable and down-to-earth sign, and in a relationship looks for a secure and unchanging base. Once Taureans get used to a particular relationship, they find it pretty difficult to make changes. This inflexibility can cause problems if there is an unexpected crisis. In love, Taureans are very sensual and expect their partners to be star performers in bed.

The Taurus Female: The Taurus woman is materialistic, and this is reflected in her choice of partners. She wants someone who can provide her with the good things of life, such as a beautiful home, beautiful clothes and beautiful jewellery. Even if she herself has a good income, she still expects her partner to top it up, so that she can afford her many shopping expeditions. She would be the last to starve for a good cause (or a good man)!

The Taurus Male: In relationships, the Taurus male is simple and down-to-earth. He wants a woman who can look after his primary needs and who will always be available for him. Taurus is usually generous and he will ensure that his partner is well provided for. However, he is not always very sensitive and often underestimates his partner's need for emotional support.

Holding on to a Taurus: Of all the signs, Taurus is easiest to hold on to. Once Taureans get into the routine of a relationship they will want to go on with it for ever and ever. Taureans will only break a relationship if their partners start doing strange and unexpected things, like serving dinner thirty seconds late.

Ideal partners: Virgo and Capricorn.
Difficult partners: Leo and Scorpio.

Positive features: Sensual, reliable and trustworthy.
Negative features: Materialistic, stubborn and unimaginative.

GEMINI

Gemini has two sides: one moment Gemini can be open and friendly, and the next, cold and detached. So it is important that the partners of Geminis are not put off by these switches. Another point to bear in mind about Gemini lovers is that they are very logical. They don't really understand emotions – instead, Geminis find it easiest to relate through words and ideas.

The Gemini Female: Gemini adjusts her conversation and body language to fit in with the people around her. As a result, men often make mistakes with her. He thinks that Gemini is interested in him, when in fact she is just being friendly. At heart, the Gemini female is looking for an exceptional man, who can steamroller her words and ideas with his sheer passion and intensity.

The Gemini Male: He often pulls women with words. He bombards her with such a massive onslaught of boasts, tall stories and excuses that she finds it difficult to say no to him. Once a woman is going out with Gemini, she may find that he is very unreliable, particularly when it comes to dates and appointments. So she will need to keep a very close eye on him.

Holding on to a Gemini: There are two ways of holding on to Geminis. One way is to give them plenty of freedom and to tolerate their unreliability and verbal diarrhoea. The other method is to come down on them like a ton of bricks and ensure that they have no freedom of action whatsoever.

Ideal partners: Libra and Aquarius,
Difficult partners: Cancer and Scorpio.

Positive features: Clear-headed, versatile and interesting.
Negative features: Two-faced, unreliable and unemotional.

CANCER

Cancer people are emotional, and in matters of love are at their most emotional. Cancers want partners who can share their inner feelings and this can only be done through a very close relationship. Cancers don't see their partners as merely lovers, but as members of the family, so people should not get involved with Cancer if they cannot cope with a high level of commitment.

The Cancer Female: The Cancer woman is warm and loving and always on hand to provide sympathy and attention. She is sensitive to her partner's feelings. When he is in trouble or feeling insecure, Cancer will immediately take on a mothering role. In return, Cancer expects total devotion from her man, and if he lets her down she will never forgive him.

The Cancer Male: Cancer really knows how to look after his partner. He will do everything to safeguard her interests and to help her out. Indeed, he will do the cooking, the washing, and take the children to school. However, he is very possessive, and his jealousy knows no limits. If another man even looks at his woman, the Cancer male is likely to tear his head off.

Holding on to a Cancer: You don't hold on to Cancers. They hold on to you, with a vice-like grip. Nonetheless, there are things that can be done to keep the relationship sweet. Stay at home as much as possible and if you are planning on going out on your own, make sure you get Cancer's permission first.

Ideal partners: Scorpio and Pisces.
Difficult partners: Libra and Aquarius.

Positive features: Warm, sympathetic and considerate.
Negative features: Unforgiving, possessive and over-emotional.

LEO

Leos are loyal and generous people, and in the right circumstances they can make perfect partners. It should be borne in mind, though, that Leos need plenty of attention. They want partners who adore them and who think that they are the centre of the universe. If Leos are ignored or criticized by their partners, they often become either angry or withdrawn.

The Leo Female: Leo knows that she is the most beautiful thing on earth and therefore expects to be treated like a film star. She thinks her partner is fortunate to have her, and expects him to make frequent demonstrations of his love and affection. Leo also expects her mate to be handsome and well-dressed, because this reflects well on her when she is out with him in public.

The Leo Male: The lion is even more arrogant than the lioness. The Leo man believes that he is God's gift to women, and he expects his partner to be in awe of his good looks, charm and charisma. Leo's ego is massive and women often fall under his magnetic spell. This is fine, provided she doesn't believe everything he says, because he is prone to exaggerate his skills.

Holding on to a Leo: Holding on to Leos is easy, once you know their weak spots. Their biggest weak spot is vulnerability to flattery. If they are upset for any reason, all a partner has to do is tell them that they are absolutely wonderful and that they are dream lovers. Leo will then beam with inflated pride.

Ideal partners: Gemini and Sagittarius.
Difficult partners: Virgo and Scorpio.

Positive features: Generous, loyal and forgiving.
Negative features: Arrogant and childish.

VIRGO

In matters of love, Virgos are able to be very honest with themselves and their partners. They know their own faults and are prepared to discuss them. In the same spirit, Virgos will point out their partner's faults. When it comes to the everyday routine of the relationship, they are punctual, and careful that all the little details are sorted out well in advance.

The Virgo Female: At heart, Virgo has a low opinion of her talents and abilities, so what she needs is a man who can make her feel good about herself and who can make her feel special. Virgo has a critical streak and when she is in a bad mood she can say some appallingly hurtful things to her lover. She doesn't mean them, so there is no need for him to take them personally.

The Virgo Male: He is usually a careful man who takes his responsibilities seriously. In a relationship, Virgo is very considerate, and will make a real effort to look after his woman. At times he may get a little too obsessed about details and start worrying unnecessarily. It is then up to his partner to help him to relax and to forget his worries.

Holding on to a Virgo: It is essential that Virgos are not messed around. They expect other people to be reliable and to stick to a promise. It is very important to turn up for appointments on time. If a partner or lover is consistently late, Virgo will eventually decide that the relationship is too stressful to continue with.

Ideal partners: Taurus and Cancer.
Difficult partners: Aries and Gemini.

Positive features: Organized, reliable and tidy.
Negative features: Critical, worried and unspontaneous.

LIBRA

Relationships are important to Libra. Somehow, Libra doesn't feel complete without a partner. However, once Librans are in a relationship, they will not be obsessed with its emotional and physical aspects. They want a nice, civilized partnership, where both sides treat each other with respect. The moment things get emotionally complicated, Libra starts backing off or backing out!

The Libra Female: Libra is charming, attractive and well-balanced. She is always looking for the perfect man, and when she thinks she's found him, she does her best to create a perfect relationship. On the surface, Libra seems weak and compliant: as a result her man often tries to take advantage of her. Fortunately, she's no fool and is quick to get rid of male parasites.

The Libra Male: The Libra man is often indecisive. This is particularly the case in matters of love, where he finds it difficult to take the initiative. When he does start to become involved with a woman, he doesn't find it easy to make a clear commitment. This is probably because Libra doesn't want to take any responsibility for the consequences of his actions.

Holding on to a Libra: Holding on to a Libra is not too difficult. After all, Libra hates fuss, especially the aggravation that is caused by the break-up of a relationship. To be absolutely certain that a relationship with a Libra will last, it is simply a matter of behaving well and avoiding crude language.

Ideal partners: Gemini and Aquarius.
Difficult partners: Taurus and Scorpio.

Positive features: Diplomatic, tactful and graceful.
Negative features: Indecisive and cowardly.

SCORPIO

Scorpios don't take relationships lightly. Once they have decided to get involved with someone, that's that. They will throw everything they've got into the relationship, and in return will expect total loyalty from a partner. Scorpios are intensely passionate and anyone that becomes romantically involved with these creatures will soon be transformed by their overwhelming emotional power.

The Scorpio Female: This woman is extremely powerful. Her partner will soon find that his life is completely controlled by her. She will want to know what he is doing with his life, his time and his money. Before long, she will be making all his key decisions for him. For instance – the time he gets up in the morning, what he wears and what job he does.

The Scorpio Male: The male probably doesn't have quite as deadly a sting as his female counterpart, but he still needs to be treated with respect. Scorpio has a magnetic personality which women find fascinating. He has a quiet confidence in his ability to pull any woman he likes, and usually this confidence is justified.

Holding on to a Scorpio: Scorpios' partners can do very little to strengthen or weaken a relationship. This is because, at the beginning of the relationship, Scorpios make a clear decision in their own minds about where they want it to go. If there is one thing that partners should avoid, it is lies. Scorpio always spots them and always punishes them.

Ideal partners: Cancer and Capricorn.
Difficult partners: Taurus and Sagittarius.

Positive features: Powerful, faithful and sincere.
Negative features: Vindictive and possessive.

SAGITTARIUS

Sagittarians need plenty of excitement in their life and quickly get bored. If a relationship fails to keep their interest, they'll leave it without a moment's hesitation. Anyone considering a relationship with a Sagittarian should ask themselves whether or not they have a personality which is sufficiently vibrant to keep them hooked.

The Sagittarius Female: This woman enjoys upsetting men. She knows how fragile male egos can be and what makes men squirm. So any man in a relationship with her needs a thick skin. Indeed, what the female Sagittarius is really looking for is a strong and self-assured man who is not only able to control her, but who can provide her life with a meaning and a purpose.

The Sagittarius Male: Although the Sagittarius man is often loud, tactless and unpredictable, he does have some positive qualities. He has a wicked sense of humour, which can enliven the most boring parties. In a relationship, Sagittarius respects his partner's need for independence and he will always encourage her to make the most of her creative talents.

Holding on to a Sagittarius: To hold on to Sagittarians it is vital *not* to hold on to them, because they value their freedom more than any relationship. If Sagittarians announce that they are going to travel the world for a year, they cannot be stopped. If you're lucky, they'll let you join in; otherwise, you'll simply have to wait for their return.

Ideal partners: Aries and Gemini.
Difficult partners: Cancer and Scorpio.

Positive features: Freedom-loving and open-minded.
Negative features: Loud, tactless and unstable.

CAPRICORN

Capricorns are reserved and slow to express their feelings. If they are interested in someone, they play a long, drawn-out game. This is because Capricorns have to be sure that they are not making a mistake. While Capricorns appreciate the need for a partner who is kind and supportive, it is also important for them to have someone who can improve their status and general position in life.

The Capricorn Female: This woman has a natural beauty which doesn't need to be boosted by make-up or plastic surgery. As a result, men often find her irresistibly attractive. However, it should be borne in mind that Capricorn hates show and pretence. She certainly won't be impressed by a man's Ferrari Testarossa – unless he can prove that he paid cash for it!

The Capricorn Male: The Capricorn man sees relationships as being akin to business partnerships. He wants his woman to do her bit for the company, whether it be balancing the books or entertaining clients. On the plus side, Capricorn values hard work, and is always prepared to compensate his partner for her time and effort.

Holding on to a Capricorn: Capricorns make their likes and dislikes clear. Their partners should, therefore, have a good idea about what to do and what not to do. The things that Capricorns appreciate most are efficiency, reliability and good financial management. Extravagance, particularly with *their* money, makes them see red.

Ideal partners: Taurus and Virgo.
Difficult partners: Aries and Libra.

Positive features: Reliable and financially astute.
Negative features: Cold and reserved.

AQUARIUS

Aquarians seldom express the full power of their feelings and prefer to communicate through words and reasoned argument. In a relationship this can present problems, because Aquarians may refuse to recognize their partner's need for emotional understanding. On a positive note, Aquarians are always prepared to talk to their partners and to listen to any ideas.

The Aquarius Female: Aquarius is stunning. She dresses to kill and her eyes can turn men to stone. In relationships, the female Aquarius does not commit herself easily, because there are few men that can really satisfy her. The man that Aquarius eventually chooses must respect her independence and understand that she sees a relationship as a close friendship, rather than an all-embracing union.

The Aquarius Male: This man likes to do things his own way and hates other people interfering with his life. Many women find him attractive and have fantasies that they can turn the mad professor into a respectable member of society. This is an impossible task. If a woman cannot accept Aquarius's eccentricities, she shouldn't involve herself with him!

Holding on to an Aquarius: Despite Aquarian claims that they don't care about other people, there is a burning need for praise and recognition. If Aquarians' partners constantly tell them what a genius they are and that their latest project is brilliant, they will never leave the relationship.

Ideal partners: Gemini and Libra.
Difficult partners: Taurus and Cancer.

Positive features: Intelligent and original.
Negative features: Aloof and unfeeling.

PISCES

The advantages and disadvantages of being in a relationship with Pisceans tend to cancel each other out. On the positive side, Pisces is warm and friendly and has no problems when it comes to expressing feelings. However, Pisceans are not always reliable or honest. They find it difficult to keep their word and, when they are in a tricky situation, are even better liars than Geminis.

The Pisces Female: The Pisces woman is seductive and attractive and she never has any difficulty finding a partner. This is just as well, because she regards relationships as being an essential part of her life. The unattached Pisces is happy to go out with the first available man she meets, provided that he doesn't mind being jilted the moment she finds someone better.

The Pisces Male: This man is a tricky customer who likes to be in two places (and sometimes two beds) at the same time. He finds it hard to make a strong commitment to any one person, and he will hedge his bets wherever possible. The reason for Pisces' approach is that he is secretly looking for the perfect woman. He'll never find her, but he always lives in hope.

Holding on to a Pisces: The key to holding on to Pisceans is not to fall for their charm and excuses. Make it absolutely clear to them that the next time they are late or dishonest they'll be dumped. Once Pisceans know that a partner can stand up to them, they will soon give some kind of a commitment.

Ideal partners: Cancer and Scorpio.
Difficult partners: Libra and Aquarius.

Positive features: Warm, friendly and sensitive.
Negative features: Unstable and untrustworthy.

4. COMPATIBILITY BETWEEN SUN SIGNS

ARIES – ARIES

Aries get on brilliantly with each other. They have a natural rapport and when it comes to romance, they light each other's fire. Relationships between Aries people tend to be easy-going, because both partners respect each other's need for freedom and independence. When two Aries are put together they are rarely bored, as they are able to stimulate each other with their limitless energy and zest for life. However, this combination of fire and fire could be problematic in that there is loads of enthusiasm, but often little direction. Big plans, grand schemes and dramatic ideas may not be practical enough to actually work!

ARIES – TAURUS

This pairing can have its disadvantages. Aries is very quick on the uptake and at times can find Taurus a little too plodding. At the same time, Taurus finds the Aries sense of humour rather upsetting. However, Aries and Taurus can learn a great deal from each other. Taurus can teach the value of patience, whilst Aries can show how important it is to be able to take the initiative. Taurus can give solid and practical grounding to the inspirational plans of Aries and, together, this could be a very fruitful and productive partnership. The earthiness of the bull is terrifically exciting to the ram, who loves the chase and is spurred on by what Taurus appears to offer.

ARIES – GEMINI

A good relationship. Aries and Gemini find it very easy to get on with each other. They find each other fascinating, and can talk for hours and hours. Sometimes Aries can be a little irrational and needs a cool, calm and collected Gemini to put some ideas into perspective. At the same time, Gemini can be all talk and no action, and can benefit from the dynamic enthusiasm that only Aries can provide. However, Aries can sometimes find Gemini's indecisiveness infuriating. If this is the case, Aries should be prepared to make up Gemini's mind for them and give them a push in the right direction. Passion could be lacking in this combination, largely because Geminis prefer to analyse and dissect their feelings rather than act upon them, but Aries can inject the spark, if only he can get a word in edgeways.

ARIES – CANCER

This is not one of the better astrological matches. Both Aries and Cancer have definite views on the way life should be lived, and as a result there can be clashes. This is made worse by the fact that both signs can be moody and so sometimes the emotional temperature within the relationship can become too hot to handle. Aries may see Cancer's concern over emotional and domestic issues as stifling his or her ability to take the initiative. At the same time, Cancer is likely to find the impulsiveness of Aries threatening. This is unlikely to be an equal relationship. If it is going to last, one side will have to give in and accept that the other person is right about absolutely everything.

Sometimes Aries can be a little irrational and needs a cool, calm, collected Gemini to put some ideas into perspective.

ARIES – LEO

Aries and Leo are both Fire signs, and as a result this relationship should be very rewarding. Together, Aries and Leo are able to generate an enormous amount of energy, and from a romantic point of view it is certainly a passionately warm combination. Both signs will want to go out and do exciting things, and their ideas and inspirations should work very well together. The only possible problem is that there might be an ego clash. Both Aries and Leo are proud signs, and they both want to feel that they are in control. So it is important that the two partners are able to make compromises. Again, as with other fiery combinations, there may be too much steam and too little substance to ideas and schemes, and as a result little productive output may be achievable.

ARIES – VIRGO

Traditionally this is one of the worst combinations, as the signs Aries and Virgo have very little in common with each other. Aries wants to be free to take the initiative, regardless of the possible risks. Virgo, on the other hand, is always worrying about the consequences of his or her actions. Aries may feel that Virgo is constantly nit-picking, and that nit-picking is getting in the way of the full enjoyment of life. However Virgos may feel that their tidy, well-organized little world is being threatened by the Aries whirlwind! The only way this relationship is going to work is if Aries is unusually timid, or if Virgo is unusually adventurous. Nevertheless, this could be a fruitful business or working relationship, in that Virgo can give practical expression to the creativity of Aries.

ARIES – LIBRA

Aries and Libra are opposite signs. They are in many ways different to each other: Aries likes to take the lead, while Libra is more interested in making compromises; Aries has a selfish streak, while Libra is always concerned about the needs of other people. Yet there is definitely a magnetic attraction between the two signs. They feel that the other person has something special, which they don't have. This union of opposites can be very productive, although it is important that both sides make some adjustments: Aries has to be more considerate and Libra has to be more assertive. Many successful marriages are to be found with this dynamic and exciting combination.

ARIES – SCORPIO

This is a very intense and passionate relationship, which will only work if both signs know exactly what they are doing. There will be an enormous amount of anger and emotion flying around, which could quickly get out of control. Indeed, there are some people who will not allow an Aries and a Scorpio to be in the same room together. If either sign is not very mature, or doesn't have much self-understanding, this is certainly a relationship to be avoided. However, if both parties are aware of their feelings and are prepared to deal with a highly charged and somewhat unpredictable relationship, this union can turn into an exciting adventure through a jungle of passion.

ARIES – SAGITTARIUS

This is a very exciting combination. Both signs are forward-thinking and constantly looking for ways of expanding their horizons. Aries and Sagittarius make excellent travel partners, because they both know how important it is to keep moving. Together, they are natural explorers, and they will be just as much at home in the South Pole as on a raft in the Pacific Ocean. However, you should beware of inviting this couple to a party. They are both natural tricksters, and delight in causing havoc. Aries and Sagittarius feed off each other's savage sense of humour and when they get going they don't care who they offend. In fact, bluntness, tactlessness and lack of social grace could characterize this coupling, but if you want the truth, that's exactly what you'll get!

ARIES – CAPRICORN

At first sight, Aries and Capricorn don't have much in common. The goat is slow and deliberate and hates loud and extravagant behaviour. At the same time, you would expect the ram to find Capricorn a little too sensible for his liking. However, in practice, Aries and Capricorn have a considerable amount of respect for each other. While they appreciate their differences, they also understand how much they can help one another. Capricorn is the planner who creates a careful strategy to achieve eventual success. It is then up to Aries to put Capricorn's plans into action. This combination is particularly good for business partnerships. When it comes to romance, however, there may not be sufficient emotional flow to keep the thing going.

ARIES – AQUARIUS

This could be a very powerful relationship: Aquarius has a clear vision of the future, while Aries people are always looking for something new to keep them amused. Aquarians need someone with initiative to realize their vision, and it may be the case that only Aries can provide the required boost.

However, Aries people should appreciate that Aquarians are very stubborn, and like to do things their own way. If Aries interferes too much with the Aquarians's plans, there could be trouble. On the other hand, Aquarians need to appreciate that some flexibility is required if they are ever going to see their plans turned into reality. They should, therefore, trust their Aries partner.

ARIES – PISCES

This is unlikely to be an easy relationship. Aries and Pisces are two signs which don't have much in common. Pisces finds it difficult to make clear decisions and is overly influenced by external circumstances. Pisces people find it difficult to be definite, and this approach tends to annoy the average Aries. Aries likes things to be simple and above-board and the emotional chaos surrounding Pisces can become very irritating. At the same time, Pisces is likely to find that Aries is too pushy. Pisceans need time to commit themselves: the Aries attitude that everything can be done on the spur of the moment may seem unreasonable. If Aries and Pisces are to have a successful relationship, this probably means that Pisces will have to accept that it will be Aries who calls all the shots, because otherwise nothing will ever get done.

TAURUS – TAURUS

This could be a rather difficult relationship: both Taureans will believe that they are right about everything and neither one will compromise. It is a bit like two Sumo wrestlers locked in eternal combat – no ground is lost, but none is gained. From a romantic point of view, there are some advantages in this match. It will certainly be very passionate and the physical aspects of the relationship will be strongly emphasized. If both partners have the same taste, then they may spend many happy hours choosing carpets and beautiful pieces of furniture, provided that there is enough money going to fuel their expensive tastes!

TAURUS – GEMINI

On the surface of it, this is not an obvious match. However, in practice, Taurus and Gemini seem to get on okay with each other. Gemini is one of the few types of people that gets Taureans to question their long-held opinions. This is because Gemini is somehow able to breach the Taurus defences. At the same time, Gemini can find Taurus fairly challenging. The Taurus physicality forces Gemini to be more body-conscious and less concerned with purely mental concerns. Geminis who are involved romantically with Taureans will at first be shocked, although they may end up being liberated from their inhibitions. Taurus can learn a great deal from Gemini, especially when it comes to thinking and acting in positive ways. Gemini can learn to be more grounded and more aware of physical requirements, such as regular eating and regular exercise.

TAURUS – CANCER

Under most circumstances, this is an easy-going relationship, which could last a very long time. Taurus and Cancer are unlikely to upset each other and they will enjoy the security and peace of mind that this relationship can offer. The lack of any challenge posed by this partnership may seem advantageous, although there is some danger that things could get a bit boring. From the point of view of marriage, this is a good combination if both Taurus and Cancer want to have a nice home, 2.4 children and to live happily ever after. However, if one partner starts wanting excitement and adventure, then this relationship rapidly falls apart. Lack of vision and an overly materialistic attitude on the part of Taurus could irritate Cancer, who is far more concerned with emotional, as opposed to material requirements.

TAURUS – LEO

Both Taurus and Leo have fairly high opinions of themselves. Taurus wants to be taken seriously, whilst Leo wants plenty of love and admiration. As a result, both partners may regard each other as being too arrogant. So in this relationship it is very important that there is a lot of self-honesty. Both signs have to accept their faults and, at the same time, listen to each other's needs. If the two start having an argument, it is vital that immediate action is taken to stop the situation getting out of control. If possible, they should bring in a third party to act as a mediator. Inflexibility and a 'might is right' attitude could be problematic, and Leos will certainly infuriate Taureans with their grand gestures, their need for so much attention and their extravagance.

TAURUS – VIRGO

Taurus and Virgo have a certain amount of sympathy for each other, because they are both Earth signs. The practical details of life matter to both of them and they will not be phased by each other's materialism. The solid and stable approach of Taurus may be very reassuring to Virgo, who often worries too much. Taurus should make a real effort to listen to Virgo, because Virgo has some very useful organizational skills, which may allow Taurus to put his or her plans into practice. From a romantic point of view, Virgos may find the impulsive sensuality of Taureans a bit threatening. However, in time they will get used to it. Taurus will respond magnificently to Virgo's gestures of love, and together this could be a very fertile, albeit routine, sort of partnership.

TAURUS – LIBRA

This is not one of the better zodiacal partnerships. While both signs share a profound sense of beauty, their idea of beauty is not quite the same. Libra is looking for a civilized order, while Taurus is interested in something altogether more sensual. Libra usually enjoys art galleries, the theatre and culture in general, whilst Taurus enjoys a hearty meal, with plenty of food and drink in a value-for-money restaurant. Libra is very concerned about good taste, and will find the Taurean crudeness far too much to handle. However, all is not lost. Librans can teach Taureans how to behave and how to moderate the worst aspects of their crude sense of humour. At the same time, Taureans can show Librans just how useful stubborn and selfish determination can be.

TAURUS – SCORPIO

Taurus and Scorpio are opposite signs. A relationship between Taurus and Scorpio can be extremely dynamic. They both have enormous resilience and together they can move mountains. However, this is not going to be an easy relationship. Both Taurus and Scorpio will want to be in control and as a result it could turn into a power struggle. Unless one side backs down, the temperature within the relationship could become too hot to handle. From a romantic point of view, this is an extremely passionate combination. Taurus will have well and truly met his match and may find his very sense of identity is eaten up by the all-consuming Scorpionic fires.

TAURUS – SAGITTARIUS

This is not an obvious combination. Taurus and Sagittarius are signs which have little in common, and there may be hardly any basis for a constructive relationship. Sagittarians need plenty of freedom and like to be able to change their minds as frequently as possible. Taureans, on the other hand, like things to be nice, safe and secure. Change is very threatening to Taurus and the desire of Sagittarius for constant variety is likely to be the cause of considerable stress. Things may be made even worse once Sagittarius spots the Taurean's Achilles heel, for Sagittarius will mercilessly tease Taurus, in the same way that a matador teases a bull. However, they had better not go too far. Once Taurus decides to attack, no one gets out alive!

TAURUS – CAPRICORN

There was a war-time cartoon, picturing Hitler the Taurus and Stalin the Capricorn walking arm in arm, each with a revolver hidden behind his back. This illustrates one kind of relationship that can exist between Taurus and Capricorn. If they feel that they can benefit from each other, then they are happy to work with each other. However, once the situation changes, they will quickly become the worst of enemies. Both signs are ambitious, and there is only room for one person on top. From a romantic point of view, this relationship is not ideal, unless the two partners want to mix plenty of business with pleasure. However, being Earth signs, they will understand each other's physical needs and, although this may be a relationship short on inspiration, it will not be short of passion.

TAURUS – AQUARIUS

It is possible that there may be some attraction between these two signs. They both appreciate the value of hard work and if they can respect each other's independence then this relationship should work very well. It is very important that Taurus doesn't preach to Aquarius, because this will quickly lead to an argument. Instead, Taurus should accept the Aquarian's individual view of the world. However, Aquarius will find it almost impossible to understand, let alone appreciate, the material requirements of Taurus: whilst idealistic Aquarius is trying to change the world and bring everlasting peace, materialistic Taurus will be revising the household budget or scrutinizing the monthly cash-flow situation.

TAURUS – PISCES

On the whole, this is a good relationship. There is a considerable amount of sympathy between these two signs and they will understand the true nature of each other's feelings. Pisces often floats away, and will appreciate the stable influence that Taurus can provide. At the same time, Pisces will not be unduly upset by the Taurean arrogant and autocratic excesses. Pisceans can slowly exert their calming influence on Taureans. Indeed, it won't be long before they have Taurus eating out of their hands. However, Taurus will have to accept the fears and vulnerability of Pisces, and take time to understand just how important their feelings and emotions are. Pisces in turn must accept that the most important thing to Taurus is stability and security. Once this has been established, the long-term potential of this relationship is second to none.

GEMINI – GEMINI

This combination could be very fruitful: the two twins will have plenty to say to each other and there will rarely be a boring moment. They will feed off each other's intellects, and as a result this could turn into something of a mutual admiration society. Although there's nothing wrong with that, when it comes to taking the initiative, there could be problems. Both Geminis will have long discussions about what should be done, but unless someone else comes along to give them a push nothing much is likely to happen. From a romantic point of view, there may also be problems. Geminis can relate at many levels to each other, but when it comes to deeper feelings they are likely to draw a blank.

GEMINI – CANCER

Gemini and Cancer have a fundamentally different view of the world. On the surface they should both be able to get on, but as the relationship gets close, they are likely to find that they cannot understand each other's moral codes. Cancer is very protective and concerned by domestic issues. Gemini doesn't really understand this and is unsympathetic to Cancer's need for security. At the same time, Gemini may find the Cancerian moodiness rather hard to handle. In terms of love, this relationship is only likely to work if Gemini is unusually considerate and Cancer is very assertive. From a business point of view, this could be a mutually satisfying partnership, as long as Cancer takes care of the books and Gemini comes up with the ideas.

GEMINI – LEO

One of the better zodiacal relationships. Gemini and Leo are two highly compatible signs. They don't threaten each other and they find it very easy to communicate. Gemini finds Leo interesting, while Leo is flattered by the attention that Gemini is prepared to give. The natural warmth that Leos generate makes Geminis feel alive, and this helps them to lose their nervousness. This in turn allows Geminis to express the true depths of their feelings and passions, so romantic harmony between these two signs is a very real possibility. The only drawback is the Leo tendency to be overly dramatic and, at times, exceptionally selfish and tactless. While Geminis can deal with this on an objective level, they may not want to live with it.

GEMINI – VIRGO

Gemini and Virgo tend to get on quite well. They are both very analytical signs, and together they are good at discussing details. This match is particularly good for business partners. Gemini will have the ideas, whilst Virgo will have the organizational skills to put them into practice. However, this relationship does have some disadvantages: Gemini's rather erratic behaviour can drive Virgo round the bend; while Virgo's over-obsession with petty details can bore Gemini to tears. From a romantic point of view, this relationship may be short on intensity and passion, but Virgo is a natural lover and can teach Gemini a thing or two.

GEMINI – LIBRA

An excellent relationship. Gemini and Libra are both Air signs and, as such, they are very rational. They are both prepared to talk their problems through and it is very unlikely that the two signs will come to blows. Both Gemini and Libra are interested in people, and together they will be able to hold wonderful parties. Indeed, both signs work best when they are in a social environment. When they are alone together things can be just a bit too easy. While they won't run out of things to say, they may both feel that there is a missing spark, which can only be provided by interaction with lots of other people. In business, this may not be an ideal partnership. Although the social side of things will swing, the more practical side could be severely neglected.

GEMINI – SCORPIO

At first sight, you wouldn't have thought that this was a particularly good match. Gemini is all talk and Scorpio is all passion, so what have they got in common? Scorpio and Gemini certainly are very different signs, and occasionally you will find Scorpios who declare their undying hatred for all Geminis. However, most Scorpios seem to get on okay with Geminis. This is because Gemini has a healthy respect for Scorpio and knows exactly how to behave in his or her presence. Indeed, it could be said that Geminis are the only people who can pick up Scorpio with their bare hands – although no one quite knows whether this is because they can avoid getting stung, or because they enjoy getting stung!

GEMINI – SAGITTARIUS

Gemini and Sagittarius are opposite signs. As such, there is a definite attraction between the two. Geminis can live too much in their heads, and need the Sagittarius energy and spontaneity to get them going. At the same time, Sagittarians can appreciate Gemini logic, which can prevent them from rushing into dangerous situations without thinking. When it comes to romance, this is an excellent combination. Sagittarius finds the Gemini reserve irresistible and once they get going they are able to defreeze all Gemini's pent-up feelings. When it comes to more practical and everyday routines, neither sign will like getting down to it: Sagittarius wants to go for a run and Gemini has a good book to read.

GEMINI – CAPRICORN

These two signs don't have much in common. Gemini's quick-silver brain may find Capricorn's approach to life rather plod-ding, while the serious Capricorn may regard Gemini as being too superficial. However, it is well worth these two making an effort to get on with each other, particularly if they are potential business partners. Gemini has the flexibility, while Capricorn has the strategy. If they put their two brains together there isn't much that they can't achieve. Romantically speaking, however, this relationship may be a bit slow off the ground, and both partners will have to be very patient if they wish to create a true and lasting bond.

GEMINI – AQUARIUS

On the surface, this is a very good relationship. Both signs have plenty of ideas and they should appreciate each other's exciting intellect. However, this is not always the case. Both signs also have an arrogant streak, which they tend to bring out in each other. They often find each other's ideas unaccept-able, and the relationship may then degenerate into a rather boring and protracted argument. It is, therefore, vital that both people are able to agree to disagree. Once that has hap-pened, the relationship can move on and, if appropriate, love may eventually be able to blossom. However, passion may be lacking, since both of them prefer to talk endlessly and discuss their feelings, rather than get stuck in!

GEMINI – PISCES

This is a very easy-going relationship. Gemini and Pisces are tolerant of each other's foibles and are able to relate on many different levels. Gemini can show Pisces the importance of clear thinking, while Pisces can introduce Gemini to the subtleties of emotional interaction. However, at times this relationship will get a bit chaotic. Gemini and Pisces can both be very unreliable time-keepers, so if the two signs are fixing up a date they should double-check that they've got the details right. Nevertheless, the two of them will eventually muddle through and then, if they can both be at the right place at the right time, romance is a distinct possibility.

CANCER – CANCER

In some ways this is a very good match. The two Cancerians will have a natural understanding of each other and on an emotional level there will be total rapport, almost bordering on the telepathic. From a romantic point of view, this is likely to be an enduring relationship. Two Cancerians who are married to each other will be putting an enormous amount of energy into the creation of a secure home-base, and their children will want for nothing. However, two Cancerians in a business partnership may run into problems. Neither will be prepared to take a risk and as a result their business may never get past the concept phase.

CANCER – LEO

This relationship might work. Cancer will give the Leo partner plenty of attention, which will of course go down very well. However, Leos like as much attention as possible, from as many different sources as possible. Cancer people might then get very jealous if their partner is the centre of other people's attention. Another problem that might crop up is the Cancer moodiness. Leo will not tolerate it, let alone understand it, and may feel that Cancer's over-emotionality is getting in the way of the serious business of having fun. If Cancer can accept that Leo likes to have space and freedom, as well as being king of the castle, and if Leo can accept that his tactlessness and bluntness is unacceptable to the crab – and they can both compromise on certain issues – then this relationship has a lot going for it.

CANCER – VIRGO

An excellent combination. Cancer and Virgo are on the same wavelength, and their priorities tend to be similar. They are looking for security, peace and quiet. The highly strung Virgo can benefit from the soothing emotionality of Cancer. Better still, Cancer will be sensitive to Virgo's obsession with health and fitness. Cancer will happily dispense the vitamin pills, aspirins and herbal teas which are part of Virgo's staple diet. In return, the Virgoan will happily go through the Cancer's accounts and reassure him or her that nothing is amiss. Cancer people are consistently supportive and helpful and, notwithstanding the occasional jealous fit and tantrum, prove themselves to be worthy partners in the long term.

CANCER – LIBRA

Cancer and Libra often bump into each other. They feel that they have a lot in common, although they are not quite sure what. Together they experiment with many different activities, hoping that they'll find the one that they both enjoy. However, it may be a vain search, unless they are both adventurous enough to try water sports which involve balance. Yes, water-skiing and windsurfing are activities which Cancer and Libra can share and enjoy. So, if Cancer and Libra have just married and want a good honeymoon destination to cement the relationship, they would be advised to go to either Malibu or Hawaii. Nevertheless, their approach to life generally is quite different: Cancer's priority is the family and those closest and he or she needs deep, close emotional commitment; Libra enjoys wide contact with a large social group, and needs plenty of space and freedom. This could cause a serious conflict.

CANCER – SCORPIO

An absolutely superb relationship, which is very unlikely to go wrong. Scorpios can at times be a little intense for their own good, and will find the reassuring stability that only Cancer can provide, to be a godsend. Scorpios can get so worked up about their own inner worries that the practical details of life, such as eating and sleeping, get forgotten. However, Cancer people can bring Scorpios down to earth and enable them to live a balanced and healthy life. From a romantic point of view, this is a brilliant match, as both partners are able to bring each other's secret passions to life. The major drawback is likely to be jealousy and insecurity on the part of Cancer. While Scorpio is a loyal and faithful person and gives no real reason for anxiety, Cancer is often beset by worries and lack of confidence. It will be up to Scorpio to be reassuring and understanding.

CANCER – SAGITTARIUS

This is not an obviously happy relationship. Cancer likes to stay at home, building a nest, while Sagittarius has to be on the move the whole time. As a result, the two signs are unlikely to see much of each other. When they do meet, there is likely to be some tension. Cancer is not going to be able to relate to the

Sagittarian restlessness, while Sagittarius will be upset by the moodiness of Cancer. The very definite space and independence requirements of Sagittarius will seriously clash with the more domestic and family needs of the crab. Cancer may wish to start a family at the same time that Sagittarius is planning the next long-distance safari. In a business partnership, the relationship might work, provided that Cancer is in charge of security and Sagittarius is responsible for overseas investments.

CANCER – CAPRICORN

As these two signs are opposite each other, there is bound to be some attraction. Both Cancer and Capricorn are down-to-earth people, who understand how important it is to be successful. They are both able to make plans for the future, and you won't catch either of them making careless mistakes. Capricorn can at times be a little dry and unemotional and can, therefore, benefit from the caring warmth of Cancer. At the same time, Cancer people tend to worry about financial security. However, with Capricorn partners they can rest assured that everything is taken care of. This is certainly a relationship which has the capacity for endurance and both signs will go out of their way to keep the relationship together.

CANCER – AQUARIUS

This is one of the most unlikely relationships possible: the signs Cancer and Aquarius have nothing in common. Cancer and Aquarius approach the world in very different ways and when they come together there is plenty of scope for disagreement. Aquarians have the reputation for being rather cold and detached; they don't like being closely tied to any one person. As such, they may find the Cancerian protectiveness and over-sentimentality too much to stomach. At the same time, Cancer might find Aquarius insensitive and callous. A great deal of compromise, broad-mindedness and tolerance will have to be offered on both sides if this combination has any hope of surviving long-term.

CANCER – PISCES

Cancer and Pisces find it easy to get on with one another. Cancer and Pisces are both Water signs, and this means that they are able to empathize with each other's feelings. Cancer and Pisces don't have to speak much to each other, because they find that feelings are a much more effective form of communication than words. The only possible problem in this relationship is that Pisces' scattiness may unsettle Cancer. When Pisces doesn't turn up to an appointment, Cancer will quickly start worrying, and imagining all sorts of terrible things. So, Pisces, be a bit more considerate! On the other hand, Pisces may get irritated by the clinginess and dependence of Cancer: a need to get away from the confines of the relationship may sweep through and completely take over the fish.

LEO – LEO

This combination may be too much. Both Leos will want to control the relationship and as a result there could be a power struggle. However, at least both signs are on the same wavelength. They both appreciate the importance of generous gestures and they will understand what makes each other tick. In a social environment it is important that both Leos stick together. That way they can soak up the praise and attention together, as a couple. Otherwise, they could end up competing for attention, which would be disastrous. However, any relationship between these two fiery signs, although short on realism, will certainly not be lacking in passion: what is lost materially will be gained emotionally.

LEO – VIRGO

Leo and Virgo have rather different attitudes. When Leos are given a present, they think it is a great gesture and are not too interested in what it is. After all, 'it's the thought that counts'. Virgos who are given a present are primarily interested in how much it cost and what its resale value is. Nonetheless, Leo and Virgo can get on. In their heart of hearts, Leos value Virgo's power of discrimination, while at the same time Virgo can learn the value of magnanimity and good grace from Leo. From a romantic point of view, this relationship can work, provided that Virgo doesn't ask too many questions, and that Leo is prepared to accommodate the tiresome habits and phobias that are typical of the average Virgo.

LEO – LIBRA

This is one the best zodiacal relationships possible. Leo and Libra get on very well with each other. There are no major causes of conflict, provided Libra realizes that Leo is a very special person who requires priority treatment. If Librans find their loyalties torn, Leo must always get first call. There is often a very powerful physical and mental attraction between these two signs, and in matters of love there is an unusually high degree of compatibility. The airy detachment and rationality of Libra blends superbly with the enthusiastic and creative fires of Leo, and together they can enjoy cultural pursuits and a hectic social life – provided that Libra never *ever* attempts to upstage the lion.

LEO – SCORPIO

Leo and Scorpio, despite their best efforts, don't get on particularly well. Leos like things to be nice and simple and find the Scorpio intensity hard to deal with. Leos often feel that their Scorpio partners are not taking them seriously enough, and, as a result, arguments ensue. At the same time, Scorpio may regard Leo as shallow and childish. The extravagance, pretentiousness and occasional hypocrisy of the lion is difficult for Scorpio to swallow. Although Scorpio admires the lion's imagination, wit and flair, domestic arrangements could be a nightmare. Leos in turn admire Scorpios, but the deep Scorpio waters tend to dampen, or even completely drench, their naïve enthusiasm and grand plans. Scorpio finds it easy to read Leo's mind and knows exactly how to manipulate him or her. At first, this may be fun, but eventually Scorpio gets bored and the lion gets angry!

LEO – SAGITTARIUS

Leo and Sagittarius are both Fire signs and, as such, they have a great deal in common. Both signs have a simple and direct view of the world and share the same spontaneous sense of fun. Their relationship is uncomplicated and there is no danger of their getting caught up in each other's power games. Leo and Sagittarius will share the same interests and their musical and artistic taste is likely to be compatible, so they will both enjoy outings to concerts, art galleries and the cinema. Romantically, this combination is excellent, and both partners will be able to enjoy a warm and passionate relationship.

LEO – CAPRICORN

At first sight, this is not a good match. Leo and Capricorn are very different and it would be hard to see them coming to any kind of agreement. However, in practice this relationship works well. Both signs see stability as very important and respect each other's sincerity. Capricorn's life can at times be a bit of a grind and he or she appreciates the Leo energy and enthusiasm. At the same time, Leo can benefit from Capricorn's earthy practicality. Capricorn will at least make sure that Leo gets out of bed in the morning, and Leo will try hard to inject some fun and laughter into the routine of the goat's life. Overall, a potentially fruitful combination, although much work is needed.

LEO – AQUARIUS

Leo and Aquarius are opposite signs, and opposite signs are often strongly attracted to each other. However, in this case it will be a more difficult match. Both signs find compromise difficult and so misunderstandings can simmer away for a considerable period of time. Leos and Aquarians both have strong beliefs, which they will not change under any circumstances. As a result, the two signs should avoid discussions about political, spiritual or philosophical matters. When it comes to romance, there is likely to be an initial attraction. However, as the relationship gets underway, certain fundamental incompatibilities are likely to make themselves felt.

LEO – PISCES

This relationship could work, if both sides are very tolerant of each other's idiosyncrasies. In particular, Pisces has to respect Leo's need for a reliable and appreciative partner. However, many Pisceans are secretly looking for a strong, larger-than-life person to sort out their life: Leos should, therefore, fit the bill. In terms of love, this is a good relationship. Pisces is easily dazzled by the lion's romantic gestures, while the lion is quickly caught in the web of passion and emotion that Pisces is so good at weaving. This combination of passionate Fire and emotional Water can work splendidly, but a distinct lack of realism and direction could be problematic, especially when it comes to household finances or business partnerships.

VIRGO – VIRGO

Two Virgos put together may drive each other round the bend! Their mutual obsession with detail is likely to spiral out of control and as a result it may be difficult for either to get anything done. Outsiders may regard their arguments as extraordinarily petty, although in a strange way the pair may enjoy these confrontations. Perhaps one of the greatest dangers of a relationship between two Virgos is that neither will take responsibility for their faults. Instead, they will blame each other. From a romantic point of view, there is certainly going to be a strong physical attraction. However, if the relationship is going to work, both Virgos will have to cultivate an enormous amount of tolerance.

VIRGO – LIBRA

This relationship is all about perfectionism. Virgo wants everything to be physically perfect, while Libra is more interested in a well-balanced social environment. If both Libra and Virgo are very organized, then this could be an excellent working partnership. Their business affairs will run smoothly and they will be brilliant when it comes to handling other people. This is a particularly good combination for running businesses involving the public, like catering, entertainment and public relations. When it comes to matters of love, this relationship may not work quite so well, because this combination is not very good for unlocking emotion and passion. However, the earthiness of Virgo will go a long way towards helping with this.

VIRGO – SCORPIO

Virgo and Scorpio get on very well. Although both signs are aware of each other's faults, they seem to tolerate them. One of the things that Scorpio and Virgo have in common is that they do not suffer fools gladly. Rather than direct their critical faculties at each other, they tend to concentrate on the people around them, so Virgo and Scorpio can spend happy hours talking about how awful their friends and enemies are. Romantically, this is a very good combination. Neither sign will rush into love, but as they get to know each other, the shoots of attachment will slowly grow. The watery nature of Scorpio will fertilize the Virgo soil, which in turn provides a solid base upon which the relationship can develop.

VIRGO – SAGITTARIUS

This is probably one of the more difficult zodiacal relationships: Virgo practicality and caution does not mix easily with Sagittarian impulsiveness and daring. Virgo and Sagittarius have very different priorities and may end up by seriously annoying each other. The caustic Virgo wit will come face to face with dynamic Sagittarian tactlessness. While this combination may work if both signs pair up as a vicious comedy duo, under most circumstances it should be avoided. There may be some irrational sexual attraction between Virgo and Sagittarius. However, this relationship should only be pursued after considerable deliberation.

VIRGO – CAPRICORN

Virgo and Capricorn are both Earth signs, and this means that they have a great deal in common. Both Virgo and Capricorn are very practical people and together they are unlikely to make many mistakes. Capricorn will appreciate Virgo's second opinions, while Virgo will be reassured by Capricorn's calm self-confidence. In terms of business partnerships this is one of the best zodiacal relationships. Romantically, it is unlikely to be exciting. However, it will be stable and will make an excellent base for the establishment of a home and a family. Since a need for stability and security is a fundamental requirement of both parties, there is little possibility that either person will mess around, unless of course, the relationship becomes intolerable.

VIRGO – AQUARIUS

At first sight, this is rather an unlikely coupling. Virgo and Aquarius are very different signs and it is doubtful that they would have much in common. However, there is some resemblance between the two: both have a callous streak, as well as a sharp tongue. They are not too concerned with sentimental niceties; they are far more interested in material substance. Both Virgo and Aquarius have a similar value system, which other, more sensitive signs may find a bit distasteful. When it comes to love, they are attracted to each other, and this relationship could work. However, neither sign will be above exploiting the other's weaknesses, particularly where money is involved.

VIRGO – PISCES

Virgo and Pisces are opposite signs. In astrology this often means that they find each other compelling. Virgo is longing to let go of all his or her worries and concerns and Pisces is a perfect example of a person who can drift and wander as he or she pleases. However, Pisces people sometimes feel that their chaos is a bit too much of a good thing and can then find Virgo's organizational ability absolutely fascinating. If Virgo and Pisces form a relationship they often copy each other. Virgo will become increasingly chaotic, while Pisces will become increasingly organized. Whether or not this is a good thing is questionable. Fundamentally, they have much in common emotionally, and many sound relationships are to be found between these two signs.

LIBRA – LIBRA

Librans get on well together and certainly seem to understand each other. They are likely to be offended by the same things and they have a similar sense of beauty. Often a truly harmonious relationship, there is, however, a danger that one or both Librans will play power games with each other. They may know each other too well and exploit one another's weaknesses. Alternatively, one Libran may manipulate the other Libran into being a fall-guy for his or her plans. In marriage, the potential is excellent and although home and family may not be top of their list of priorities, a lot of time will be spent having fun, socializing, travelling and generally getting to know the four corners of the earth.

LIBRA – SCORPIO

On the surface, this is not an easy relationship. The endless flitting and flirting of Libra may really wind Scorpio up. It will all be a bit too insincere and frivolous for the fixed intensity of Scorpio. Scorpios find it hard to understand the superficiality of this Air sign, and will eventually discover that

Librans don't operate on a deep enough level when it comes to their emotions and deepest feelings. Libra, being a civilized person who likes to talk things out, may be freaked out by the brooding emotion which is so characteristic of Scorpio. An enormous amount of compromise and tolerance will be needed here, and it may well be that with the passage of time, each will discover a more compatible partner.

LIBRA – SAGITTARIUS

On the whole, a very good relationship. Some Librans may be a bit concerned by the tactlessness of Sagittarius, although a disruptive Libra will be positively enthralled by his fiery irreverence. Libra wit and Sagittarius bravado is an exciting combination, and almost guaranteed to get any party going. Romantically, there is much in common – the fiery nature of Sagittarius burns rapidly in the air of Libra, and any relationship will be quick to get off the ground. Neither sign is cautious, and will not hesitate to take the plunge if there is enough excitement and stimulation on offer. Businesswise, there may be too much movement and too little grounding, which could have serious long-term consequences.

LIBRA – CAPRICORN

There is a definite fascination between Libra and Capricorn. They may feel an affinity with each other – that both want the same things out of life. Both like getting ahead by manipulating their environment, though at the end of the day they may both realize that their priorities are ultimately different. While Librans want to accept their vision of the world, and are particularly appreciative of former enemies who have 'seen the light', Capricorns prefer using people to destroy each other. So Libra may betray a confidence as part of a game, whilst Capricorn will do this to remove a rival. Love-wise, the embers of desire will smoulder slowly and grand passion is unlikely.

LIBRA – AQUARIUS

Libra and Aquarius have a lot to say to each other and they may find that their ideas are very similar. An example of such a relationship was between Libra Margaret Thatcher and Aquarius Ronald Reagan. They cemented a 'special' relationship between Britain and the US, based on common ideals. In some cases, although certainly not with Reagan and Thatcher, Aquarius may find Libra a little too superficial, particularly when Libra changes his or her ideas for social reasons. Romantically, the Libra – Aquarius relationship may never quite take off, but if it does it will have excellent endurance capabilities, and each person will find the other appreciative and supportive.

LIBRA – PISCES

An interesting combination, as both Libra and Pisces are good at adapting. However, Libra adapts with his or her mind and Pisces adapts with his or her feelings, and at the end of the day this may create a conflict of purpose. Libra may be rather overwhelmed by the tide of emotion that Pisces can generate, and it may be that Pisces is able to confuse and upset Libra's very fine sense of equilibrium. However, a manipulative Libra might well be able to ensnare Pisces in one of his or her many power games. An interesting Libra – Pisces combination was Margaret Thatcher and Pisces Mikhail Gorbachev. He certainly managed to charm the British Prime Minister, and she was the first Western leader who recognized that he was a man who 'we could do business with'.

SCORPIO – SCORPIO

A perfect relationship. After all, the only people who truly understand Scorpios are other Scorpios. Scorpios appreciate that not everything has to be spoken and they can, therefore, understand each other's silences. The Scorpio – Scorpio relationship is likely to be one of the most intense and passionate combinations possible, and if the vast amounts of feeling generated by the relationship can be managed and controlled, then the prospects look excellent. The only drawbacks could be stubborness and inflexibility. Both people will always believe they are right, and it may be impossible to introduce the right amount of flexibility and moderation into this rather extreme combination.

SCORPIO – SAGITTARIUS

On the surface, not an easy relationship. The loud tactlessness of Sagittarius may offend the sensitivities of Scorpio, and Scorpio may find the Sagittarian's relentless quest for action a bit too much. Sagittarius may find the silence of Scorpio rather daunting, and may be unsure how to inject life into the relationship. On the other hand, they both have a lot to give each other: Scorpios appreciate the way in which Sagittarians can get them out of their shell; at the same time, Scorpios can teach Sagittarians a lot about the value of reserve. This could be a learning relationship, but after the lessons have been passed, both parties may graduate on to more suitable partners.

SCORPIO – CAPRICORN

Scorpio and Capricorn are both quite reserved, so they are not likely to offend each other too much. This is a very civilized combination and, moreover, an excellent combination for getting things done. Capricorn business acumen and Scorpio finely tuned intuition should work very well together, and together they will be able to accomplish great things. However, the relationship may lack passion – at least from Scorpio's point of view. And it is possible that Capricorn may not quite understand the depths to which the Scorpionic emotion can reach, and may unwittingly hurt or offend Scorpio, which could subsequently lead to difficulties in the relationship. However, this is a compatible combination, and the chance of a lasting attachment developing is very high.

SCORPIO – AQUARIUS

There is certainly a degree of fascination between Scorpio and Aquarius and, on the whole, they will respect each other's deeply held beliefs. However, Aquarius may be irritated by Scorpio's reluctance to discuss his or her feelings. On the other hand, Scorpio may find Aquarius a bit on the cold side and be unable to comprehend the austere, detached and often clinical approach that Aquarius offers when trying to understand emotional or personal problems. As both signs are very fixed in their beliefs they could get dead-locked. Even so, both are humanitarian and compassionate people and will do extremely well together in business, or in work where charitable causes are concerned.

SCORPIO – PISCES

A very good combination. If anyone is going to suss out a Scorpio it is going to be a Pisces. Both Scorpio and Pisces understand the true value of feelings and will be able to give each other a great deal of emotional support. The main danger with this relationship is that the feelings of Scorpio and Pisces may get mixed up with each other, with the result that the relationship gets a bit chaotic; a solid grounding really is a most definite requirement. Too much emotion, not enough practicality and, in many cases, a distinct lack of positive action or optimism could be another drawback, although the exceptional compatibility between these two people is likely to compensate for this.

SAGITTARIUS – SAGITTARIUS

Sagittarius is one of the more difficult signs to typecast: no two Sagittarians are ever quite the same. They will have the same basic drive, but the emphasis will always be slightly different. And, as a result of this, Sagittarians are not always going to get on that well together. One of them will be stronger and more outrageous and this could cause friction and rivalry. However, if two Sagittarians do find that they get on and that they are on the same wavelength, then it could be a very exciting relationship. Sports and outdoor activities will be the common ground, but a restlessness and unwillingness to commit could work for or against this relationship. Much depends on the respective ages and on other horosocope factors

SAGITTARIUS – CAPRICORN

Probably not the easiest of relationships. Capricorn might regard Sagittarius as silly and frivolous, while Sagittarius will see Capricorn as rather boring and uninspired. Sagittarius needs people who can keep the buzz going, and your average Capricorn is not going to be the life and soul of the party. Indeed, Sagittarius may find Capricorn to be a little on the depressing side. But pity poor Capricorns! They like to go about life in a slow and methodical way, and the unpredictability of Sagittarius is surely going to be quite upsetting at times.

However, if the Sagittarian initiative, creativity and imagination can be harnessed by Capricorn and used in practical, organized ways, this partnership has a lot going for it on a business level.

SAGITTARIUS – AQUARIUS

A very constructive relationship. Each one is going to give the other what he or she doesn't have. Aquarians can get a bit set in their ways, and do need the occasional jolt to show them that there is more to life than their rigid little ideas. Sagittarians certainly know how to give that jolt, although they should of course watch that they don't push Aquarius too far. However, Aquarians will probably keep their cool under the Sagittarian onslaught, which may force them to stand back and question their whole strategy. As well as being compatible as far as day-to-day interests and long-term goals are concerned, this is also a highly compatible partnership on an emotional level, which can only be good news!

SAGITTARIUS – PISCES

Something quite undefinable happens when Sagittarius meets Pisces: for one thing, there is a kind of attraction, and perhaps both may feel that they have met their match. Both know about change and both are capable of extreme unreliability. Pisceans may be able to mould themselves to every passing initiative of Sagittarians, which the latter may find quite infuriating – because they find it difficult to get a positive reaction out of Pisces! However, a strong Pisces will be able to handle Sagittarius, providing the support and understanding which may be lacking in other signs.

CAPRICORN – CAPRICORN

A very cool relationship. From a business point of view, it is probably quite good, at least from an administrative angle. However, there may be a certain lack of imagination in this combination. Two Capricorns won't get too excited about anything and as a result they might get into a creative and inspirational rut. Although they will see each other's point of view, from a romantic perspective, this may not be the most passionate of relationships: one thinks it would be more of a marriage of convenience. However, since Capricorn is an Earth sign and is both fertile and productive, there is Every reason to believe that in the fullness of time a close union may develop, which could survive the traumas of modern life quite easily.

CAPRICORN – AQUARIUS

Another cool affair. Neither Capricorns nor Aquarians are noted for their passion, although this should make a good business relationship. Aquarius has the ideas and Capricorn has the organizing ability, so they will be able to get things done in quite a cold and ruthless way. Capricorn – Aquarius is not a particularly emotional combination, and romantically there may be similar problems as with Capricorn – Capricorn: little real understanding or rapport, and consequently little intimacy and emotional exchange. Though perhaps this time Aquarius might see Capricorn as being a little dull, and Capricorn might regard Aquarius as a bit too idealistic.

CAPRICORN – PISCES

With a bit of work on both sides, this relationship should work very well. Pisces can be a bit out of control at times, and drift off on cloud nine; the Capricorn sense of reality could provide a useful anchor. At the same time, the emotions of Pisces may be a new experience for the goat, and perhaps Pisces can help Capricorn let go of all that locked-up feeling. However, if one or both sides are not prepared to change, it could be difficult. Capricorn might find the Piscean untogetherness intolerable, and Pisces may not be able to handle the cold unresponsiveness of his Capricorn partner.

AQUARIUS – AQUARIUS

Aquarians do have a certain understanding of each other, although an Aquarian relationship could become a bit of a mutual admiration society. After all, they can inspire each other with their brilliant ideas. The most important thing about the Aquarius – Aquarius relationship is that neither partner will get in the other's way – they will respect each other's space. It may not be the most wonderfully emotional of relationships, but then the cooler Aquarians do see feelings as being rather crude and uncivilized. Aquarians particularly dislike displays of emotional intensity, and generally prefer partners or lovers who respond in the same detached and objective fashion as themselves.

AQUARIUS – PISCES

Not at first sight the easiest of relationships, although clever Pisceans, who have learnt to intuitively understand what makes their partners tick, may be able to make it work. Aquarius Ronald Reagan and Pisces Gorbachev seemed to get on well – so much so, that together they ended the Cold War and removed the threat of global annihilation. If Aquarius can show Pisces the value of detachment, and stop Pisces from getting over-involved emotionally, and if in turn Pisces can dissolve some of the Aquarian reservations, then this relationship could work well. But usually it will be a bit of a struggle.

PISCES – PISCES

Two Pisces together is quite a thought! From an emotional point of view, this should be one of the ultimate relationships, and it is likely that their two identities will merge. They will feel each other's feelings and know what each other is thinking. It is probable that one of the two Pisces is going to be of the organized, businesslike type, because otherwise they would never get anything done. The Pisces – Pisces relationship may well have a spiritual touch to it, and it is possible that one or both partners will believe that they knew each other in a previous incarnation.

....

THE PLANETS

5. THE PLANETS IN THE SKY

We have now taken a detailed look at Sun signs (often referred to as star signs – the signs you read in your daily paper).

As you have seen, the sign which the Sun is placed in at birth gives us a lot of information about the personality. It tells us about people's aims and ambitions, about their romantic potential and even about commonly occurring events in their lives. However, the Sun is not the whole story. There are other planets in the solar system, and if you want to give a really accurate reading of someone's horoscope, you will have to take these into account as well.

Apart from the Earth, there are eight planets which revolve around the Sun: Mercury, Venus, Mars, Jupiter, Saturn, Uranus, Neptune and Pluto. All of these planets are used by astrologers to describe the personality and to make predictions. As well as the planets, astrologers also take note of the Moon, a body which revolves around the Earth. Technically speaking, the Moon is a satellite of the Earth, rather than a planet. However, for convenience's sake, we will in future be grouping it with the rest of the planets.

Each of the planets represents a different part of the

personality. For example, Venus represents the way we relate to other people, while Mercury represents the way we communicate. By looking at the position of all the planets at the moment of birth, we can get a precise picture of how the different parts of the personality work. So, if you were looking at someone's horoscope, and this person was particularly concerned about relationships, you would immediately home in on the position of Venus.

When we talk about the position of the planets in the horoscope, we are talking about the sign and house position. As we explained in Chapter One, the position of each planet in your horoscope is determined at the time of your birth. To use the example of the roulette wheel once again: when the wheel stops spinning, the ball falls in a certain sector of the wheel and on a certain number. The same thing happens in the horoscope.

At the moment of birth, the planets (Sun, Moon, Mercury, Venus, Mars, Jupiter, Saturn, Uranus, Neptune and Pluto) fall in a certain sector of the wheel (the house of the horoscope) and on a certain number (the sign of the zodiac). This is where they stay. They form the horoscope which astrologers use throughout life as a base for their predictions and character analyses. The signs are: Aries, Taurus, Gemini, Cancer, Leo, Virgo, Libra, Scorpio, Sagittarius, Capricorn, Aquarius and Pisces. The houses are: first house, second house, third house, fourth house, fifth house, sixth house, seventh house, eighth house, ninth house, tenth house, eleventh house, twelfth house.

As you can see, each individual horoscope for each different person is very different. The chances of having a horoscope exactly the same as another person's, with each planet in exactly the same sector of the horoscope and in the same zodiacal sign, are not that high. Unless, of course, two people are born at exactly the same time and place as each other, in which case, all the planets have fallen in the same sector and on the same number of that roulette wheel. Later in the book you will be finding out about houses. For the moment, we are just going to stick to signs.

Although all the planets travel through the twelve signs of the zodiac continuously, around and around the belt of the zodiac, it is their position in the sky when we were born – at that precise moment – which determines our character and destiny. As you will soon see, these sign positions have a profound effect on our personalities. Before we do anything else, we must show you how to discover them.

DISCOVERING THE SIGN POSITIONS OF THE PLANETS

Example: Jimi Hendrix, the great American guitarist. His planets were positioned in the following signs:

Date of birth: 27 November 1942, in Seattle, USA

Planet	Sign
Sun	Sagittarius
Moon	Cancer
Mercury	Sagittarius
Venus	Sagittarius
Mars	Scorpio
Jupiter	Cancer
Saturn	Gemini

INTERPRETING THE SIGN POSITIONS OF THE PLANETS

In the following few chapters (Six to Twelve) we give a detailed description of each of the planets, followed by interpretations of their meanings when they are positioned in each sign of the zodiac.

The meanings of the Sun signs have already been given in Chapter Two. In other words, the meanings that we give to the Sun when it falls in each different sign of the zodiac. We have described the Sun signs in a separate section because these are the signs with which most people are familiar. The Sun sign is the same as your star sign, the sign that you read in your daily paper.

As for the planets Uranus, Neptune and Pluto – they are grouped together in Chapter Twelve. They are less important than the other seven planets and their meanings apply more to large groups or generations of people, than to individuals, because Uranus, Neptune and Pluto move very slowly. Uranus stays in the same sign for seven years, Neptune for about thirteen years and Pluto for even longer. To take an example: nearly everyone born between 1956 and 1971 had their Pluto in Virgo! So the sign position of Uranus, Neptune and Pluto affects a whole generation, rather than the individual.

Jimi Hendrix

We will now continue with the example of Jimi Hendrix, and explore his Venus in Sagittarius.

First, have a look at Chapter Eight on Venus. Read the description of the planet at the beginning. You will see that this description doesn't just tell us about the way people relate to one another, it also tells us about a person's sense of beauty, art, clothes and sometimes appearance. In the horoscope of a man, Venus often describes the sort of woman he is attracted to.

Everyone has Venus in their horoscope. This means that everyone has a way of relating and an attitude to clothes and beauty. However it is the *sign position* of Venus which describes the particular *way* in which an individual relates, as well as their particular attitude to clothes and beauty.

Have a look at the section of Chapter Eight which covers the various sign placements. Go down to the entry on Venus in Sagittarius. You will see that this is a very exciting position. People with Venus in Sagittarius want to relate to people who can provide them with new horizons. This was no doubt reflected in Jimi Hendrix's attitude to his social life. Although this entry does not say anything specific about art, you can pick out certain key words, like 'exciting', 'unpredictable' and 'exotic'. Having done that, you can use these words to describe the art that he would be interested in, as well as the music that he produced.

Let's look at another planet in Jimi Hendrix's horoscope. He had Mars in Scorpio. Mars is the planet of assertion and aggression. Everyone asserts themselves somehow – however well or badly. The sign position of Mars will tell you precisely *how* an individual asserts himself. As you can see from Chapter Nine on Mars, Scorpio is a very powerful sign for Mars to be in. Jimi Hendrix would have been someone who asserted himself well, and who usually got what he wanted. As Mars rules male sexuality, one would have expected many women to find his sheer intensity to be magnetically attractive.

Now that you have looked at a couple of planets in a famous person's horoscope, work out the sign positions of your own planets. You can then look up the meanings of these positions. We sincerely hope that you will be encouraged and inspired by these meanings and that they will help you to tune into your true potential. Don't worry if some of the descriptions are a little negative. We all have our weak spots, and once we are aware of them we can take active measures to avoid their pitfalls.

6. THE MOON

The Moon is nearly as important as the Sun. It describes the emotions and the way we instinctively respond to new situations. The Moon is also connected to the past and to memories of the past. Women tend to become more like their Moon sign and less like their Sun sign as they grow older and more mature.

When assessing someone's character, the importance of the Moon should never be underestimated. The Moon's position describes a person's physical magnetism, creativity, imagination, and often the way in which a person deals with the public. It represents our emotions, our spontaneous reactions, our moods, loves, hates and fears. Ancient astrologers assigned great importance to the Moon: coins from the reign of Emperor Augustus depict a goat (the symbol of Capricorn). Capricorn was his Moon sign, indicating that the Romans were more interested in Moon signs than Sun signs.

The Moon influences many aspects of our lives. The tides

are affected by the magnetic pull of the Moon on the Earth, and meteorologists take its position into account when predicting certain weather conditions. Because the Moon takes a month to complete its cycle, it is often connected with women's cycle of menstruation. From a medical point of view, it is often considered dangerous to have an operation at the time of a Full Moon, because the body bleeds more. It has also been suggested that the Full Moon coincides with increased admissions to psychiatric wards. So, all things considered it is not surprising that the Moon plays a crucial role in determining our character and our destiny.

The Family and Childhood: If you want to know about someone's childhood and their family background, it is essential to look at the Moon. However, you must be careful. If you delve deeply into the Moon's position, you could dig up some very sensitive information, which needs to be treated with tact and discretion.

Social Life: The Moon is often associated with the way people respond to social situations. By looking at the Moon's placing you can tell how spontaneous and how confident people feel in a crowd. There is little doubt that to deal effectively with the public you do need a strong, well-placed Moon.

Relationships: It is often said that what men want in a relationship is a mother, rather than a wife or girlfriend. In astrology, the Moon in a man's horoscope represents both his mother and his ideal woman. So a man with Moon in Virgo, as we shall see, may expect his wife to be just as well-organized as his mother.

FINDING YOUR MOON SIGN

Finding your Moon sign is very easy. All you have to do is follow three simple steps. We'll use the example of Princess

Diana to show you how it is done. As we go through the three steps for Princess Diana, apply each step to yourself, so that you can find your own personal Moon sign.

Step One

In this step it is necessary to find the Moon number. If you look at the Moon number table (table 1), you will see that all the days of the year are listed. Look up your birth date on this table, and then read off the Moon number for that date.

Princess Diana was born on 1 July 1961. If we look down the Moon number table, we see that the number next to both 1 and 2 July is 9. So we know that Princess Diana's Moon number is 9. It doesn't matter about the year of birth when looking at the Moon number table. If Princess Diana had been born on 1 July in any other year, her Moon number would still have been 9.

Just to get you into practice, look up the Moon number of someone born on 5 December. You will find it is 6. Now, look up your own Moon number.

Step Two

Now that you know your Moon number, turn to the Moon sign table (table 2). On the left of the table there is the heading 'Birth Year'. You will see that the different years of the twentieth century are divided up into birth year groups, ranging from group 1, which contains 1900, 1919, 1938, 1957, 1976 and 1995, to group 19, which contains 1918, 1937, 1956, 1975, and 1994. You have to find your year of birth, so look through the groups and see which one contains your year. For example, Princess Diana was born in 1961. You will find that 1961 is in group 5.

You will have no difficulty finding your birth year group. However, to make it even easier for you, we have divided the years into three columns. Years between 1900 and 1937 are in the first, left-hand column, those between 1938 and 1975 are in the second, middle column, and years from 1976 onwards are in the third column, which is the right-hand one.

Since 1961 is between 1938 and 1975, we know that Princess Diana's birth year will be found in column 2.

We hope you have now found out your birth year group. Before we move on to the final step, look up the birth year group for someone born in 1932.

1932 is in column 1 and is in group 14.

Step Three

You now know your Moon number and your birth year group. You can now look up your Moon sign. You will see that each group has twelve signs attached to it. To save space, we have written out the first three letters of each sign. You will find a key to these abbreviations on page xiv. If your Moon number is 1, then the first sign on the left will be your Moon sign. If your Moon number is 2, then the second sign from the left will be your Moon sign, and so on.

Let's have a look at group 1. If someone's birth year group is group 1 and their Moon number is 1, then their Moon sign will be Capricorn (Cap). Princess Diana's Moon number is 9 and her birth year group is 5. Look down to group 5, and then read off the ninth sign. You will see that the table says 'Aqu' (Aquarius). So Princess Diana's Moon is in Aquarius.

You can now find your own Moon sign, without effort or tears. Remember:

1. Find your Moon number on the Moon number table.
2. Find your birth year group on the Moon sign table.
3. Then read across the signs given for your birth year group, until you find the one which matches up with your Moon number.

Just to be absolutely sure, let's try one more example: what is the Moon sign of someone born on 5 May 1987? First, look

Table 1 **Moon Number Table**

Jan			Apr		
	1, 2	1		1, 2	5
	3, 4	2		3, 4	6
	5, 6	3		5, 6	7
	7, 8	4		7, 8	8
	9, 10	5		9, 10, 11	9
	11, 12	6		12, 13	10
	13, 14	7		14, 15, 16	11
	15, 16, 17	8		17, 18	12
	18, 19	9		19, 20, 21	1
	20, 21	10		22, 23	2
	22, 23, 24	11		24, 25	3
	25, 26	12		26, 27, 28	4
	27, 28, 29	1		29, 30	5
	30, 31	2			

Feb			May		
	1, 2	3		1, 2	6
	3, 4	4		3, 4	7
	5, 6	5		5, 6	8
	7, 8	6		7, 8	9
	9, 10, 11	7		9, 10	10
	12, 13	8		11, 12, 13	11
	14, 15	9		14, 15, 16	12
	16, 17, 18	10		17, 18	1
	19, 20	11		19, 20	2
	21, 22, 23	12		21, 22, 23	3
	24, 25	1		24, 25	4
	26, 27, 28	2		26, 27	5
	29	3		28, 29	6
				30, 31	7

Mar			June		
	1, 2	3		1, 2	8
	3, 4	4		3, 4	9
	5, 6	5		5, 6, 7	10
	7, 8	6		8, 9	11
	9, 10	7		10, 11, 12	12
	11, 12	8		13, 14	1
	13, 14	9		15, 16, 17	2
	15, 16, 17	10		18, 19	3
	18, 19	11		20, 21	4
	20, 21, 22	12		22, 23	5
	23, 24, 25	1		24, 25	6
	26, 27	2		26, 27	7
	28, 29	3		28, 29, 30	8
	30, 31	4			

Table 1 **Moon Number Table** contd

Jul				Oct		
	1, 2	9			1, 2	1
	3, 4	10			3, 4	2
	5, 6, 7	11			5, 6	3
	8, 9	12			7, 8, 9	4
	10, 11, 12	1			10, 11	5
	13, 14	2			12, 13	6
	15, 16	3			14, 15	7
	17, 18	4			16, 17	8
	19, 20	5			18, 19	9
	21, 22, 23	6			20, 21	10
	24, 25	7			22, 23, 24	11
	26, 27	8			25, 26	12
	28, 29	9			27, 28, 29	1
	30, 31	10			30, 31	2

Aug				Nov		
	1	10			1, 2, 3	3
	2, 3	11			4, 5	4
	4, 5, 6	12			6, 7	5
	7, 8	1			8, 9	6
	9, 10	2			10, 11	7
	11, 12, 13	3			12, 13	8
	14, 15	4			14, 15	9
	16, 17	5			16, 17, 18	10
	18, 19	6			19, 20	11
	20, 21	7			21, 22, 23	12
	22, 23	8			24, 25	1
	24, 25	9			26, 27, 28	2
	26, 27, 28	10			29, 30	3
	29, 30	11				
	31	12				

Sept				Dec		
	1, 2	12			1, 2	4
	3, 4	1			3, 4	5
	5, 6, 7	2			5, 6	6
	8, 9	3			7, 8, 9	7
	10, 11	4			10, 11	8
	12, 13	5			12, 13	9
	14, 15	6			14, 15	10
	16, 17	7			16, 17	11
	18, 19	8			18, 19, 20	12
	20, 21, 22	9			21, 22	1
	23, 24	10			23, 24, 25	2
	25, 26, 27	11			26, 27	3
	28, 29	12			28, 29	4
	30	1			30, 31	5

Table 2 **Moon Sign Table**

	BIRTH YEAR			MOON NUMBER					
	Col. 1	Col. 2	Col. 3	1	2	3	4	5	6
Group 1	1900 – 1919	1938 – 1957	1976 – 1995	Cap	Aqu	Pis	Ari	Tau	Gem
Group 2	1901 – 1920	1939 – 1958	1977 – 1996	Tau	Gem	Can	Leo	Vir	Lib
Group 3	1902 – 1921	1940 – 1959	1978 – 1997	Lib	Sco	Sag	Cap	Aqu	Pis
Group 4	1903 – 1922	1941 – 1960	1979 – 1998	Aqu	Pis	Ari	Tau	Gem	Can
Group 5	1904 – 1923	1942 – 1961	1980 – 1999	Gem	Can	Leo	Vir	Lib	Sco
Group 6	1905 – 1924	1943 – 1962	1981	Sco	Sag	Cap	Aqu	Pis	Ari
Group 7	1906 – 1925	1944 – 1963	1982	Pis	Ari	Tau	Gem	Can	Leo
Group 8	1907 – 1926	1945 – 1964	1983	Leo	Vir	Lib	Sco	Sag	Cap
Group 9	1908 – 1927	1946 – 1965	1984	Sag	Cap	Aqu	Pis	Ari	Tau
Group 10	1909 – 1928	1947 – 1966	1985	Ari	Tau	Gem	Can	Leo	Vir
Group 11	1910 – 1929	1948 – 1967	1986	Vir	Lib	Sco	Sag	Cap	Aqu
Group 12	1911 – 1930	1949 – 1968	1987	Cap	Aqu	Pis	Ari	Tau	Gem
Group 13	1912 – 1931	1950 – 1969	1988	Gem	Can	Leo	Vir	Lib	Sco
Group 14	1913 – 1932	1951 – 1970	1989	Lib	Sco	Sag	Cap	Aqu	Pis
Group 15	1914 – 1933	1952 – 1971	1990	Pis	Ari	Tau	Gem	Can	Leo
Group 16	1915 – 1934	1953 – 1972	1991	Can	Leo	Vir	Lib	Sco	Sag
Group 17	1916 – 1935	1954 – 1973	1992	Sco	Sag	Cap	Aqu	Pis	Ari
Group 18	1917 – 1936	1955 – 1974	1993	Ari	Tau	Gem	Can	Leo	Vir
Group 19	1918 – 1937	1956 – 1975	1994	Leo	Vir	Lib	Sco	Sag	Cap

Table 2 **Moon Sign Table** contd

	BIRTH YEAR			MOON NUMBER					
	Col. 1	Col. 2	Col. 3	7	8	9	10	11	12
Group 1	1900 – 1919	1938 – 1957	1976 – 1995	Can	Leo	Vir	Lib	Sco	Sag
Group 2	1901 – 1920	1939 – 1958	1977 – 1996	Sco	Sag	Cap	Aqu	Pis	Ari
Group 3	1902 – 1921	1940 – 1959	1978 – 1997	Ari	Tau	Gem	Can	Leo	Vir
Group 4	1903 – 1922	1941 – 1960	1979 – 1998	Leo	Vir	Lib	Sco	Sag	Cap
Group 5	1904 – 1923	1942 – 1961	1980 – 1999	Sag	Cap	Aqu	Pis	Ari	Tau
Group 6	1905 – 1924	1943 – 1962	1981	Tau	Gem	Can	Leo	Vir	Lib
Group 7	1906 – 1925	1944 – 1963	1982	Vir	Lib	Sco	Sag	Cap	Aqu
Group 8	1907 – 1926	1945 – 1964	1983	Aqu	Pis	Ari	Tau	Gem	Can
Group 9	1908 – 1927	1946 – 1965	1984	Gem	Can	Leo	Vir	Lib	Sco
Group 10	1909 – 1928	1947 – 1966	1985	Lib	Sco	Sag	Cap	Aqu	Pis
Group 11	1910 – 1929	1948 – 1967	1986	Pis	Ari	Tau	Gem	Can	Leo
Group 12	1911 – 1930	1949 – 1968	1987	Can	Leo	Vir	Lib	Sco	Sag
Group 13	1912 – 1931	1950 – 1969	1988	Sag	Cap	Aqu	Pis	Ari	Tau
Group 14	1913 – 1932	1951 – 1970	1989	Ari	Tau	Gem	Can	Leo	Vir
Group 15	1914 – 1933	1952 – 1971	1990	Vir	Lib	Sco	Sag	Cap	Aqu
Group 16	1915 – 1934	1953 – 1972	1991	Cap	Aqu	Pis	Ari	Tau	Gem
Group 17	1916 – 1935	1954 – 1973	1992	Tau	Gem	Can	Leo	Vir	Lib
Group 18	1917 – 1936	1955 – 1974	1993	Lib	Sco	Sag	Cap	Aqu	Pis
Group 19	1918 – 1937	1956 – 1975	1994	Aqu	Pis	Ari	Tau	Gem	Can

at the Moon number table. The Moon number for 5 May is 8. Now look at the Moon sign table: the birth year group of 1987 is in group 12. Read across the signs of group 12, until you come to the eighth sign, which is Leo. Leo is the Moon sign for someone born on 5 May 1987.

THE MEANING OF THE MOON IN EACH SIGN OF THE ZODIAC

Moon in Aries (Idi Amin)

The Moon in Aries is often afraid of emotional confinement, and people who have this Moon position dislike other people telling them what to do. Moon in Aries people want to be free to express the full power of their emotions, regardless of the consequences. As a result they often say and do things which they later regret. Once they have decided that they want something, they want it immediately, and quickly get angry if anyone stands in their path. Overall, these people need to think before they act and try to cultivate the virtue of patience.

Moon in Taurus (Karl Marx)

This is a wonderful sign for the Moon to be in. The Moon in Taurus is very down-to-earth and has a natural appreciation of physical beauty. The senses are very important and these people have a refined sense of touch. People with this Moon position are generally at their best in the countryside, where they can see, smell and touch the beauty of nature. When relating to other people, body contact is very important, even if it is only the shake of a hand or a gentle kiss. It is through such contact that the Moon in Taurus tunes into someone's real personality.

Moon in Gemini (Benito Mussolini)

This is a very communicative position for the Moon to be in. People who have the Moon in Gemini are sociable, witty and great fun to be with. At the same time, they are likely to have excellent writing skills: indeed, many professional writers have their Moons in Gemini. Talking makes them feel emotionally comfortable and when they are unable to express themselves, they quickly become nervous. On the whole, the Moon in Gemini likes to keep conversation at a fairly light level and if other people start talking about difficult issues, the Moon will be quick to change the subject.

Moon in Cancer (John Thaw)

The Moon works very well when it is in the sign of Cancer. Nurturing and mothering come naturally, and people with this Moon position are especially good at building a stable home-base for themselves and their family. When they find the right relationship, their lives really blossom and they therefore find it easy to embrace the security of married life. There is no doubt that the Moon in Cancer is able to bring enormous strength and support into any relationship, and this more than compensates for occasional bouts of over-possessiveness or jealousy.

Moon in Leo (David Bowie)

The Moon in Leo radiates a generous warmth, which friends and family find attractive and reassuring. There is no doubt that this is a very good-natured position for the Moon, who always thinks the best of other people. When mistakes are made, the Moon in Leo is slow to condemn and quick to give another chance. However, people with this Moon position are intensely proud and, if they are not given the attention and appreciation which they deserve, the Moon will become

Nurturing and mothering come naturally to people with the Moon in Cancer.

genuinely upset. So they should make sure that they are always in a position where other people can't fail to notice their brilliance.

Moon in Virgo (Greta Garbo)

The Moon in Virgo is very conscious of the physical environment. People with this Moon position quickly pick up on small details and are disturbed when they see things which are out of place or out of order. Their bodies really do matter and people with the Moon in Virgo are careful to ensure that their diet is balanced and healthy. They don't have to be told how important it is to eat plenty of fresh fruit and vegetables. However, at times they may underestimate how sensitive they are to the chemical additives so often found in today's food.

Moon in Libra (Henry Kissinger)

At an emotional level, harmony is very important. People with a Libra Moon want those around them to get on with each other and find arguments and aggravation extremely distressing. When people are fighting, their immediate response is to act as a peacemaker and, as a result, the Moon in Libra makes an excellent diplomat. So, if they are ever stuck for a job, they could apply to the United Nations! In all dealings, these people will do their best to be scrupulously fair, and if with children, are always careful to ensure that they are treated the same and that one doesn't benefit at the expense of another.

Moon in Scorpio (Uri Geller)

This is a complicated position for the Moon to be in. This is a very secretive Moon position and these people will go out of their way to hide their true feelings. As a result, personal relationships can be problematic. They are often not prepared to share the true depth of their feelings with a partner and it is, therefore, difficult for a relationship to become really close. However, they do have a natural ability to delve into other people's lives and would make excellent detectives or psychologists.

Moon in Sagittarius (Rod Stewart)

Moon in Sagittarius people are impulsive and spontaneous. They have a wonderful sense of humour and often find themselves becoming the life and soul of a party. On an emotional level, they need plenty of space, particularly if they live in a city or in a crowded house or flat, and at the first signs of claustrophobia they'll head for the countryside or the nearest park. For some strange reason, the Moon in Sagittarius can be a bit gullible and these people should not believe everything they are told.

Moon in Capricorn (John Major)

Security is very important. If these people don't have a stable emotional or financial base to fall back on, they start worrying. As a result, the Moon works hard to safeguard the future and avoids taking unnecessary risks. At gut level, those with this Moon position are very good at evaluating whether or not projects are going to be successful, and this means that their business and financial advice is much sought after. However, in relationships the Moon in Capricorn finds it hard to express true feelings and it is unlikely that they will find true and lasting love before the age of thirty.

Moon in Aquarius (Mikhail Gorbachev)

The Moon in Aquarius responds very well to group situations. People with the Moon in Aquarius like having lots of different people around them, and their open and gregarious behaviour ensures that they are always tremendously popular. One of the

Moon's greatest virtues is a natural understanding of the plight of those less fortunate. As a result, these people can be very effective as charity workers. From a romantic point of view, they are logical and detached and want a partner to be as much a friend as a lover.

Moon in Pisces (Paul Newman)

The Moon in Pisces is a comfortable position, and usually denotes gentle and compassionate people who are very sensitive to the emotional undercurrents around. The Moon quickly picks up on other people's feelings and when someone is worried or is in trouble the Moon in Pisces is usually the first to know about it. It is, therefore, important that they don't get too caught up in other people's feelings. They should try to be a little more detached and do their best to create secure emotional boundaries for themselves.

7. MERCURY

Mercury is the planet of communications and of intellect. Its position in the horoscope gives information about the way someone thinks and organizes their ideas. Mercury also tells us about the manner in which someone communicates. It can, therefore, tell us about a person's speech and writing skills.

Career: Mercury can tell you how well someone is coping with the organizational demands of their working life or career. For example, Mercury in Virgo is usually on top of the paperwork, while Mercury in Pisces may be drowning in it. Mercury's position is also important for careers which require good communication skills.

Social Life: The position of Mercury can tell you about someone's social life, as well as the kind of people he likes to mix with. In some signs, particularly Cancer, Scorpio and Capricorn, Mercury is very choosey about friends. However, Mercury in the Air signs (Gemini, Libra and Aquarius) and

Fire signs (Leo, Aries and Sagittarius) tends to be a lot more open.

Special Talents: Everyone has special talents and one of the jobs of the astrologer is to find them out. If you want to tap into them, it is a good idea to look at Mercury. So, Mercury placed in Gemini might indicate writing talents; in Pisces, poetic and artistic talents; in Aquarius or Scorpio, psychic gifts.

HOW TO FIND YOUR MERCURY SIGN

This is very easy, and so we don't expect you to have any problems.

Step One

Simply turn to the Mercury group finder (table 3) and look across the top row to find the column which contains your year of birth. Then look down the list of figures until you find your particular year. If you then look at the far left-hand column, you will see your group number.

For example, if you were born on 10 May 1965, you would look down the fourth column, labelled '1960–1979', then down that list until you reached '1965'. Looking at the left-hand column, you would see that your group number was 6.

Step Two

To find your sign position, turn to the Mercury group tables (table 4), and look for your date of birth under the relevant group table. If you were born on 10 May 1965, for example, you would look under group 6, where you would find that your birth date comes between the dates '11 March–16 May'. On your date of birth, therefore, Mercury was in Aries.

Table 3 Mercury Group Finder

	1900-1919	1920-1939	1940-1959	1960-1979	1980-1999
Group 1	1900	1920	1940	1960	1980
Group 2	1901	1921	1941	1961	1981
Group 3	1902	1922	1942	1962	1982
Group 4	1903	1923	1943	1963	1983
Group 5	1904	1924	1944	1964	1984
Group 6	1905	1925	1945	1965	1985
Group 7	1906	1926	1946	1966	1986
Group 8	1907	1927	1947	1967	1987
Group 9	1908	1928	1948	1968	1988
Group 10	1909	1929	1949	1969	1989
Group 11	1910	1930	1950	1970	1990
Group 12	1911	1931	1951	1971	1991
Group 13	1912	1932	1952	1972	1992
Group 14	1913	1933	1953	1973	1993
Group 15	1914	1934	1954	1974	1994
Group 16	1915	1935	1955	1975	1995
Group 17	1916	1936	1956	1976	1996
Group 18	1917	1937	1957	1977	1997
Group 19	1918	1938	1958	1978	1998
Group 20	1919	1939	1959	1979	1999

Table 4 **Mercury Group Tables**

Group 1

Jan 1–Jan 3	Sag
Jan 4–Jan 22	Cap
Jan 23–Feb 8	Aqu
Feb 9–Apr 15	Pis
Apr 16–May 4	Ari
May 5–May 18	Tau
May 19–Jun 2	Gem
Jun 3–Jun 30	Can
Jul 1–Jul 5	Leo
Jul 6–Aug 10	Can
Aug 11–Aug 26	Leo
Aug 27–Sep 11	Vir
Sep 12–Oct 1	Lib
Oct 2–Dec 7	Sco
Dec 8–Dec 26	Sag
Dec 27–Dec 31	Cap

Group 2

Jan 1–Jan 14	Cap
Jan 15–Feb 1	Aqu
Feb 2–Feb 24	Pis
Feb 25–Mar 17	Aqu
Mar 18–Apr 9	Pis
Apr 10–Apr 26	Ari
Apr 27–May 10	Tau
May 11–May 28	Gem
May 29–Aug 3	Can
Aug 4–Aug 18	Leo
Aug 19–Sep 4	Vir
Sep 5–Sep 27	Lib
Sep 28–Oct 21	Sco
Oct 22–Nov 10	Lib
Nov 11–Nov 30	Sco
Dec 1–Dec 19	Sag
Dec 20–Dec 31	Cap

Group 3

Jan 1–Jan 7	Cap
Jan 8–Mar 14	Aqu
Mar 15–Apr 2	Pis
Apr 3–Apr 17	Ari
Apr 18–May 2	Tau
May 3–Jul 10	Gem
Jul 11–Jul 26	Can
Jul 27–Aug 10	Leo
Aug 11–Aug 29	Vir
Aug 30–Nov 4	Lib
Nov 5–Nov 23	Sco
Nov 24–Dec 12	Sag
Dec 13–Dec 31	Cap

Group 4

Jan 1–Jan 1	Cap
Jan 2–Jan 19	Aqu
Jan 20–Feb 14	Cap
Feb 15–Mar 8	Aqu
Mar 9–Mar 25	Pis
Mar 26–Apr 9	Ari
Apr 10–May 2	Tau
May 3–May 10	Gem
May 11–Jun 14	Tau
Jun 15–Jul 3	Gem
Jul 4–Jul 17	Can
Jul 18–Aug 2	Leo
Aug 3–Aug 26	Vir
Aug 27–Sep 16	Lib
Sep 17–Oct 10	Vir
Oct 11–Oct 28	Lib
Oct 29–Nov 15	Sco
Nov 16–Dec 5	Sag
Dec 6–Dec 31	Cap

Table 4 **Mercury Group Tables** contd

Group 9

Jan 1–Jan 13	Cap
Jan 14–Feb 1	Aqu
Feb 2–Feb 19	Pis
Feb 20–Mar 17	Aqu
Mar 18–Apr 8	Pis
Apr 9–Apr 24	Ari
Apr 25–May 8	Tau
May 9–May 27	Gem
May 28–Jun 28	Can
Jun 29–Jul 11	Gem
Jul 12–Aug 2	Can
Aug 3–Aug 16	Leo
Aug 17–Sep 3	Vir
Sep 4–Sep 26	Lib
Sep 27–Oct 16	Sco
Oct 17–Nov 9	Lib
Nov 10–Nov 29	Sco
Nov 30–Dec 18	Sag
Dec 19–Dec 31	Cap

Group 10

Jan 1–Jan 5	Cap
Jan 6–Mar 13	Aqu
Mar 14–Apr 1	Pis
Apr 2–Apr 16	Ari
Apr 17–May 1	Tau
May 2–Jul 9	Gem
Jul 10–Jul 24	Can
Jul 25–Aug 8	Leo
Aug 9–Aug 28	Vir
Aug 29–Nov 3	Lib
Nov 4–Nov 21	Sco
Nov 22–Dec 11	Sag
Dec 12–Dec 31	Cap

Group 11

Jan 1–Jan 1	Cap
Jan 2–Jan 14	Aqu
Jan 15–Feb 14	Cap
Feb 15–Mar 7	Aqu
Mar 8–Mar 24	Pis
Mar 25–Apr 7	Ari
Apr 8–Jun 14	Tau
Jun 15–Jul 2	Gem
Jul 3–Jul 16	Can
Jul 17–Aug 1	Leo
Aug 2–Aug 27	Vir
Aug 28–Sep 10	Lib
Sep 11–Oct 9	Vir
Oct 10–Oct 26	Lib
Oct 27–Nov 14	Sco
Nov 15–Dec 4	Sag
Dec 5–Dec 31	Cap

Group 12

Jan 1–Feb 9	Cap
Feb 10–Feb 28	Aqu
Mar 1–Mar 15	Pis
Mar 16–Apr 1	Ari
Apr 2–May 1	Tau
May 2–May 14	Ari
May 15–Jun 8	Tau
Jun 9–Jun 23	Gem
Jun 24–Jul 8	Can
Jul 9–Jul 27	Leo
Jul 28–Oct 2	Vir
Oct 3–Oct 19	Lib
Oct 20–Nov 7	Sco
Nov 8–Dec 1	Sag
Dec 2–Dec 12	Cap
Dec 13–Dec 31	Sag

Table 4 **Mercury Group Tables** contd

Group 5

Jan 1–Feb 12	Cap
Feb 13–Mar 2	Aqu
Mar 3–Mar 18	Pis
Mar 19–Apr 3	Ari
Apr 4–Jun 10	Tau
Jun 11–Jun 26	Gem
Jun 27–Jul 10	Can
Jul 11–Jul 28	Leo
Jul 29–Oct 4	Vir
Oct 5–Oct 21	Lib
Oct 22–Nov 9	Sco
Nov 10–Dec 1	Sag
Dec 2–Dec 23	Cap
Dec 24–Dec 31	Sag

Group 6

Jan 1–Jan 13	Sag
Jan 14–Feb 4	Cap
Feb 5–Feb 22	Aqu
Feb 23–Mar 10	Pis
Mar 11–May 16	Ari
May 17–Jun 3	Tau
Jun 4–Jun 18	Gem
Jun 19–Jul 3	Can
Jul 4–Jul 26	Leo
Jul 27–Aug 16	Vir
Aug 17–Sep 9	Leo
Sep 10–Sep 27	Vir
Sep 28–Oct 14	Lib
Oct 15–Nov 3	Sco
Nov 4–Dec 31	Sag

Group 7

Jan 1–Jan 9	Sag
Jan 10–Jan 28	Cap
Jan 29–Feb 15	Aqu
Feb 16–Mar 3	Pis
Mar 4–Apr 1	Ari
Apr 2–Apr 16	Pis
Apr 17–May 11	Ari
May 12–May 26	Tau
May 27–Jun 9	Gem
Jun 10–Jun 27	Can
Jun 28–Sep 3	Leo
Sep 4–Sep 19	Vir
Sep 20–Oct 7	Lib
Oct 8–Oct 29	Sco
Oct 30–Nov 20	Sag
Nov 21–Dec 12	Sco
Dec 13–Dec 31	Sag

Group 8

Jan 1–Jan 2	Sag
Jan 3–Jan 21	Cap
Jan 22–Feb 7	Aqu
Feb 8–Apr 15	Pis
Apr 16–May 3	Ari
May 4–May 18	Tau
May 19–Jun 2	Gem
Jun 3–Aug 10	Can
Aug 11–Aug 26	Leo
Aug 27–Sep 11	Vir
Sep 12–Oct 1	Lib
Oct 2–Dec 7	Sco
Dec 8–Dec 26	Sag
Dec 27–Dec 31	Cap

Table 4 **Mercury Group Tables** contd

Group 13

Jan 1–Jan 12	Sag
Jan 13–Feb 2	Cap
Feb 3–Feb 20	Aqu
Feb 21–Mar 7	Pis
Mar 8–May 14	Ari
May 15–May 31	Tau
Jun 1–Jun 14	Gem
Jun 15–Jun 29	Can
Jun 30–Sep 7	Leo
Sep 8–Sep 23	Vir
Sep 24–Oct 11	Lib
Oct 12–Oct 31	Sco
Nov 1–Dec 31	Sag

Group 14

Jan 1–Jan 6	Sag
Jan 7–Jan 25	Cap
Jan 26–Feb 11	Aqu
Feb 12–Mar 2	Pis
Mar 3–Mar 15	Ari
Mar 16–Apr 17	Pis
Apr 18–May 7	Ari
May 8–May 22	Tau
May 23–Jun 5	Gem
Jun 6–Jun 25	Can
Jun 26–Jul 28	Leo
Jul 29–Aug 11	Can
Aug 12–Aug 30	Leo
Aug 31–Sep 15	Vir
Sep 16–Oct 4	Lib
Oct 5–Oct 31	Sco
Nov 1–Nov 6	Sag
Nov 7–Dec 10	Sco
Dec 11–Dec 30	Sag
Dec 31–Dec 31	Cap

Group 15

Jan 1–Jan 17	Cap
Jan 18–Feb 4	Aqu
Feb 5–Apr 12	Pis
Apr 13–Apr 29	Ari
Apr 30–May 14	Tau
May 15–May 30	Gem
May 31–Aug 7	Can
Aug 8–Aug 22	Leo
Aug 23–Sep 7	Vir
Sep 8–Sep 28	Lib
Sep 29–Nov 4	Sco
Nov 5–Nov 10	Lib
Nov 11–Dec 3	Sco
Dec 4–Dec 23	Sag
Dec 24–Dec 31	Cap

Group 16

Jan 1–Jan 10	Cap
Jan 11–Mar 17	Aqu
Mar 18–Apr 6	Pis
Apr 7–Apr 21	Ari
Apr 22–May 6	Tau
May 7–Jul 13	Gem
Jul 14–Jul 30	Can
Jul 31–Aug 14	Leo
Aug 15–Sep 1	Vir
Sep 2–Nov 7	Lib
Nov 8–Nov 26	Sco
Nov 27–Dec 15	Sag
Dec 16–Dec 31	Cap

Table 4 **Mercury Group Tables** contd

Group 17

Jan 1–Jan 3	Cap
Jan 4–Feb 2	Aqu
Feb 3–Feb 14	Cap
Feb 15–Mar 10	Aqu
Mar 11–Mar 28	Pis
Mar 29–Apr 12	Ari
Apr 13–Apr 29	Tau
Apr 30–Jul 6	Gem
Jul 7–Jul 20	Can
Jul 21–Aug 5	Leo
Aug 6–Aug 26	Vir
Aug 27–Sep 29	Lib
Sep 30–Oct 10	Vir
Oct 11–Oct 30	Lib
Oct 31–Nov 18	Sco
Nov 19–Dec 7	Sag
Dec 8–Dec 31	Cap

Group 18

Jan 1–Feb 12	Cap
Feb 13–Mar 3	Aqu
Mar 4–Mar 20	Pis
Mar 21–Apr 4	Ari
Apr 5–Jun 12	Tau
Jun 13–Jun 28	Gem
Jun 29–Jul 12	Can
Jul 13–Jul 29	Leo
Jul 30–Oct 5	Vir
Oct 6–Oct 23	Lib
Oct 24–Nov 11	Sco
Nov 12–Dec 1	Sag
Dec 2–Dec 28	Cap
Dec 29–Dec 31	Sag

Group 19

Jan 1–Jan 13	Sag
Jan 14–Feb 6	Cap
Feb 7–Feb 24	Aqu
Feb 25–Mar 12	Pis
Mar 13–Apr 2	Ari
Apr 3–Apr 10	Tau
Apr 11–May 16	Ari
May 17–Jun 5	Tau
Jun 6–Jun 19	Gem
Jun 20–Jul 4	Can
Jul 5–Jul 25	Leo
Jul 26–Aug 23	Vir
Aug 24–Sep 10	Leo
Sep 11–Sep 28	Vir
Sep 29–Oct 15	Lib
Oct 16–Nov 4	Sco
Nov 5–Dec 31	Sag

Group 20

Jan 1–Jan 10	Sag
Jan 11–Jan 30	Cap
Jan 31–Feb 16	Aqu
Feb 17–Mar 4	Pis
Mar 5–May 12	Ari
May 13–May 28	Tau
May 29–Jun 11	Gem
Jun 12–Jun 28	Can
Jun 29–Sep 4	Leo
Sep 5–Sep 20	Vir
Sep 21–Oct 8	Lib
Oct 9–Oct 30	Sco
Oct 31–Nov 24	Sag
Nov 25–Dec 13	Sco
Dec 14–Dec 31	Sag

THE MEANING OF MERCURY IN EACH SIGN OF THE ZODIAC

The sign position of Mercury will describe a person's mind, as well as the way he or she communicates. It will be particularly important to have a detailed look at Mercury when you are dealing with questions of education, career and money.

Mercury in Aries (Omar Sharif)

These people like communicating and enjoy the sound of their own voice. They have opinions about most things, which are expressed at any opportunity. These attributes can be useful, particularly in careers such as politics and journalism. However, some caution is required. Mercury in Aries people don't always think their ideas through properly, and if they start arguing with someone more intelligent or more knowledgeable than themselves, they can come badly unstuck. Once they are involved in an unwinnable argument it is practically impossible for them to back down, and they sometimes end up by making total fools of themselves.

Mercury in Taurus (Selina Scott)

Taurus is one of the better sign placements for Mercury. Mercury in Taurus people have good powers of concentration and tend to think carefully before opening their mouths. If you are talking to people with this sign placement, you will find that they listen carefully to what you say and will notice immediately if you contradict yourself. So don't get into an argument with Mercury in Taurus, unless you are really sure of your facts. The communication skills of this person are further improved by the fact that Taurus usually gives Mercury a very clear voice and sometimes a pronounced musical ability.

Mercury in Gemini (Ross Perot)

A very versatile mind is characteristic of Mercury in Gemini, who can deal with many different things simultaneously. Indeed, having a conversation with Mercury in Gemini people can be quite exhausting, because they love changing the subject in mid-sentence. This is because their brains are several steps ahead of their voices. One phrase you will hardly ever hear Mercury in Gemini say is 'I don't know'. This is because they know a bit about most things, whether it be nuclear physics or minor league Bulgarian football. If they really don't know anything about a subject, then they'll make up a few facts, rather than admit ignorance.

Mercury in Cancer (Princess Diana)

People with Mercury in Cancer have vivid imaginations, which they are able to express very well. This expression can be very creative, which is why Mercury in Cancer is often prominent in the horoscopes of artists and poets. Cancer is a sign which is frequently associated with the past, and when Mercury is placed here it can indicate a keen interest in history and tradition. It also gives an excellent memory. If you know someone with this sign placement, get them to talk about their early child-hood, because they will usually be able to remember it in extraordinary detail.

Mercury in Leo (Bill Clinton)

Mercury doesn't work that well in Leo. People who have Mercury in this sign can be rather inflexible, particularly when it comes to ideas. They will never admit that they are wrong in public, because this would involve too much loss of face. Occasionally they will make such an admission in private, but only to a very close friend, whose discretion can be relied on. It is probably the case that Mercury in Leo people should aim to be a little less dogmatic and a little more open to the

A very versatile mind is characteristic of Mercury in Gemini, who can deal with many different things simultaneously.

opinions of people around them. In this way, they will be able to benefit from the knowledge and experience of others.

Mercury in Virgo (Madonna)

This is a brilliant position for Mercury. Mercury in Virgo has a good head for detail and usually finds it easy to deal with money and other material matters. Very clear ideas about the true value of things is a natural talent, and this means that Mercury in Virgo is a skilled financial negotiator. These people are excellent interior designers: they know what looks right and have a good colour sense. If you are planning on redecorating your home, make sure that you invite one of them round to give you the benefit of their good taste.

Mercury in Libra (Britt Ekland)

Libra is a very social sign and anyone who has their Mercury placed here is likely to be obsessed with other people and their problems. Mercury finds solitude difficult to deal with, and will attempt to have as active a social life as possible. Mercury in Libra people are gossips. They will want to know what other people are doing and they will enjoy spreading rumours. People with this sign position are very good at organizing parties – they know exactly who to invite and who not to invite. Mercury is also a brilliant matchmaker and any dating agency run by someone with Mercury in Libra is bound to succeed.

Mercury in Scorpio (Prince Charles)

Mercury in Scorpio people have minds like laser beams. They focus all their power on one thing at a time, without getting distracted by unnecessary details. Once Mercury in Scorpio people have started a task, they stay with it until the very end. When it comes to communication, Mercury in Scorpio is very persuasive. Other people are fascinated by this intensity, in the same way that a rabbit is mesmerized by a fox. It is because of this talent that people with this sign position make excellent salesmen and publicity agents. As a final word, you may also find that Mercury in Scorpio bestows marked psychic abilities.

Mercury in Sagittarius (Jodie Foster)

This is not one of the better signs for Mercury to be in. Mercury in Sagittarius often has ideas which are unrealistic and may find it very difficult to handle the details of these ideas. The mind starts going all over the place, and these people can end up getting hopelessly confused. In a social setting, Mercury in Sagittarius people have an easier time, provided that they avoid the temptation to shoot their mouth off. Meeting new people is tremendous fun and a spontaneous sense of humour can be appealing, if a little unsophisticated.

Mercury in Capricorn (Charles Dickens)

Mercury in Capricorn people have good business minds. They are able to concentrate on the practical details of a project and ignore anything which is irrelevant. As a result, Mercury in Capricorn people often tell other people to stop beating about the bush and to get to the point. People with this sign placement are not great communicators: they don't talk for the sake of it and hate small-talk. However, Mercury in Capricorn often has a sharp, though rather dry, sense of humour. This usually manifests in vicious one-liners, which can leave victims reeling.

Mercury in Aquarius (Les Dawson)

Mercury in Aquarius has an original mind and enjoys experimenting with new ideas and new lifestyles. Mercury in Aquarius is usually one step ahead of other people, and if you want to know about the latest fashion, ask Mercury in Aquarius. While they like to give the impression that they are open-minded, this isn't always the case. They don't like being contradicted or lectured to. Anyone that doesn't see their point of view is unlikely to be tolerated. Somewhat surprisingly, Aquarius is one of the most psychic placings for Mercury, and people with this sign position are often telepathic.

Mercury in Pisces (Ursula Andress)

Mercury doesn't work too well in Pisces. As a result, these people often find logical thought rather difficult, usually because they are too emotional. When communicating with other people, Mercury in Pisces people don't always make themselves clear and this can lead to dangerous misunderstandings. So they should always make sure that they have been understood properly, even if this means repeating themselves. On the plus side, Mercury in Pisces is a very artistic and creative sign and often makes excellent artists or actors.

8. VENUS

The position of Venus informs us about all kinds of relationships, whether they are romantic, social, or professional. It also tells us about what kind of environment makes people feel comfortable. When it comes to musical and artistic tastes, it is always essential to look at Venus.

Relationships: Venus is the love planet and her sign provides information about the way people conduct their love lives. For example, Venus in Aquarius is fairly detached, while in Scorpio, Venus is intensely passionate. In a man's horoscope Venus, like the Moon, describes the qualities he looks for in the opposite sex.

Art and Culture: The sign position of Venus describes people's attitude to the arts. Taurus and Libra are particularly refined signs for Venus. They have exquiste taste and hate music and art which lacks harmony. Venus in Gemini or Sagittarius, on the other hand, often has rather unusual likes and dislikes.

Appearance: Venus is a good indicator of both physical appearance and dress sense. If Venus is well placed, then someone's dress sense should be quite good. However, if Venus is in a sign such as Aries or Virgo it may be necessary to think twice before wearing a particular garment or applying a particular shade of lipstick.

FINDING YOUR VENUS SIGN

In order to find the sign position of your Venus, you need to look at the Venus group finder and the eight Venus group tables. The steps for finding the sign in which your Venus is placed are very simple. We will take you through these steps, using the example of Princess Diana:

Step One

Look at the Venus group finder (table 5). You will see that the left-hand column lists eight groups: group 1, group 2, group 3, group 4, group 5, group 6, group 7 and group 8. You need to find out which group contains your year of birth. If you read across from the group names, you can see that each one covers a row of years. So, for group 1, you can read 1900 (on the left), after that, 1908, and after that, 1916, etc. All the other years in this row belong to group 1.

Now find your year of birth, and see what group it is in. To help you find your birth date, we have labelled each column of dates. The left-hand column is labelled '1900–1907'. This tells you that all the dates in the left-hand column are between 1900 and 1907. The next column is labelled '1908–1915', which tells you that the dates in that column are between those years.

Run your finger along the top row of dates, above the group 1 row, and find the range in which you were born. Then look down, and find your exact birth year. You can then see what group it is in.

Table 5 **Venus Group Finder**

	1900-1907	1908-1915	1916-1923	1924-1931	1932-1939
Group 1	1900	1908	1916	1924	1932
Group 2	1901	1909	1917	1925	1933
Group 3	1902	1910	1918	1926	1934
Group 4	1903	1911	1919	1927	1935
Group 5	1904	1912	1920	1928	1936
Group 6	1905	1913	1921	1929	1937
Group 7	1906	1914	1922	1930	1938
Group 8	1907	1915	1923	1931	1939

	1940-1947	1948-1955	1956-1963	1964-1971
Group 1	1940	1948	1956	1964
Group 2	1941	1949	1957	1965
Group 3	1942	1950	1958	1966
Group 4	1943	1951	1959	1967
Group 5	1944	1952	1960	1968
Group 6	1945	1953	1961	1969
Group 7	1946	1954	1962	1970
Group 8	1947	1955	1963	1971

	1972-1979	1980-1987	1988-1995	1996-1999
Group 1	1972	1980	1988	1996
Group 2	1973	1981	1989	1997
Group 3	1974	1982	1990	1998
Group 4	1975	1983	1991	1999
Group 5	1976	1984	1992	
Group 6	1977	1985	1993	
Group 7	1978	1986	1994	
Group 8	1979	1987	1995	

Table 6 **Venus Group Tables**

Group 1

Jan 1–Jan 17	Aqu
Jan 18–Feb 10	Pis
Feb 11–Mar 7	Ari
Mar 8–Apr 3	Tau
Apr 4–May 7	Gem
May 8–Jun 23	Can
Jun 24–Aug 3	Gem
Aug 4–Sep 7	Can
Sep 8–Oct 5	Leo
Oct 6–Oct 31	Vir
Nov 1–Nov 25	Lib
Nov 26–Dec 19	Sco
Dec 20–Dec 31	Sag

Group 2

Jan 1–Jan 12	Sag
Jan 13–Feb 5	Cap
Feb 6–Mar 1	Aqu
Mar 2–Mar 25	Pis
Mar 26–Apr 18	Ari
Apr 19–May 12	Tau
May 13–Jun 6	Gem
Jun 7–Jun 30	Can
Jul 1–Jul 25	Leo
Jul 26–Aug 19	Vir
Aug 20–Sep 13	Lib
Sep 14–Oct 9	Sco
Oct 10–Nov 5	Sag
Nov 6–Dec 6	Cap
Dec 7–Dec 31	Aqu

Group 3

Jan 1–Apr 6	Aqu
Apr 7–May 4	Pis
May 5–May 31	Ari
Jun 1–Jun 26	Tau
Jun 27–Jul 21	Gem
Jul 22–Aug 15	Can
Aug 16–Sep 9	Leo
Sep 10–Oct 3	Vir
Oct 4–Oct 27	Lib
Oct 28–Nov 20	Sco
Nov 21–Dec 13	Sag
Dec 14–Dec 31	Cap

Group 4

Jan 1–Jan 7	Cap
Jan 8–Jan 31	Aqu
Feb 1–Feb 24	Pis
Feb 25–Mar 20	Ari
Mar 21–Apr 14	Tau
Apr 15–May 10	Gem
May 11–Jun 6	Can
Jun 7–Jul 7	Leo
Jul 8–Nov 9	Vir
Nov 10–Dec 7	Lib
Dec 8–Dec 31	Sco

Table 6 **Venus Group Tables** contd

Group 5

Jan 1–Jan 2	Sco
Jan 3–Jan 27	Sag
Jan 28–Feb 20	Cap
Feb 21–Mar 16	Aqu
Mar 17–Apr 9	Pis
Apr 10–May 3	Ari
May 4–May 28	Tau
May 29–Jun21	Gem
Jun 22–Jul 16	Can
Jul 17–Aug 9	Leo
Aug 10–Sep 2	Vir
Sep 3–Sep 27	Lib
Sep 28–Oct 21	Sco
Oct 22–Nov 15	Sag
Nov 16–Dec 10	Cap
Dec 11–Dec 31	Aqu

Group 6

Jan 1–Jan 4	Aqu
Jan 5–Feb 1	Pis
Feb 2–Mar 14	Ari
Mar 15–Mar 30	Tau
Mar 31–Jun 4	Ari
Jun 5–Jul 6	Tau
Jul 7–Aug 3	Gem
Aug 4–Aug 29	Can
Aug 30–Sep 23	Leo
Sep 24–Oct 18	Vir
Oct 19–Nov 11	Lib
Nov 12–Dec 5	Sco
Dec 6–Dec 29	Sag
Dec 30–Dec 31	Cap

Group 7

Jan 1–Jan 22	Cap
Jan 23–Feb 15	Aqu
Feb 16–Mar 11	Pis
Mar 12–Apr 4	Ari
Apr 5–Apr 28	Tau
Apr 29–May 23	Gem
May 24–Jun 17	Can
Jun 18–Jul 13	Leo
Jul 14–Aug 8	Vir
Aug 9–Sep 6	Lib
Sep 7–Oct 15	Sco
Oct 16–Nov 7	Sag
Nov 8–Dec 31	Sco

Group 8

Jan 1–Jan 5	Sco
Jan 6–Feb 5	Sag
Feb 6–Mar 4	Cap
Mar 5–Mar 29	Aqu
Mar 30–Apr 24	Pis
Apr 25–May19	Ari
May 20–Jun 12	Tau
Jun 13–Jul 7	Gem
Jul 8–Jul 31	Can
Aug 1–Aug 25	Leo
Aug 26–Sep 18	Vir
Sep 19–Oct 12	Lib
Oct 13–Nov 5	Sco
Nov 6–Nov 29	Sag
Nov 30–Dec 23	Cap
Dec 24–Dec 31	Aqu

For example, Princess Diana was born in 1961. Look along the very top row of the middle group on p. 132, until you find the box labelled '1956–1963'. Then look down until you find the year 1961. Then look across to the left of the table, and you will see that this year is in group 6. This is Princess Diana's Venus group.

Step Two

You can see that there are eight Venus group tables each with their group number written at the top. Once you know what someone's Venus group is, you can find the appropriate table. You then read down the table until you find the dates between which the birthday falls.

When you are looking at the Venus group tables, you will see that the year is not listed. This is because we are now only looking at the day and the month of birth.

Princess Diana's Venus is in group 6, so look at the table headed 'Group 6'. Princess Diana was born on 1 July, so look down the group 6 table until you find the dates between which she was born. You will eventually come to the dates 'Jun 5 – Jul 6'. 1 July is between 5 June and 6 July, so this is the right place. You can then read off the abbreviation 'Tau' (Taurus) which means that Diana has her Venus in Taurus.

Let's try another example. If someone was born on 30 May 1962, where would their Venus be?

Turn to the Venus group finder and find 1962 on the very top row of the middle group. This will take you to the box with '1956–1963' written in it. Now go down the column, until you find the year 1962. Read across and you will see that 1962 is in group 7. Now turn to the Venus group table headed 'Group 7'. Look down this table, until you find the entry 'May 24 – Jun 17', because 30 May is between these dates. You can now see that Venus was in Cancer on 30 May 1962.

THE MEANING OF VENUS IN EACH SIGN OF THE ZODIAC

Venus in Aries (Bianca Jagger)

Venus is a soft and gentle planet, and when placed in assertive Aries doesn't always work best. Venus in Aries people are not usually very subtle and in relationships they tend to take the initiative. Sometimes Venus in Aries may act too quickly, without taking into account a partner's needs and feelings, so a little more sensitivity may be required. When it comes to dress sense, Venus in Aries people like to wear clothes which make them stand out in a crowd. However, before buying a daring costume, they should always get a second opinion.

Venus in Taurus (Nicola Pagett)

Taurus is a great place for Venus. Venus in Taurus has excellent taste and enjoys the good things in life. Very attractive, Venus in Taurus usually has a beautiful voice and graceful movements. Their dress sense is always perfect, and you will rarely see Venus in Taurus looking anything but immaculate. In the area of close relationships, Venus in Taurus is rather physical. Plenty of body contact is important and sexual fulfilment is vital. The main disadvantage of Venus in Taurus is extravagance, a love of shopping and very often an inability to keep hold of financial reality.

Venus in Gemini (Joan Collins)

Gemini is a sign which likes plenty of variety and when Venus is here you often find people who enjoy a varied social life. A person with this sign position is certainly good at making friends and has a natural ability to make conversation. When applying for jobs, Venus in Gemini is particularly brilliant at interviews. When it comes to relationships, Venus in Gemini can present problems, however. There is a tendency to get bored

Venus in Taurus has excellent taste and enjoys the good things in life.

with other people very easily, and the idea of having one life-long partner can be difficult to handle. This is particularly the case if partners are inflexible and set in their ways.

Venus in Cancer (Adam Faith)

Venus in Cancer can be very emotional, even if this doesn't seem to be the case on the surface. These people quickly pick up on other people's feelings and are often keen to help those who appear to be in trouble. In relationships, Venus in Cancer is responsive to a partner's needs and is usually good at creating a secure and loving home base. Perhaps the main disadvantage of Venus in Cancer people is that they can be a little too sentimental. Once they start expressing their feelings, they don't know when to stop and the end result can be nothing short of embarrassing.

Venus in Leo (Dame Barbara Cartland)

Leo is a proud sign, and when Venus is placed here it usually indicates someone who is very conscious of outer appearances. Venus in Leo wants to be noticed and admired, and in social situations is easily flattered. In relationships, Venus in Leo people want partners who not only give them plenty of attention, but who also look good. Indeed, they want someone who they can show off to other people. Venus in Leo does have some good points, too. Venus can be very generous and can show enormous loyalty to family and friends. Provided, of course, that they show the same loyalty in return.

Venus in Virgo (Ingrid Bergman)

Virgo is not one of Venus' better sign placements. Venus in Virgo people are very concerned about details, and will be quick to home in on a partner's every fault. Venus finds it difficult to enjoy love for its own sake. This may be because love is seen as something which has a price tag. At worst, Venus in Virgo will weigh up the material pros and cons of a relationship before deciding whether to pursue the matter further. The sexual aspects of any relationship are important, however, often to the exclusion of everything, except money.

Venus in Libra (Peter Sellers)

A person with Venus in Libra is extremely civilized. Venus in Libra knows how to behave in any social situation and is usually very popular. Good behaviour is important; Venus in Libra is slow to forgive people who are rude, ungrateful or bad-mannered. When it comes to dress sense, these people never have any problems. They always know exactly the right things to wear and can never be accused of being over- or underdressed. Relationships are important, too. Whatever Venus in Libra people might say in public, they always need to have a devoted partner by their side.

Venus in Scorpio (Charles Manson)

Scorpio is a very intense and private sign. Venus finds it difficult to function easily when placed here. Venus in Scorpio people can be too emotional for their own good and in relationships can be jealous and possessive. For some reason they find it difficult to have complete trust in a partner and this in turn prevents them from expressing the full power of their passions and emotions. On the positive side, those with Venus in Scorpio hate injustice and will often go out of their way to fight for people who are disadvantaged or who are the victims of prejudice.

Venus in Sagittarius (Margaret Thatcher)

Venus in Sagittarius is a very exciting sign placement. These people are always looking for new horizons and this is reflected in their choice of friends. Venus wants to be surrounded by people who are both inspiring and entertaining. Venus doesn't like staying in one place for too long and is happiest in exotic and tropical locations. Having a relationship with Venus in Sagittarius people can be hard work, because their behaviour is unpredictable. However, if you are prepared to follow Venus to the ends of the earth, you should be okay. One final point: people with Venus in Sagittarius tend to have appalling dress sense.

Venus in Capricorn (Indira Gandhi)

Venus in Capricorn tends to be rather reserved. Venus doesn't like show, and these people are always careful not to be extravagant in the way they dress and make themselves up. However, this shouldn't hide the fact that status is important. Venus in Capricorn people want a partner who will reflect well on them and who will contribute to their eventual success. From a career point, those with this sign placement are very good at handling other people and make brilliant personnel officers.

Venus in Aquarius (Victoria Principal)

Aquarius is a sign which is often rather detached, and when the planet of love is placed here you find people who like to keep their distance. Not for them, sentimental, mushy relationships. Venus in Aquarius finds all that romantic stuff too much to handle. If Venus in Aquarius people are going to enter into a relationship, they expect their partners to respect their freedom. Indeed, they are probably going to expect their partner to be a friend as much as a lover. When it comes to dress sense, Venus in Aquarius likes to wear clothes which are exciting, original and even futuristic.

Venus in Pisces (Martin Luther King)

Pisces is one of the best signs for Venus. People with Venus in Pisces are very comfortable with their feelings. They find it easy to relate to others in a natural and spontaneous way. This placement often indicates pronounced creative talents, and you will find that many artists, dancers, singers and actors have Venus in Pisces. In the area of relationships, Venus in Pisces people make wonderful partners. They are warm and sympathetic, finding it easy to express love and affection. The only problem with Venus in Pisces is that they can be a little lazy and self-indulgent.

9. MARS

Mars is an energetic planet which describes the way we assert ourselves. Emotionally, Mars is important, because it shows how our raw energy is expressed. Mars can indicate hidden anger, especially in Taurus or Cancer. Mars is also a very physical planet and is often very strong in the horoscopes of sportsmen.

Career: In order to be successful in one's career it is vital that there is a certain amount of self-assertion. If you want to look at someone's career potential, it is always worth looking at Mars. If Mars is poorly placed, particularly in Libra, it may be necessary to take an assertiveness training course.

Relationships: Mars is connected with male sexuality and is important when considering relationships. In a man's chart it will tell you about the way he approaches relationships. If Mars is in Aries or Scorpio he may well be the domineering type. In a woman's chart, Mars is often descriptive of her perfect lover.

Physical Activity: Many people are worried that they are not taking enough exercise and they may want an astrologer to tell them what activities they should be doing. In order to give this kind of advice you should look at Mars. You might see that Mars is in Libra, and then suggest a team sport, like football.

HOW TO FIND YOUR MARS SIGN

Step One

Turn to the Mars group finder (table 7), and look along the top row of dates until you find the date which contains your year of birth. Next, look down that column, until you find your particular year of birth. In the column on the far left, you will see your group number.

To use the example of 10 May 1965: 1965 falls in the fifth row of dates ('1960–1974'). If you look down that column, you will see that 1965 belongs to group 6.

Step Two

Turn to the Mars group tables (table 8), and find the position of Mars by looking for your date of birth under the relevant group number. For example, in the group 6 table, 1965 is contained in the second column of dates ('1923–1974'), and because 10 May comes between 28 March and 11 June, we can see that Mars is in Virgo.

Table 7 **Mars Group Finder**

	1900-1914	1915-1929	1930-1944	1945-1959	1960-1974	1975-1989	1990-1999
Group 1	1900	1915	1930	1945	1960	1975	1990
Group 2	1901	1916	1931	1946	1961	1976	1991
Group 3	1902	1917	1932	1947	1962	1977	1992
Group 4	1903	1918	1933	1948	1963	1978	1993
Group 5	1904	1919	1934	1949	1964	1979	1994
Group 6	1905	1920	1935	1950	1965	1980	1995
Group 7	1906	1921	1936	1951	1966	1981	1996
Group 8	1907	1922	1937	1952	1967	1982	1997
Group 9	1908	1923	1938	1953	1968	1983	1998
Group 10	1909	1924	1939	1954	1969	1984	1999
Group 11	1910	1925	1940	1955	1970	1985	
Group 12	1911	1926	1941	1956	1971	1986	
Group 13	1912	1927	1942	1957	1972	1987	
Group 14	1913	1928	1943	1958	1973	1988	
Group 15	1914	1929	1944	1959	1974	1989	

THE MEANING OF MARS THROUGH EACH SIGN OF THE ZODIAC

Mars is the planet of assertion and his sign placing will tell you about the ways in which people assert themselves. It is often connected with passion, so if you want to know about romantic matters it is worth looking at Mars's position.

Mars in Aries (Vladimir Ilyich Lenin)

Mars has a special connection with Aries. When you find Mars in Aries in a horoscope it is a sure sign that you are dealing with a dynamic and assertive person who enjoys taking the

Table 8 **Mars Group Tables**

Group 1	1900-1922	1923-1974	1975-1999
Jan 1-Jan 5	Cap	Sag	Sco
Jan 6-Feb 13	Aqu	Cap	Sag
Feb 14-Mar 24	Pis	Aqu	Cap
Mar 25-May 2	Ari	Pis	Aqu
May 3-Jun 10	Tau	Ari	Pis
Jun 11-Jul 22	Gem	Tau	Ari
Jul 23-Sep 7	Can	Gem	Tau
Sep 8-Nov 11	Leo	Can	Gem
Nov 12-Dec 26	Vir	Leo	Can
Dec 27-Dec 31	Leo	Can	Gem

Group 2	1900-1922	1923-1974	1975-1999
Jan 1-Apr 22	Leo	Can	Gem
Apr 23-Jun 19	Vir	Leo	Can
Jun 20-Aug 9	Lib	Vir	Leo
Aug 10-Sep 24	Sco	Lib	Vir
Sep 25-Nov 6	Sag	Sco	Lib
Nov 7-Dec 16	Cap	Sag	Sco
Dec 17-Dec 31	Aqu	Cap	Sag

Group 3	1900-1922	1923-1974	1975-1999
Jan 1-Jan 24	Aqu	Cap	Sag
Jan 25-Mar 4	Pis	Aqu	Cap
Mar 5-Apr 11	Ari	Pis	Aqu
Apr 12-May 20	Tau	Ari	Pis
May 21-Jun 30	Gem	Tau	Ari
Jul 1-Aug 13	Can	Gem	Tau
Aug 14-Sep 30	Leo	Can	Gem
Oct 1-Nov 30	Vir	Leo	Can
Dec 1-Dec 31	Lib	Vir	Leo

Group 4	1900-1922	1923-1974	1975-1999
Jan 1-Feb 11	Lib	Vir	Leo
Feb 12-May 18	Vir	Leo	Can
May 19-Jul 16	Lib	Vir	Leo
Jul 17-Sep 3	Sco	Lib	Vir
Sep 4-Oct 16	Sag	Sco	Lib
Oct 17-Nov 26	Cap	Sag	Sco
Nov 27-Dec 31	Aqu	Cap	Sag

Group 5	1900-1922	1923-1974	1975-1999
Jan 1-Jan 4	Aqu	Cap	Sag
Jan 5-Feb 11	Pis	Aqu	Cap
Feb 12-Mar 21	Ari	Pis	Aqu
Mar 22-Apr 29	Tau	Ari	Pis
Apr 30-Jun 9	Gem	Tau	Ari
Jun 10-Jul 22	Can	Gem	Tau
Jul 23-Sep 6	Leo	Can	Gem
Sep 7-Oct 26	Vir	Leo	Can
Oct 27-Dec 25	Lib	Vir	Leo
Dec 26-Dec 31	Sco	Lib	Vir

Group 6	1900-1922	1923-1974	1975-1999
Jan 1-Mar 27	Sco	Lib	Vir
Mar 28-Jun 11	Lib	Vir	Leo
Jun 12-Aug 10	Sco	Lib	Vir
Aug 11-Sep 25	Sag	Sco	Lib
Sep 26-Nov 5	Cap	Sag	Sco
Nov 6-Dec 14	Aqu	Cap	Sag
Dec 15-Dec 31	Pis	Aqu	Cap

Table 8 **Mars Group Tables** contd

Group 7	1900-1922	1923-1974	1975-1999
Jan 1–Jan 22	Pis	Aqu	Cap
Jan 23–Mar 1	Ari	Pis	Aqu
Mar 2–Apr 9	Tau	Ari	Pis
Apr 10–May 21	Gem	Tau	Ari
May 22–Jul 3	Can	Gem	Tau
Jul 4–Aug 17	Leo	Can	Gem
Aug 18–Oct 4	Vir	Leo	Can
Oct 5–Nov 23	Lib	Vir	Leo
Nov 24–Dec 31	Sco	Lib	Vir

Group 8	1900-1922	1923-1974	1975-1999
Jan 1–Jan 19	Sco	Lib	Vir
Jan 20–Aug 27	Sag	Sco	Lib
Aug 28–Oct 11	Cap	Sag	Sco
Oct 12–Nov 21	Aqu	Cap	Sag
Nov 22–Dec 30	Pis	Aqu	Cap
Dec 31–Dec 31	Ari	Pis	Aqu

Group 9	1900-1922	1923-1974	1975-1999
Jan 1–Feb 7	Ari	Pis	Aqu
Feb 8–Mar 19	Tau	Ari	Pis
Mar 20–Apr 30	Gem	Tau	Ari
May 1–Jun 13	Can	Gem	Tau
Jun 14–Jul 29	Leo	Can	Gem
Jul 30–Sep 14	Vir	Leo	Can
Sep 15–Nov 1	Lib	Vir	Leo
Nov 2–Dec 19	Sco	Lib	Vir
Dec 20–Dec 31	Sag	Sco	Lib

Group 10	1900-1922	1923-1974	1975-1999
Jan 1–Feb 9	Sag	Sco	Lib
Feb 10–Apr 12	Cap	Sag	Sco
Apr 13–Jul 2	Aqu	Cap	Sag
Jul 3–Aug 24	Cap	Sag	Sco
Aug 25–Oct 21	Aqu	Cap	Sag
Oct 22–Dec 3	Pis	Aqu	Cap
Dec 4–Dec 31	Ari	Pis	Aqu

Group 11	1900-1922	1923-1974	1975-1999
Jan 1–Jan 14	Ari	Pis	Aqu
Jan 15–Feb 25	Tau	Ari	Pis
Feb 26–Apr 10	Gem	Tau	Ari
Apr 11–May 25	Can	Gem	Tau
May 26–Jul 10	Leo	Can	Gem
Jul 11–Aug 26	Vir	Leo	Can
Aug 27–Oct 12	Lib	Vir	Leo
Oct 13–Nov 28	Sco	Lib	Vir
Nov 29–Dec 31	Sag	Sco	Lib

Group 12	1900-1922	1923-1974	1975-1999
Jan 1–Jan 13	Sag	Sco	Lib
Jan 14–Feb 28	Cap	Sag	Sco
Feb 29–Apr 14	Aqu	Cap	Sag
Apr 15–Jun 2	Pis	Aqu	Cap
Jun 3–Dec 5	Ari	Pis	Aqu
Dec 6–Dec 31	Tau	Ari	Pis

Table 8 **Mars Group Tables** contd

Group 13	1900-1922	1923-1974	1975-1999
Jan 1–Jan 28	Tau	Ari	Pis
Jan 29–Mar 17	Gem	Tau	Ari
Mar 18–May 4	Can	Gem	Tau
May 5–Jun 21	Leo	Can	Gem
Jun 22–Aug 7	Vir	Leo	Can
Aug 8–Sep 23	Lib	Vir	Leo
Sep 24–Nov 8	Sco	Lib	Vir
Nov 9–Dec 22	Sag	Sco	Lib
Dec 23–Dec 31	Cap	Sag	Sco

Group 14	1900-1922	1923-1974	1975-1999
Jan 1–Feb 3	Cap	Sag	Sco
Feb 4–Mar 16	Aqu	Cap	Sag
Mar 17–Apr 26	Pis	Aqu	Cap
Apr 27–Jun 6	Ari	Pis	Aqu
Jun 7–Jul 20	Tau	Ari	Pis
Jul 21–Sep 20	Gem	Tau	Ari
Sep 21–Oct 28	Can	Gem	Tau
Oct 29–Dec 31	Gem	Tau	Ari

Group 15	1900-1922	1923-1974	1975-1999
Jan 1–Feb 10	Gem	Tau	Ari
Feb 11–Apr 9	Can	Gem	Tau
Apr 10–May 31	Leo	Can	Gem
Jun 1–Jul 19	Vir	Leo	Can
Jul 20–Sep 5	Lib	Vir	Leo
Sep 6–Oct 20	Sco	Lib	Vir
Oct 21–Dec 3	Sag	Sco	Lib
Dec 4–Dec 31	Cap	Sag	Sco

initiative. Mars in Aries is direct and to the point and doesn't shy away from fights and confrontations. This is usually a good thing, although there are times when a lack of tact leads to unnecessary arguments. When it comes to love, Mars in Aries is not very subtle. Once these people are attracted to a person, that's it. They will make their intentions loud and clear and certainly won't be interested in a long, drawn-out courtship.

Mars in Aries is direct and to the point and doesn't shy away from fights and confrontations.

148

Mars in Taurus (Josef Stalin)

Mars is a fast, energetic planet and wants quick results. Mars, therefore, doesn't work very well when placed in slow-moving Taurus. A person with Mars in Taurus often finds that it is difficult to make things happen, particularly when it comes to career and finance. As a result, Mars in Taurus often has a hidden anger and impatience, which can erupt in wild displays of temper. Mars in Taurus needs to be a little more relaxed, and shouldn't worry if things take longer than expected. This sign position is also very stubborn, and once these people have made up their minds on something, they will not budge.

Mars in Gemini (Al Pacino)

Mars in Gemini has an enormous amount of nervous energy. Mars is constantly fidgeting and tends to get bored very easily. The usual way that Mars in Gemini people express themselves is through words, and when they talk they are fulfilled and free, especially when they are involved in heated arguments. However, Mars in Gemini people do have to be careful what they say. Very often, they say things in the heat of the moment which they later regret. People with Mars in Gemini often have very good writing skills. Ideal professions are speech-writing and journalism.

Mars in Cancer (Humphrey Bogart)

Cancer is not one of the better sign placements for Mars. Mars in Cancer finds it difficult to be assertive in the correct way. Very often this is because the timing is wrong. Mars fails to take initiatives at the right time and gets angry and offensive at the wrong time. This suggests that Mars in Cancer people are not always in control of their own emotions. However, it is not all bad: in relationships, they are very protective of their loved ones and are always there in a crisis. They are also likely to be very good at do-it-yourself jobs around the home.

Mars in Leo (President Boris Yeltsin)

Mars in Leo people tend to have fairly big egos. They believe that they know best, and when their talents are questioned will be quick to defend themselves. In their heart of hearts, Mars in Leo people believe that they are the centre of the universe and if friends and colleagues are prepared to accept this, they will be treated with kindness and consideration. It should be appreciated that Mars in Leo people want to be able to do whatever they want, and if anyone tells them otherwise, they will refuse to listen. Although this sign position can be uncontrollable, flattery can occasionally calm them down.

Mars in Virgo (Henry VIII)

Virgo is a very organized sign and when Mars is placed here we often find people who are obsessed with ordering and tidying up their environment. While Mars in Virgo people often have amazing administrative skills, they have be careful that they don't take this too far. After all, there is no point in details for the sake of them. Indeed, these people will sometimes tidy things up because they cannot think of anything better to do with their time. In which case they need to redirect their energy into something more constructive – like exercise or charity work.

Mars in Libra (Sigmund Freud)

Libra is not a good place for Mars to be in. Mars is the planet of assertion, while Libra is the sign of compromise. As a result, Mars in Libra may find it difficult to take the initiative. Mars in Libra people will constantly be thinking about other people's interests and, in the process, may forget about their own needs. On the plus side, they tend to have good social skills. They don't rock the boat and are often able to patch things up between warring factions. It is not surprising, therefore, that this placement makes for effective diplomats and marriage guidance counsellors.

Mars in Scorpio (Jimi Hendrix)

Mars in Scorpio people are usually very powerful. They know exactly what they want out of life and are able to achieve their aims with ruthless efficiency. One of the reasons that these people are so successful is that they are discreet. They don't usually tell everyone what they are doing, but instead get on quietly with the job. Mars in Scorpio people are very passionate, and usually have powerful desires. Once they have set their eyes on someone, that's that! They will always achieve their target. One other thing to bear in mind about Mars in Scorpio is that they never forgive and they never forget!

Mars in Sagittarius (Richard Nixon)

People with this sign placement are usually very active. They find it impossible to keep still for two seconds, and are at their best when involved in some kind of sporting activity. Mars in Sagittarius is fond of travelling and enjoys going on activity holidays which involve a certain amount of danger. Hang-gliding and shark-wrestling are particular favourites. Another way that Mars in Sagittarius people express themselves is through their rather bold sense of humour. They love making people laugh and, if necessary, will resort to rather tasteless practical jokes.

Mars in Capricorn (Albert Einstein)

Mars is exalted in Capricorn. This means that Mars in Capricorn often does very well in life. They understand the meaning of hard work and, once they get involved in something, will see it through to the end. While most people with this sign placing will fit this description, there are people with Mars in Capricorn who are different. Rather than being interested in hard work, in this instance Mars is obsessed with the pursuit of pleasure, regardless of the consequences. Mars believes that life is short and that you might as well make the most of it while you are still alive.

Mars in Aquarius (Lauren Bacall)

Mars in Aquarius people are great individualists. They like to run their lives in their own way at their own pace, and very rarely listen to other people. Often, Mars in Aquarius has unusual interests, like UFO-spotting or pre-Reformation Flemish church music. This is one of the least aggressive sign placings for Mars, although it should not necessarily be seen as weak. Mars in Aquarius people just do what they want, without making a big fuss about it. However, Mars is frequently an idealist and will often campaign for a better world.

Mars in Pisces (Marilyn Monroe)

Mars can work well in Pisces, provided that the energy is used in exactly the right way. Mars in Pisces people should avoid taking direct initiatives, because they will usually fail. Instead, Mars should be more subtle. If they are involved in a fight with someone, they should be patient and give themselves plenty of time to discover his or her weaknesses. Mars in Pisces has a natural affinity with water and, if possible, should live by the sea. If not, they can at least take up hobbies which bring them close to the water, such as fishing, sailing or windsurfing.

10. JUPITER

Jupiter is the planet of expansion. Its position in the horoscope indicates the areas in which we reach out for new horizons. So Jupiter can, therefore, describe some of our greatest ambitions. From a more negative point of view, Jupiter can highlight excessive and unrealistic behaviour patterns.

Career: Jupiter gives valuable information about someone's career. Jupiter tells you about a person's hopes regarding career, as well as the way he or she functions in a professional environment. So Jupiter in Aquarius or Pisces may see their work as a contribution to humanity, while in Capricorn he or she may take a more selfish approach.

Money: If you want to know about someone's overall financial state, then Jupiter is one of the planets to look at. When Jupiter is in Cancer, Virgo or Capricorn, it can indicate a responsible attitude towards money. However, in the Fire signs (Aries, Leo or Sagittarius) they often over-commit themselves.

Spirituality: Jupiter is a spiritual planet and its position gives us clues about someone's spiritual beliefs. Jupiter in Earth signs (Taurus, Virgo and Capricorn) finds it difficult to take things on trust and wants concrete evidence that higher forces exist. By contrast, Jupiter in Scorpio, Sagittarius or Pisces is prepared to rely on faith.

HOW TO FIND YOUR JUPITER SIGN

It is very easy to find out where your Jupiter is – all you need to do is to look at the Jupiter tables (table 9), which contain five different tables of birth year dates. One table contains the dates from 1900–1924, the next table contains the dates from 1925–1949, and so on.

Simply pick the table which includes your own year of birth, then run your finger down the table to locate the row in which your birthday falls. For example, suppose you were born on 7 November 1956: the year 1956 falls in the table labelled '1950–1969'. You then find the row in which 7 November falls – the twelfth row from the top. Next to this row you will see the abbreviation 'Vir' (Virgo). So, this person's Jupiter was positioned in the sign of Virgo on 7 November 1956. Isn't it easy? Now discover your own Jupiter sign.

THE MEANING OF JUPITER IN EACH SIGN OF THE ZODIAC

By looking at the sign position of Jupiter you will get an idea of where someone's expansive energies are going to be expressed. It is particularly important to check up on Jupiter's position when you are considering career, money and spirituality.

Table 9 **Jupiter Tables**

1900–1924

1 Jan 1900–18 Jan 1901	Sag
19 Jan 1901– 6 Feb 1902	Cap
7 Feb 1902–19 Feb 1903	Aqu
20 Feb 1903–29 Feb 1904	Pis
1 Mar 1904– 8 Aug 1904	Ari
9 Aug 1904–31 Aug 1904	Tau
1 Sep 1904– 7 Mar 1905	Ari
8 Mar 1905–20 Jul 1905	Tau
21 Jul 1905– 4 Dec 1905	Gem
5 Dec 1905– 9 Mar 1906	Tau
10 Mar 1906–30 Jul 1906	Gem
31 Jul 1906–18 Aug 1907	Can
19 Aug 1907–11 Sep 1908	Leo
12 Sep 1908–11 Oct 1909	Vir
12 Oct 1909–11 Nov 1910	Lib
12 Nov 1910– 9 Dec 1911	Sco
10 Dec 1911– 2 Jan 1913	Sag
3 Jan 1913–21 Jan 1914	Cap
22 Jan 1914– 3 Feb 1915	Aqu
4 Feb 1915–11 Feb 1916	Pis
12 Feb 1916–25 Jun 1916	Ari
26 Jun 1916–26 Oct 1916	Tau
27 Oct 1916–12 Feb 1917	Ari
13 Feb 1917–29 Jun 1917	Tau
30 Jun 1917–12 Jul 1918	Gem
13 Jul 1918– 1 Aug 1919	Can
2 Aug 1919–26 Aug 1920	Leo
27 Aug 1920–25 Sep 1921	Vir
26 Sep 1921–26 Oct 1922	Lib
27 Oct 1922–24 Nov 1923	Sco
25 Nov 1923–17 Dec 1924	Sag
18 Dec 1924–31 Dec 1924	Cap

1925–1949

1 Jan 1925– 5 Jan 1926	Cap
6 Jan 1926–17 Jan 1927	Aqu
18 Jan 1927– 5 Jun 1927	Pis
6 Jun 1927–10 Sep 1927	Ari
11 Sep 1927–22 Jan 1928	Pis
23 Jan 1928– 3 Jun 1928	Ari
4 Jun 1928–12 Jun 1929	Tau
13 Jun 1929–26 Jun 1930	Gem
27 Jun 1930–16 Jul 1931	Can
17 Jul 1931–10 Aug 1932	Leo
11 Aug 1932– 9 Sep 1933	Vir
10 Sep 1933–10 Oct 1934	Lib
11 Oct 1934– 8 Nov 1935	Sco
9 Nov 1935– 1 Dec 1936	Sag
2 Dec 1936–19 Dec 1937	Cap
20 Dec 1937–13 May 1938	Aqu
14 May 1938–29 Jul 1938	Pis
30 Jul 1938–29 Dec 1938	Aqu
30 Dec 1938–11 May 1939	Pis
12 May 1939–29 Oct 1939	Ari
30 Oct 1939–20 Dec 1939	Pis
21 Dec 1939–15 May 1940	Ari
16 May 1940–26 May 1941	Tau
27 May 1941– 9 Jun 1942	Gem
10 Jun 1942–30 Jun 1943	Can
1 Jul 1943–25 Jul 1944	Leo
26 Jul 1944–24 Aug 1945	Vir
25 Aug 1945–24 Sep 1946	Lib
25 Sep 1946–23 Oct 1947	Sco
24 Oct 1947–14 Nov 1948	Sag
15 Nov 1948–12 Apr 1949	Cap
13 Apr 1949–27 Jun 1949	Aqu
28 Jun 1949–30 Nov 1949	Cap
1 Dec 1949–31 Dec 1949	Aqu

Table 9 **Jupiter Tables** *contd*

1950–1969

1 Jan 1950–14 Apr 1950	Aqu
15 Apr 1950–14 Sep 1950	Pis
15 Sep 1950– 1 Dec 1950	Aqu
2 Dec 1950–21 Apr 1951	Pis
22 Apr 1951–28 Apr 1952	Ari
29 Apr 1952– 9 May 1953	Tau
10 May 1953–23 May 1954	Gem
24 May 1954–12 Jun 1955	Can
13 Jun 1955–16 Nov 1955	Leo
17 Nov 1955–17 Jan 1956	Vir
18 Jan 1956– 7 Jul 1956	Leo
8 Jul 1956–12 Dec 1956	Vir
13 Dec 1956–19 Feb 1957	Lib
20 Feb 1957– 6 Aug 1957	Vir
7 Aug 1957–13 Jan 1958	Lib
14 Jan 1958–20 Mar 1958	Sco
21 Mar 1958– 6 Sep 1958	Lib
7 Sep 1958–10 Feb 1959	Sco
11 Feb 1959–24 Apr 1959	Sag
25 Apr 1959– 5 Oct 1959	Sco
6 Oct 1959– 1 Mar 1960	Sag
2 Mar 1960– 9 Jun 1960	Cap
10 Jun 1960–25 Oct 1960	Sag
26 Oct 1960–14 Mar 1961	Cap
15 Mar 1961–11 Aug 1961	Aqu
12 Aug 1961– 3 Nov 1961	Cap
4 Nov 1961–25 Mar 1962	Aqu
26 Mar 1962– 3 Apr 1963	Pis
4 Apr 1963–11 Apr 1964	Ari
12 Apr 1964–22 Apr 1965	Tau
23 Apr 1965–20 Sep 1965	Gem
21 Sep 1965–16 Nov 1965	Can
17 Nov 1965– 5 May 1966	Gem
6 May 1966–27 Sep 1966	Can
28 Sep 1966–15 Jan 1967	Leo
16 Jan 1967–22 May 1967	Can
23 May 1967–18 Oct 1967	Leo
19 Oct 1967–26 Feb 1968	Vir
27 Feb 1968–15 Jun 1968	Leo
16 Jun 1968–15 Nov 1968	Vir
16 Nov 1968–30 Mar 1969	Lib
31 Mar 1969–15 Jul 1969	Vir
16 Jul 1969–16 Dec 1969	Lib
17 Dec 1969–31 Dec 1969	Sco

1970–1999

1 Jan 1970–29 Apr 1970	Sco
30 Apr 1970–15 Aug 1970	Lib
16 Aug 1970–13 Jan 1971	Sco
14 Jan 1971– 4 Jun 1971	Sag
5 Jun 1971–11 Sep 1971	Sco
12 Sep 1971– 6 Feb 1972	Sag
7 Feb 1972–24 Jul 1972	Cap
25 Jul 1972–25 Sep 1972	Sag
26 Sep 1972–22 Feb 1973	Cap
23 Feb 1973– 7 Mar 1974	Aqu
8 Mar 1974–18 Mar 1975	Pis
19 Mar 1975–25 Mar 1976	Ari
26 Mar 1976–22 Aug 1976	Tau
23 Aug 1976–16 Oct 1976	Gem
17 Oct 1976– 3 Apr 1977	Tau
4 Apr 1977–20 Aug 1977	Gem
21 Aug 1977–30 Dec 1977	Can
31 Dec 1977–11 Apr 1978	Gem
12 Apr 1978– 4 Sep 1978	Can
5 Sep 1978–28 Feb 1979	Leo
1 Mar 1979–19 Apr 1979	Can
20 Apr 1979–28 Sep 1979	Leo
29 Sep 1979–26 Oct 1980	Vir
27 Oct 1980–26 Nov 1981	Lib
27 Nov 1981–25 Dec 1982	Sco
26 Dec 1982–19 Jan 1984	Sag
20 Jan 1984– 6 Feb 1985	Cap
7 Feb 1985–20 Feb 1986	Aqu
21 Feb 1986– 2 Mar 1987	Pis
3 Mar 1987– 8 Mar 1988	Ari
9 Mar 1988–21 Jul 1988	Tau
22 Jul 1988–30 Nov 1988	Gem
1 Dec 1988–10 Mar 1989	Tau
11 Mar 1989–30 Jul 1989	Gem
31 Jul 1989–17 Aug 1990	Can
18 Aug 1990–11 Sep 1991	Leo
12 Sep 1991–10 Oct 1992	Vir
11 Oct 1992– 9 Nov 1993	Lib
10 Nov 1993– 8 Dec 1994	Sco
9 Dec 1994– 2 Jan 1996	Sag
3 Jan 1996–21 Jan 1997	Cap
22 Jan 1997– 3 Feb 1998	Aqu
4 Feb 1998–12 Feb 1999	Pis
13 Feb 1999–27 Jun 1999	Ari
28 Jun 1999–22 Oct 1999	Tau
23 Oct 1999–31 Dec 1999	Ari

Table 9 **Jupiter Tables** contd

Jupiter in Aries (Salvador Dali)

Jupiter in Aries people see themselves as pioneers. They like to feel that they are the first to do something and are never afraid of taking a step into the unknown. Very often, these people have strong principles, which they are not afraid of expressing. This is particularly the case when they believe that people or institutions have done something which is unjust or unfair. In their careers, Jupiter in Aries need a high degree of independence. They need to be able to act on their own initiative, without having to seek prior approval from their superiors.

Jupiter in Taurus (Pablo Picasso)

This is one of the more materialistic sign placements for Jupiter. Jupiter in Taurus people understand the importance of money and are keen to create a secure financial base for themselves. In their careers, they are usually successful. Areas where Jupiter can really excel include banking, property and building. Jupiter in Taurus also has a natural affinity with nature, and can gain enormous satisfaction from gardening and long walks in the country. Indeed, the environment is important to Jupiter in Taurus people and they will do all they can to protect it.

Jupiter in Gemini (Jackie Onassis)

Gemini is not one of the better places for Jupiter to be placed. This is because Jupiter is the planet of big ideas and finds it difficult to cope with the endless questions asked by Gemini. Under these circumstances, Jupiter in Gemini people often lack a clear vision about what they want for the future. Their ideas and opinions change from day to day and they may be very unsure about their religious beliefs. However, every cloud has a silver lining: Jupiter in Gemini is unlikely to be dogmatic about anything and will always give other people a fair hearing.

Jupiter in Cancer (Laurence Olivier)

Jupiter in Cancer is likely to be stable and secure. These people understand the importance of family life and will be able to create a happy and loving home for their nearest and dearest. They have a deep respect for the past and are somewhat wary of modern ideas. As a result, they can have a reputation for being a bit too traditional and old-fashioned. When it comes to diet, Jupiter Cancer is fond of food and drink. This may mean that they put on a bit of excess weight. Not to worry. Regular swimming will quickly burn it off.

Jupiter in Leo (Omar Sharif)

Jupiter in Leo is warm-hearted and generous. These people think the best of their friends and are usually prepared to give them the benefit of the doubt. In social situations, Jupiter in Leo is frequently the centre of attention, without having to try. There can be little doubt that Jupiter in Leo people have a fairly high opinion of themselves and tend to believe that they are right about most things. However, they will do their best to avoid arguments. If they hear someone say things that they disagree with, they are unlikely to interfere: they'll just smile to themselves in silent arrogance.

Jupiter in Virgo (HRH Princess Michael of Kent)

Virgo is a very detailed and organized sign, and it is probably not the best place for optimistic and expansive Jupiter. Jupiter in Virgo people get so concerned with details that it is often difficult for them to realize all their ambitions. There are some positive features of this approach to life, however. These people are good with money and unlikely to over-commit themselves financially. They will also be good at giving other people business advice. Another side to Jupiter in Virgo is their interest in health and nutrition. These people make excellent doctors, nurses, dieticians and fitness instructors.

Jupiter in Libra (Dolly Parton)

Jupiter in Libra is very interested in other people. To make the most out of their potential, they need to have an active social life, and in their careers they work best in a team. It is probably also true that Jupiter in Libra people need to be in a close relationship. When they are single, they feel that they are not quite a whole person and will, therefore, look for someone who can fill the gap. One of the most positive qualities of Jupiter in Libra is that they are absolutely fair. They believe that people should be treated equally, regardless of the circumstances.

Jupiter in Scorpio (David Bowie/Ronald Reagan)

Jupiter in Scorpio people have powerful beliefs, which they will never compromise. These beliefs can cover a wide spectrum, including religion, philosophy and politics. However, they don't really like talking about their opinions, unless it is with someone for whom they have total respect. When it comes to religion, people with Jupiter in Scorpio tend to have a healthy attitude to death. They don't see it as an end, but a natural process of transformation. As a result, many people with Jupiter in Scorpio in their horoscopes believe in reincarnation.

Jupiter in Sagittarius (Marlon Brando)

Sagittarius is a brilliant sign for Jupiter to be in. Jupiter in Sagittarius is a natural optimist. However bad things may seem on the surface, these people always believe that they will turn out okay. In their careers, Jupiter in Sagittarius have immense vision and, if they are able to follow their instincts, are often very successful. Nevertheless, they do need a fair amount of variety in their lives, and it is important that they don't stay in one place for too long. They should make a special effort to go on regular holidays, because otherwise they become irritable.

Jupiter in Capricorn (Adolf Hitler)

This is a tricky sign for Jupiter to be placed in. Jupiter in Capricorn people are not idealistic and tend to see everything in terms of their own needs, rather than other people's. They have very little faith in the goodness of human nature and believe that people are only motivated by punishment and reward. So it is not surprising that if these people have a religious bent, they usually believe that sinners roast for eternity in hell. On the plus side, Jupiter in Capricorn has excellent business and financial skills and is good at looking after number one.

Jupiter in Sagittarius people need a fair amount of variety in their lives and it is important that they don't stay in one place for too long.

Jupiter in Aquarius (Norman Fowler)

Jupiter in Aquarius people are idealists. They believe that the world can be turned into a better place, if only people can learn to trust each other. It is very important for them to feel part of a wider group of people and as result they are constantly looking for ways of improving their social life. Unfortunately, they are often let down. Their friends don't always live up to their high expectations, and at times their good nature is taken advantage of. However, this needn't be a problem, if only they could be a little more choosy in whom they trust and confide.

Jupiter in Pisces (HRH Princess Anne)

Pisces is a lucky sign for Jupiter to be in. Jupiter in Pisces people have a natural sensitivity to what is going on around them, both in their immediate environment and in the world at large. When Jupiter in Pisces people hear about a news event happening thousands of miles away, they immediately understand it, without having to know the precise facts. They are also very sympathetic to the needs of their friends, family and colleagues and can always be relied on for help and advice. When it comes to career matters, this sign position makes for good counsellors and priests.

11. SATURN

Saturn is the planet of restriction and discipline. His position tells us what is holding us back, not just in the present, but also in the past. So Saturn may describe obstacles we had to face in our childhood. Saturn also indicates the things we take most seriously, and the things we find hardest to achieve.

Career: Saturn usually tells us about our capacity for hard work. If Saturn is placed in Capricorn or Aquarius this usually means that it should be fairly easy to deal with the demands of one's career. However, in other signs, particularly in the Fire signs (Aries, Leo or Sagittarius), it may be more difficult to settle down to a hard routine.

Fears: To be truly successful in life we need to face our fears. Saturn represents these fears. So people with Saturn in Water signs (Cancer, Scorpio or Pisces) may find it difficult to deal with the darker side of their own feelings. However, once they have accepted their anger or hatred, they may feel much more healthy and creative.

Relationships: If you want a really in-depth look at the way someone functions within a relationship, it is always worth looking at Saturn's position. It can tell you what people hold back from their partners, as well as what they fear from close, romantic involvements.

HOW TO FIND YOUR SATURN SIGN

Of all the planets so far, Saturn is the easiest to find. There are only three tables (table 10): one contains the years from 1900 to 1949, the second contains the years from 1950 to 1999. The third lists the years from 2000 to 2010. Simply choose the relevant table – that is, the one which contains your year of birth – then run your finger down until you locate the row which contains your date of birth. To use the example of a person born on 7 November 1956: 1956 falls in the second table (1950–1999), and 7 November falls in the eighth row from the top. This row has the abbreviation 'Sag' next to it, so this person has Saturn positioned in the sign of Sagittarius. Isn't it easy? Now find your own Saturn sign.

THE MEANING OF SATURN IN EACH SIGN OF THE ZODIAC

Saturn can be thought of as the planet of restriction. So by looking at Saturn's placement through the signs, you can get information about the kinds of obstacles that people have to face. Saturn can also give information about their fears, as well as the way they discipline themselves.

Table 10 **Saturn Tables**

1900–1949

1 Jan 1900–20 Jan 1900	Sag
21 Jan 1900–18 Jul 1900	Cap
19 Jul 1900–16 Oct 1900	Sag
17 Oct 1900–19 Jan 1903	Cap
20 Jan 1903–12 Apr 1905	Aqu
13 Apr 1905–16 Aug 1905	Pis
17 Aug 1905– 8 Jan 1906	Aqu
9 Jan 1906–19 Mar 1908	Pis
20 Mar 1908–16 May 1910	Ari
17 May 1910–14 Dec 1910	Tau
15 Dec 1910–19 Jan 1911	Ari
20 Jan 1911– 6 Jul 1912	Tau
7 Jul 1912–30 Nov 1912	Gem
1 Dec 1912–26 Mar 1913	Tau
27 Mar 1913–24 Aug 1914	Gem
25 Aug 1914– 6 Dec 1914	Can
7 Dec 1914–11 May 1915	Gem
12 May 1915–17 Oct 1916	Can
18 Oct 1916– 7 Dec 1916	Leo
8 Dec 1916–24 Jun 1917	Can
25 Jun 1917–12 Aug 1919	Leo
13 Aug 1919– 7 Oct 1921	Vir
8 Oct 1921–19 Dec 1923	Lib
20 Dec 1923 – 5 Apr 1924	Sco
6 Apr 1924 – 13 Sep 1924	Lib
14 Sep 1924– 2 Dec 1926	Sco
3 Dec 1926–15 Mar 1929	Sag
16 Mar 1929– 4 May 1929	Cap
5 May 1929–29 Nov 1929	Sag
30 Nov 1929–23 Feb 1932	Cap
24 Feb 1932–12 Aug 1932	Aqu
13 Aug 1932–19 Nov 1932	Cap
20 Nov 1932–14 Feb 1935	Aqu
15 Feb 1935–24 Apr 1937	Pis
25 Apr 1937–17 Oct 1937	Ari
18 Oct 1937–13 Jan 1938	Pis
14 Jan 1938– 5 Jul 1939	Ari
6 Jul 1939–21 Sep 1939	Tau
22 Sep 1939–19 Mar 1940	Ari
20 Mar 1940– 8 May 1942	Tau
9 May 1942–19 Jun 1944	Gem
20 Jun 1944– 2 Aug 1946	Can
3 Aug 1946–18 Sep 1948	Leo
19 Sep 1948– 2 Apr 1949	Vir
3 Apr 1949–29 May 1949	Leo
30 May 1949–31 Dec 1949	Vir

1950–1999

1 Jan 1950–20 Nov 1950	Vir
21 Nov 1950– 7 Mar 1951	Lib
8 Mar 1951–13 Aug 1951	Vir
14 Aug 1951–22 Oct 1953	Lib
23 Oct 1953–12 Jan 1956	Sco
13 Jan 1956–13 May 1956	Sag
14 May 1956–10 Oct 1956	Sco
11 Oct 1956– 5 Jan 1959	Sag
6 Jan 1959– 3 Jan 1962	Cap
4 Jan 1962–23 Mar 1964	Aqu
24 Mar 1964–16 Sep 1964	Pis
17 Sep 1964–15 Dec 1964	Aqu
16 Dec 1964– 3 Mar 1967	Pis
4 Mar 1967–29 Apr 1969	Ari
30 Apr 1969–18 Jun 1971	Tau
19 Jun 1971– 9 Jan 1972	Gem
10 Jan 1972–21 Feb 1972	Tau
22 Feb 1972– 1 Aug 1973	Gem
2 Aug 1973– 7 Jan 1974	Can
8 Jan 1974–18 Apr 1974	Gem
19 Apr 1974–16 Sep 1975	Can
17 Sep 1975–14 Jan 1976	Leo
15 Jan 1976– 4 Jun 1976	Can
5 Jun 1976–16 Nov 1977	Leo
17 Nov 1977– 4 Jan 1978	Vir
5 Jan 1978–26 Jul 1978	Leo
27 Jul 1978–20 Sep 1980	Vir
21 Sep 1980–28 Nov 1982	Lib
29 Nov 1982– 6 May 1983	Sco
7 May 1983–24 Aug 1983	Lib
25 Aug 1983–16 Nov 1985	Sco
17 Nov 1985–13 Feb 1988	Sag
14 Feb 1988– 9 Jun 1988	Cap
10 Jun 1988–11 Nov 1988	Sag
12 Nov 1988– 6 Feb 1991	Cap
7 Feb 1991–20 May 1993	Aqu
21 May 1993–29 Jun 1993	Pis
30 Jun 1993–28 Jan 1994	Aqu
29 Jan 1994– 6 Apr 1996	Pis
7 Apr 1996– 8 Jun 1998	Ari
9 Jun 1998–25 Oct 1998	Tau
26 Oct 1998–28 Feb 1999	Ari
1 Mar 1999–31 Dec 1999	Tau

Table 10 **Saturn Tables** contd

2000–2010	
1 Jan 2000– 9 Aug 2000	Tau
10 Aug 2000–15 Oct 2000	Gem
16 Oct 2000–20 Apr 2001	Tau
21 Apr 2001– 3 Jun 2003	Gem
4 Jun 2003–16 Jul 2005	Can
17 Jul 2005– 2 Sep 2007	Leo
3 Sep 2007–29 Oct 2009	Vir
30 Oct 2009– 7 Apr 2010	Lib
8 Apr 2010–21 Jul 2010	Vir
22 Jul 2010–31 Dec 2010	Lib

Saturn in Aries (Leon Trotsky)

Aries is not one of the easier sign placements for Saturn. Saturn in Aries people often believe that circumstances beyond their control are holding them back, preventing them from reaching their full potential. As a result, Saturn in Aries has a fair amount of hidden anger, which explodes every few years in a volcano of energy. The lesson that Saturn in Aries people have to learn is patience, and they need to accept that everything takes time – that all their aims can't be achieved at once. To find inner peace, it is recommended that Saturn in Aries takes up yoga or meditation.

Saturn in Taurus (John Lennon)

Taurus is an Earth sign, and Saturn in Taurus is usually concerned about material matters. Saturn in Taurus people are never quite satisfied that they have enough money, and this can mean that they are prepared to work hard in order to safeguard their position. These people are often also very concerned about their body, and will regard a healthy diet and vigorous exercise as being very important. Indeed, they are fond of telling people about their many plans to lose weight and get fit. Unfortunately, these plans rarely materialize.

Saturn in Gemini (Mick Jagger)

Gemini is one of the luckiest sign placings for Saturn. Saturn in Gemini is usually very intelligent, able to put logic before feelings. Their worst trait is that they are pretty intolerant of people who aren't as clever as they are. If Saturn in Gemini people think that someone is a fool, they will treat that person with utter contempt and rudeness. Saturn in Gemini is probably on best form when reading or studying. In social situations they don't know how to function properly, and can come over as being terribly detached, almost to the point of iciness.

Saturn in Cancer (Napoleon Bonaparte)

Cancer is a sign often connected with the home. Saturn in Cancer, therefore, regards home matters as very, very important. Having a stable domestic environment and a supporting family is also important, and these people will put an enormous amount of effort into achieving this aim. Saturn in Cancer will often go so far as to persist with a difficult marriage, just to keep the family unit together. On a deep level, many people with Saturn in Cancer feel that they are never quite happy where they are living. Somehow, Saturn always believes that the grass might be greener somewhere else.

Saturn in Leo (Ludwig van Beethoven)

There are probably better signs for Saturn to be in than Leo. This is because heavy-going Saturn finds Leo a little too frivolous. Saturn in Leo people are desperate to be taken seriously, and often find that they are not given sufficient attention. This puts them in a difficult position. Either they make a fuss and risk looking stupid – or say nothing and risk being further ignored. The best way around this problem is for Saturn in Leo not to get so worried about other people. They should get on with their own lives and let their achievements speak for themselves.

Saturn in Virgo (Pope John Paul II)

Saturn in Virgo tends to be very organized. These people understand the importance of a stable routine and often work to a strict schedule. This means that they are able to get an enormous amount done. However, it is important that they don't get so concerned with details that they forget their wider goals in life. Virgo is a sign which is often connected with health and hygiene and Saturn placed in Virgo is often very concerned that the environment is spotlessly clean. As far as career is concerned, Saturn in Virgo people often make excellent public health officials.

Saturn in Libra (George Bush)

Saturn works well in Libra. People who have Saturn in Libra are usually quite balanced and able to cope with the demands that society puts on them. When it comes to handling other people, they are aware of their responsibilities. They will keep their word and always lend a hand to someone in need. However, they will never martyr themselves. They know that they have to look after their own interests if they are to be of any use to others. As far as career is concerned, Saturn in Libra makes excellent judges or lawyers.

Saturn in Scorpio (Queen Elizabeth II)

Saturn in Scorpio tends to take life rather seriously. These people find it difficult to let go and enjoy themselves and are often on the look-out for rivals and hidden enemies. It is not easy to gain the trust of Saturn in Scorpio people, because they will always suspect your motives. And if you offend or betray Saturn in Scorpio you will almost certainly live to regret it.

Scorpio is a sign which is often associated with the mystical side of life, and people with Saturn placed here are often fascinated by the occult, the supernatural and astrology.

Saturn in Sagittarius (Sandy Lyle)

Saturn in Sagittarius can often bring a profound restlessness. Sagittarius is a sign which thrives on movement, travel and variety, and Saturn in this sign can lead to a feeling of being trapped. This is particularly the case if Saturn is often indoors, particularly in an office environment. To be on best form, Saturn in Sagittarius should get outside as much as possible, preferably in the countryside. These people sometimes have very strong opinions, which they are keen to impose on other people. This is usually because one of the parents has been too strict.

Saturn in Capricorn (John McEnroe)

Capricorn is one of the best sign positions for Saturn. Saturn in Capricorn is ambitious and capable of working extremely hard. However, these people don't expect immediate results for their efforts and are prepared to spend a long time building up their position. This approach explains why people with this sign placement often have a slow start to their careers. In fact, it is often only when they hit their mid to late thirties that Saturn in Capricorn people start to establish themselves. After that there is no stopping them and it is only a matter of time before they reach the pinnacles of achievement.

Saturn in Aquarius (Wolfgang Amadeus Mozart)

Saturn feels at home in Aquarius. A person with this sign position is usually very intelligent and able to make a positive contribution to society. While Saturn in Aquarius is an idealistic placement, these people do appreciate that the world cannot

Saturn in Capricorn people don't expect immediate results for their efforts and are prepared to spend a long time building up their position.

be changed without dedication and hard work. Sometimes the ideas that Saturn in Aquarius comes up with seem a little frightening. However, there is no need to worry. If you allow them to explain themselves in full, you will quickly come round to their point of view. Saturn in Aquarius makes excellent politicians, prophets or professors.

Saturn in Pisces (Vanessa Redgrave)

Saturn in Pisces is looking for a quiet life. These people don't like complicated scenes, particularly where emotions are involved, and will do anything they can to find peace and security. Saturn in Pisces people are not great risk-takers and are afraid of things that they don't understand. So you will very rarely find them getting involved with witchcraft and black magic. Despite their fear of emotions, Saturn in Pisces people are extremely sensitive. They care about other people, and if friends are going through a genuine crisis they are capable of being very sympathetic and caring.

12. URANUS, NEPTUNE AND PLUTO

Uranus, Neptune and Pluto were only discovered in the last two hundred years, so the ancient astrologers knew nothing of their existence. It is possible to look at a horoscope without using them at all, although if you do this you may be missing out on some important details.

The sign positions of Uranus, Neptune and Pluto are not usually of personal significance. Instead, they describe the generation to which someone belongs. In the following sections on Uranus, Neptune and Pluto, we describe the general characteristics of the planets and list their meanings through the signs. You will notice that for Neptune and Pluto we don't list all the twelve sign positions. This is because these planets move so slowly that there are certain signs which they do not go through during the twentieth century.

If you read something about your Uranus, Neptune or Pluto which you disagree with, don't worry. What we have written are generalizations which describe generations as a whole. There will always be people within a generation who don't conform to its general characteristics.

BUILDING A GENERATION PROFILE WITH URANUS, NEPTUNE AND PLUTO

When you are looking at an individual horoscope, you may want to build up a profile of that person's generation. In order to do this, you must look at the sign positions of their Uranus, Neptune and Pluto. Having done that, you can look up the sign meanings that are provided later in this chapter. Occasionally you may find that the sign meanings appear to be giving very different meanings. What this means is that the generation you are looking at is torn between conflicting planetary energies.

One thing to bear in mind when looking at generations is that, in astrology, they change very quickly. For example, someone born in 1955 has Uranus in Cancer, Neptune in Libra and Pluto in Leo. Someone else, born a year later in 1956, would have Uranus in Leo, Neptune in Scorpio and Pluto in Virgo. Normally, we think of people of different generations as being of very different ages. In astrology it is not the age that counts, but the positions of the planets. So astrologers would regard the 1956 person as being in a completely different generation from the one born in 1955.

Let's look at Madonna's horoscope, to show how a generation profile works. She was born in 1958, when Uranus was in Leo, Neptune was in Scorpio and Pluto was in Virgo. Now these positions don't necessarily describe her personally. After all, most people between 1956 and 1962 would have these same Uranus, Neptune and Pluto positions. These positions describe in general terms the majority of people born during these six years. You can see what kind of styles this generation are interested in, as well as some of their likes and dislikes.

If we look up the meanings of Madonna's Uranus, Neptune and Pluto, we find the following:

Uranus in Leo This generation has high hopes for itself. It wants to do something special, which the world recognizes it for. Such recognition will come, but often slowly.

Neptune in Scorpio These people are very aware of the sexuality around them. At the same time crime and poverty upset them and they are often pessimistic about the future.

Pluto in Virgo As a group, people with Pluto in Virgo believe

173

that they can establish their authority through argument and criticism. They are also obsessed with health matters.

In the case of Uranus in Leo, we see that Madonna has had no problem getting the recognition that is so important to this placement. It seems that she has made a generational planet personal to her. Indeed, it is very often the case that famous and successful people are able to do this. They become the spokesmen and -women for a generation. So if you want to be very successful, make sure that you act in a way which accords with your Uranus, Neptune and Pluto signs.

With her Neptune in Scorpio, Madonna is part of a generation which is very concerned about sexual issues. Sexual themes and imagery are very much part of her creative expression. So again, this has become a focus for the feelings of the Neptune in Scorpio generation. Like many people born in the late fifties and sixties, health matters are important to Madonna, and she is known to take a lot of exercise.

HOW TO FIND YOUR URANUS, NEPTUNE AND PLUTO SIGNS

These tables are dead easy. There is only one table for each of these planets. Simply run your finger down each table to locate your year of birth, then look at the abbreviation on the right-hand side of that row. For example, a person born on 7 November 1956 will have Uranus in Leo. On row 23 of the Uranus table (table 11) we see that 7 November 1956 falls within the dates 10 June 1956–1 November 1961. And on the right-hand side we see 'Leo'.

This same person has Neptune in Scorpio. On the Neptune table (table 12), 7 November 1956 falls in row 18, because it falls within the dates 19 October 1956–15 June 1957. And on the right-hand side of that row, we see 'Sco' – the abbreviation for Scorpio.

Finally, our example person has Pluto in Virgo. In the Pluto

Table 11 **Uranus Table**

1900–1999

1 Jan 1900–20 Dec 1904	Sag
21 Dec 1904–30 Jan 1912	Cap
31 Jan 1912– 4 Sep 1912	Aqu
5 Sep 1912–11 Nov 1912	Cap
12 Nov 1912–31 Mar 1919	Aqu
1 Apr 1919–16 Aug 1919	Pis
17 Aug 1919–22 Jan 1920	Aqu
23 Jan 1920–31 Mar 1927	Pis
1 Apr 1927– 3 Nov 1927	Aqu
4 Nov 1927–12 Jan 1928	Pis
13 Jan 1928– 6 Jun 1934	Ari
7 Jun 1934– 9 Oct 1934	Tau
10 Oct 1934–27 Mar 1935	Ari
28 Mar 1935– 7 Aug 1941	Tau
8 Aug 1941– 4 Oct 1941	Gem
5 Oct 1941–14 May 1942	Tau
15 May 1942–30 Aug 1948	Gem
31 Aug 1948–12 Nov 1948	Can
13 Nov 1948– 9 Jun 1949	Gem
10 Jun 1949–24 Aug 1955	Can
25 Aug 1955–27 Jan 1956	Leo
28 Jan 1956– 9 Jun 1956	Can
10 Jun 1956– 1 Nov 1961	Leo
2 Nov 1961– 9 Jan 1962	Vir
10 Jan 1962– 9 Aug 1962	Leo
10 Aug 1962–28 Sep 1968	Vir
29 Sep 1968–20 May 1969	Lib
21 May 1969–23 Jun 1969	Vir
24 Jun 1969–20 Nov 1974	Lib
21 Nov 1974– 1 May 1975	Sco
2 May 1975– 7 Sep 1975	Lib
8 Sep 1975–16 Feb 1981	Sco
17 Feb 1981–20 Mar 1981	Sag
21 Mar 1981–16 Nov 1981	Sco
17 Nov 1981–14 Feb 1988	Sag
15 Feb 1988–26 May 1988	Cap
27 May 1988– 2 Dec 1988	Sag
3 Dec 1988– 1 Apr 1995	Cap
2 Apr 1995– 8 Jun 1995	Aqu
9 Jun 1995–11 Jan 1996	Cap
12 Jan 1996–31 Dec 1999	Aqu

Table 12 **Neptune Table**

1900–1999

1 Jan 1900–19 Jul 1901	Gem
20 Jul 1901–25 Dec 1901	Can
26 Dec 1901–21 May 1902	Gem
22 May 1902–23 Sep 1914	Can
24 Sep 1914–14 Dec 1914	Leo
15 Dec 1914–19 Jul 1915	Can
20 Jul 1915–19 Mar 1916	Leo
20 Mar 1916– 1 May 1916	Can
2 May 1916–21 Sep 1928	Leo
22 Sep 1928–18 Feb 1929	Vir
19 Feb 1929–24 Jul 1929	Leo
25 Jul 1929– 3 Oct 1942	Vir
4 Oct 1942–16 Apr 1943	Lib
17 Apr 1943– 2 Aug 1943	Vir
3 Aug 1943–24 Dec 1955	Lib
25 Dec 1955–11 Mar 1956	Sco
12 Mar 1956–18 Oct 1956	Lib
19 Oct 1956–15 Jun 1957	Sco
16 Jun 1957– 5 Aug 1957	Lib
6 Aug 1957– 4 Jan 1970	Sco
5 Jan 1970– 2 May 1970	Sag
3 May 1970– 6 Nov 1970	Sco
7 Nov 1970–18 Jan 1984	Sag
19 Jan 1984–22 Jun 1984	Cap
23 Jun 1984–20 Nov 1984	Sag
21 Nov 1984–28 Jan 1998	Cap
29 Jan 1998–22 Aug 1998	Aqu
23 Aug 1998–27 Nov 1998	Cap
28 Nov 1998–31 Dec 1999	Aqu

Table 13 **Pluto Table**

1900–1999

1 Jan 1900–10 Sep 1912	Gem
11 Sep 1912–19 Oct 1912	Can
20 Oct 1912– 9 Jul 1913	Gem
10 Jul 1913–27 Dec 1913	Can
28 Dec 1913–26 May 1914	Gem
27 May 1914– 6 Oct 1937	Can
7 Oct 1937–24 Nov 1937	Leo
25 Nov 1937– 3 Oct 1938	Can
4 Oct 1938– 7 Feb 1939	Leo
8 Feb 1939–13 Jun 1939	Can
14 Jun 1939–19 Oct 1956	Leo
20 Oct 1956–14 Jan 1957	Vir
15 Jan 1957–18 Aug 1957	Leo
19 Aug 1957–11 Apr 1958	Vir
12 Apr 1958–10 Jun 1958	Leo
11 Jun 1958– 4 Oct 1971	Vir
5 Oct 1971–16 Apr 1972	Lib
17 Apr 1972–29 Jul 1972	Vir
30 Jul 1972– 5 Nov 1983	Lib
6 Nov 1983–18 May 1984	Sco
19 May 1984–27 Aug 1984	Lib
28 Aug 1984–16 Jan 1995	Sco
17 Jan 1995–20 Apr 1995	Sag
21 Apr 1995–10 Nov 1995	Sco
11 Nov 1995–31 Dec 1999	Sag

table (table 13), 7 November 1956 falls in row 12, between the dates 20 October 1956–14 January 1957. On the right-hand side of that row we see the abbreviation 'Vir', which stands for Virgo.

This is really simple – now find your own Uranus, Neptune and Pluto signs.

Uranus is the planet of disruption. It is often connected with earthquakes and explosions. Uranus also represents anything which is new and original. Its position through the signs of the zodiac will tell us how a generation wants to be special and to rebel from the rest of society.

We have not gone into great detail with these descriptions because they are not personal, unlike the Sun, Moon, Mercury, Venus, Mars, Jupiter and Saturn. They are generational descriptions.

Uranus in Aries

This generation is keen to assert its independence. They are unhappy with existing forms of authority and they hate it when politicians meddle in their lives.

Uranus in Taurus

The Uranus in Taurus generation has unusual ideas about money and property, which may threaten the established order. They may also be musical innovators.

Uranus in Gemini

A brilliant generation, who are open-minded and who think up more than their fair share of good ideas. This group is highly influential in the field of art and culture.

Uranus in Cancer

Many of this generation are attracted to alternative living and to communal life. While these people are anxious to be different, circumstances may force them to conform.

Uranus in Leo

This generation has high hopes for itself. It wants to do something special, which the world recognizes it for. Such recognition will come, but often slowly.

Uranus in Virgo

Uranus in Virgo often likes to express its individuality by criticizing other people's creativity, rather than by creating anything positive of its own.

Uranus in Libra

This generation has unorthodox views about marriage and relationships. It shows its originality by being in unusual relationships with unusual people.

Uranus in Scorpio

An extremely powerful generation, who believe that their emotional and sexual energy can, in some way best known to themselves, cause revolutionary change.

Uranus in Sagittarius

Uranus in Sagittarius people are likely to have a major impact on society. They are true visionaries, whose ideas are nothing short of brilliant.

Uranus in Capricorn

This generation is extremely down-to-earth. It believes that there is no point in talking about changing the world unless you've got the guns and the political will.

Uranus in Aquarius

The Uranus in Aquarius generation is surprisingly narrow-minded, and is often intolerant of people who have ideas which differ from its own.

Uranus in Pisces

The generation with Uranus in Pisces often find it difficult to create change of their own. Instead they are likely follow prevailing fashions.

Neptune is often associated with confusion, deception, chaos and disorganization. On a more positive note, it can represent sprirituality and people's desire to merge with something higher and greater than themselves. So it is often linked with psychic and supernatural phenomena.

As with Uranus, the descriptions given are brief, because they apply more to generations than to individuals.

Neptune in Gemini

This generation are often strongly influenced by the ideas of politicians and the popular press. Sometimes it is difficult for them to think for themselves.

Neptune in Cancer

The generation born when Neptune was in Cancer are often great patriots. They sometimes think that their country is so wonderful that they want to worship it.

Neptune in Leo

Leo is a creative sign for Neptune to be in, and people of this generation tend to have a powerful imagination which can be used in both their writing and their painting.

Neptune in Virgo

The Neptune in Virgo generation may find things like paper-work and bureaucracy hard to deal with. They quickly find themselves being swamped by it.

Neptune in Libra

A very idealistic generation, especially about relationships. They believe that the power of love can transport them to heaven and back. If only they could find the right partner.

Neptune in Scorpio

These people are very aware of the sexuality around them. At the same time crime and poverty upset them, and they are often pessimistic about the future.

Neptune in Sagittarius

Sagittarius is one of the most optimistic signs that Neptune can be in. This generation wants to enjoy life to the full, without fear or regret.

Neptune in Capricorn

Capricorn is not the best place for Neptune. The Neptune in Capricorn generation may be too practical and too concerned with money for its own good.

Neptune in Aquarius

This generation will be very humanitarian. They will believe in the fundamental good nature of mankind, and will put into action a radically new way of running society.

PLUTO

Pluto is sometimes regarded as the planet of obsession. Its sign position can therefore describe the kinds of things which generations of people get obsessed about. It is also linked to things which are hidden, as well as to the way individuals and groups express their need to be in control.

As with Uranus and Neptune, the descriptions given are brief.

Pluto in Gemini

The Pluto in Gemini generation may be obsessed with the need to get their message across to a wider audience. They may also find themselves magnetically attracted to dictators.

Pluto in Cancer

Those with Pluto in Cancer tend to be preoccupied by their country. It may represent something which they not only have to fight for, but also die for.

Pluto in Leo

This generation has a great belief in its own power. They feel they can take control of destiny and break away from the grip of tradition and of authority.

Pluto in Virgo

As a group, people with Pluto in Virgo believe that they can establish their authority through argument and criticism. They are also obsessed with health matters.

Pluto in Libra

Relationships are often on the mind of the Pluto in Libra generation. They want to be transformed by relationships, but they are also afraid of this transformation.

Pluto in Scorpio

The Pluto in Scorpio generation (today's generation) want to get to the bottom of the mysteries of life and death. So they are likely to be particularly concerned by spiritual matters.

Pluto in Sagittarius

Those people with Pluto in Sagittarius (from late 1995 onwards) will be obsessed with the idea that society and other people are holding them back. As a result they may be a generation of rebels.

Section Three

··

THE ELEMENTS

13. THE FOUR ELEMENTS

Up until a few centuries ago, it was believed that everything could be divided up into four elements: Fire, Earth, Air and Water. Anything burning was Fire, anything solid was Earth, anything which was a gas or a wind was Air. All liquids were Water. So when you make a cup of coffee, you take a cup from the shelf, which is solid, and is therefore made of Earth. The spoonful of instant coffee you put into the cup is also solid, and is Earth. The hot water you put into the cup is a liquid, and is obviously Water. To make the water hot in the first place you may have had to boil a kettle on a stove. If you had been using a gas cooker, this would have required a flame, which is Fire. Once you have made the cup of coffee, you would notice steam coming off it. This is a gas, and in ancient times would have been classified as Air.

It would certainly be very simple if all aspects of our world could be divided up into Fire, Earth Air and Water. Unfortunately, modern science has shown that this is not the case, and that matter is divided up into several hundred different elements, like carbon, oxygen, gold, copper and iron. As a result of this discovery, most people stopped thinking of their world

185

in terms of the four elements. However, there was one group of people who continued to use them. They were astrologers.

Although astrologers accept that the world is not literally divided into four elements, they do believe that the signs of the zodiac can be classified in terms of Fire, Earth, Air and Water. The Fire signs are Aries, Leo and Sagittarius, the Earth signs are Taurus, Virgo and Capricorn, the Air signs are Gemini, Libra and Aquarius, and the Water signs are Cancer, Scorpio and Pisces.

This does not mean that all the Fire signs are on fire, or that all the Earth signs are solid as a rock. Rather, the images of Fire, Earth, Air and Water help us to understand the sign.

So, if we take the Earth Signs, we can say that these signs are quite materialistic. They like to have solid facts and details in front of them. They are the 'acquirers' of the zodiac.

The Air Signs, on the other hand, need plenty of variety in their lives: they enjoy moving from place to place and from person to person. Rather like the wind, which is always on the move. They are the 'thinkers' of the zodiac.

The Fire Signs, however, like adventure, challenge and change. If they are confined by people or situations they become easily disheartened. These people are incredibly enthusiastic, gregarious and spontaneous. They are the 'doers' of the zodiac.

The Water Signs need emotional security – usually in the form of a deep understanding with a lover or partner. It is their feelings and emotions which motivate them. Life without intensity is like no life at all. They are the 'feeling' types of the zodiac.

The four elements can be seen as four different ways of dealing with the world, and can be used to describe people's personalities. Broadly speaking, Fire signs are about 'action', Earth signs are about 'touch', Air signs are about 'thought' and Water signs are about 'emotion'.

Once you find out what the strongest element in someone's

horoscope is, you are able to categorize him or her in terms of the elements. People who have Air as the principal element in their horoscope are likely to live through their thoughts. They will spend a lot of time thinking, and it may be easier for them to talk about something, rather than actually do it. This contrasts with Fire people, who believe that actions speak louder than words.

DISCOVERING THE STRONGEST ELEMENT IN A HOROSCOPE

Step One

The first thing you need to do is to work out the sign positions of the first seven planets in someone's horoscope. (When it comes to elements, the positions of Uranus, Neptune and Pluto are not taken into account.)

If we take the example of Madonna, we find that at the moment of her birth the seven planets were in the following signs:

> Sun: Leo
> Moon: Virgo
> Mercury: Virgo
> Venus: Leo
> Mars: Taurus
> Jupiter: Libra
> Saturn: Sagittarius

Step Two

Note the element of the sign in which each of the planets in the horoscope is positioned. Madonna has:

> Sun in Leo, which is a Fire sign
> Moon in Virgo, which is an Earth sign
> Mercury in Virgo, which is another Earth Sign.

Venus in Leo, which is a Fire sign
Mars in Taurus, which is an Earth sign
Jupiter in Libra, which is an Air sign
Saturn in Sagittarius, which is a Fire sign

The elements of Madonna's planets:

Sun: Fire
Moon: Earth
Mercury: Earth
Venus: Fire
Mars: Earth
Jupiter: Air
Saturn: Fire

Step Three

Once you know what the elements of the first seven planets in the horoscope are, it is a matter of counting them up. The element which has the most planets in it is the one which is the strongest. Madonna has three planets in Fire signs (Sun, Venus and Saturn), three planets in Earth signs (Moon, Mercury and Mars), one planet in an Air Sign (Jupiter), and no planets in Water signs.

So in Madonna's case we have a tie. Both the Fire and Earth signs are strongly represented, with three planets in each. When there are two or three elements which seem to be equally strong, check to see which of these tying elements has the Sun in it. In Madonna's horoscope Fire and Earth appear equally strong, but she is regarded as a Fire person because her Sun is in Leo, which is a Fire sign.

To take another example of a tie situation, if the Sun is the only one of the seven planets which is in a particular element, then you look at the Moon's element instead. You might find that someone has the Sun in an Earth sign, the Moon, Mercury and Venus in Air Signs, and Mars, Jupiter and Saturn in Water Signs. This gives us three planets in Water signs, and three in Air signs. Which of these two elements is strongest? Looking at the Sun's element is not much help, because it is neither Water nor Air. So we look at the Moon. It is in an Air Sign, so Air must be the strongest element.

Step Four: Interpreting the Strongest Element

In the next section you will find detailed descriptions of the four elements. When you have worked out someone's strongest element, turn to this section and read about the effect of this element on his or her personality.

Usually the strongest element will be the same as the element of the Sun sign. This means that in most cases these element descriptions will be enlarging on what you already know about the Sun sign. If you are working out someone's horoscope and you find that the strongest element is different from the element of the Sun sign, then it is possible that this person may not be a typical example of his or her Sun sign.

Let's take an example of a man with his planets in the following positions:

> Sun in Gemini (Air)
> Moon in Scorpio (Water)
> Mercury in Cancer (Water)
> Venus in Cancer (Water)
> Mars in Capricorn (Earth)
> Jupiter in Cancer (Water)
> Saturn in Scorpio (Water)

This person has his Sun in Gemini. You would expect him to be versatile and to get bored easily. Gemini is an Air sign, so he would have plenty of ideas and he would tend to relate to the world with his brain rather than with his feelings. Perhaps he might be a little aloof and detached, particularly when it came to the area of close relationships.

Well, if you said all this, without looking at his overall elemental balance, you might be wrong! He has five planets in

Water signs (Moon, Mercury, Venus, Jupiter and Saturn), one planet in an Air sign (Sun), and one in a Earth sign. So water is very much his strongest element. He is therefore likely to be emotional and to make judgements on the basis of his feelings, rather than his thoughts.

THE FOUR ELEMENTS IN DETAIL

The Fire Signs (Aries, Leo, Sagittarius)

Action is vital to Fire signs. They don't like waiting for things to happen and are usually prepared to take the initiative. Once Fire people have embarked on a particular project, they will throw an enormous amount of energy at it. This means that they often get very fast results. This applies to every aspect of their lives, from career through to love life and social life, so it is not surprising that Fire people are exciting to have around.

If you are planning on holding a party, it is always a good idea to invite plenty of Fire people. They can really set things on fire with their enthusiasm and sense of fun. If things are not moving fast enough, Fire will always know what to do. Sometimes Fire will quite literally set things on fire. One Fire person we know motivates people by flicking lighted matches at them.

Fire is a natural leader. Fire people inspire those around them, and in a crisis they really come into their own. This is because they don't spend ages thinking about possible courses of action, but instinctively know what needs to be done. This ability to make good use of their instincts means that Fire is often the right person in the right place at the right time.

An example of such a person is Winston Churchill, who had his Sun in Sagittarius and his Moon in Leo. In the late 1930s everyone was writing off his political career, including the astrologers. In fact, one astrologer said of Churchill in 1936:

'One of the greatest literary figures of his generation; his ultimate fame will rest on literature and not on his political career.' Only four years later, Churchill became British Prime Minister, because he was seen as the only man that could rescue Britain from the impending threat of Nazi invasion.

However, when looking at Fire it should be borne in mind that Fire needs support. A fire cannot burn on its own; it needs fuel to feed off and oxygen to breath with. It is therefore vital that Fire people are surrounded by people, both at home and at work, who can provide them with support and encouragement. If this support and encouragement is lacking, Fire people begin to lose confidence. They start becoming withdrawn and even inhibited. When Fire gets into this state it is very difficult to get them to snap out of it. Kind words won't be much use, and they certainly won't listen to other people's suggestions. No, the best thing to do is to let time take its course. Eventually, some wild and unexpected event will happen, which will spark the Fire person's energy and enthusiasm. Then it will be business as usual.

The Earth Signs (Taurus, Virgo, Capricorn)

Of all the signs of the zodiac, the Earth signs are the most closely connected to the material world. This is the world which we reach out to and touch. People whose horoscope contains a lot of planets in Earth signs tend to judge things by what they look and feel like. Ideas and vague feelings are simply not enough.

At the crudest level, this can mean that Earth people are not satisfied by promises such as 'the cheque's in the post'. They are only happy when they can physically feel the money, in cash, in their grubby little hands. It is, therefore, not surprising that people who are very Earthy are fond of saying: 'a bird in the hand is worth two in the bush.'

At the highest level, Earth is about nature and the soil. After all, there is nothing more down to earth than the earth itself.

Earth appreciates real, natural beauty and is not interested in shallow pretence. Earth is quick to see through surface appearances, which can be a little upsetting for other signs.

A Leo who likes to make extravagant gestures, such as giving expensive presents, may be asked by the Earthy Virgo how much it all costs. The Aquarian architect who has just designed the ultimate futuristic development may be told by the Capricorn director of finance to cut his costs by half. He might also be told by the Taurus chairperson of the local environment protection group that the project can't go ahead because there is a protected wood in the way. Get it?

Earth is about the material world in the widest sense. Some Earthy people see this in terms of money; others see it in terms of the natural world.

The body is usually very important to Earth. This is not surprising, considering that this element is about touch and physical sensation. Earth people often spend a lot of time looking after their bodies. They may try to look and feel their best and to be as beautiful as possible. This often involves plenty of exercise, as well as careful attention to diet and hygiene. The body is also important when it comes to relating to other people. Earth people regard touch and physical contact as vital, because it is proof that other people exist and that other people love and care for each other.

One problem that Earth people often have is that an abuse of the power entrusted to them can take place. Examples in history include Hitler, Lenin and Robespierre (all Taureans), Ivan the Terrible (Virgo) and Stalin and Mao Tse Tung (both Capricorns). The reason that Earth people are given power in the first place is because they seem so responsible and hardworking, and are efficient administrators. By the time people realize that Earth also has a dictatorial streak, it is too late. The first firing squads are already claiming their victims.

The Air Signs (Gemini, Libra, Aquarius)

Air signs are the thinking signs. This doesn't mean that Air is more intelligent than the other signs, but rather that Air people tend to relate to the world through their thoughts. Conversation is often important to Air and they like to talk things out.

Air people tend to regard things like emotions as a little messy. They find the nitty-gritty of the real, material world rather crude. Indeed, Air people see themselves as being detached from the mundane problems that the other signs have to face in their day-to-day existences.

Words matter to Air and they are adept at using them to get out of difficult situations. If things are getting too emotional, words can be used to diffuse the situation. This may at times give Air the reputation for being a little cold. Everything is just a bit too rational, and anything, including the deepest feelings, can easily be explained away. However, in certain situations, where two people are about to tear each other to bits, the timely intervention of Air, with his cool rationality, might be just the ticket.

Nevertheless, there are other times when emotions are important: The Pisces whose cat has just been run over by a bus needs a bit of sympathy and understanding. If Pisces (Water) seeks out the support of an unfeeling Gemini, she might be reassured with words such as 'Cheer up! Cats are only pieces of emotional furniture. You can always buy another one, unless you'd prefer to buy a radio cassette recorder. Anyway, look on the bright side. You're saving a fortune in cat food.'

On the surface of it, Air certainly seems to be in control. Air people hardly ever talk about their inner feelings, and they like giving the impression that they don't need anyone else's help or support. Well, this image is false. Air may have a well-developed sense of logic and reason, but on an emotional level, is often painfully immature. The reason these people avoid emotion is because they can't deal with it. They may be secretly desperate to express their real feelings, if only they could find a way.

In the area of relationships, Air is most comfortable when the emphasis is on conversation and ideas. So Air people make good friends, provided that you don't make emotional demands on them. In close relationships the situation is different. Air is not a natural romantic, and will find it difficult to express love and affection spontaneously. It is therefore very important that their partners are patient. Partners should take time to build up a safe and trusting environment. With a bit of luck, this will allow Air people to let go of their true feelings.

The Water Signs (Cancer, Scorpio, Pisces)

Water people have very powerful emotions. They feel everything which goes on around them, and are extremely sensitive to other people's moods. When Water people talk, they are not just listening to the words of the conversation, they are also tuning into the subtle, non-verbal signals which are being given. So when you are talking to Water people, don't think you can hide anything from them. Waters' intuition will tell them that you are not being entirely honest, and it is for this reason that Water people make excellent policemen and customs officers.

If you have a problem which is difficult for you to discuss, then your best bet is to find a Water person. Water people are caring and understanding, and you will be able to rely on their tact and discretion. Water won't bombard you with questions. Instead, they will listen to what you are saying, often without making any comments or judgements. While this is very beneficial for you, you should be careful to unburden your problems on Water only if you have to. This is because Water people can often be too sensitive for their own good. They may allow themselves to be swamped by other people's problems and, in the process, forget about their own needs.

Traditionally the Water signs are known as the 'mute' signs. After all, crabs (Cancer), scorpions (Scorpio) and fish (Pisces) are animals which make very little noise. So they often don't say much – perhaps because they know that feelings can't be communicated by words. Water may be happier to sit back and then tune into whatever is going on around. Perhaps this also means that, unlike Air, who shoots his mouth off whenever the opportunity arises, Water will only say something when it really matters.

Many astrology books give the impression that the Water signs have their heads in the clouds and are incapable of dealing with the real world. This impression is misleading. Water can be very perceptive. Once they have learnt to trust their feelings, it is difficult to pull the wool over their eyes. At the same time, Water is good at tuning into wider trends, and this can enable them to spot business opportunities. Rupert Murdoch, the media tycoon, is a Water person, with his Sun in Pisces. The Water enables him to understand what the public wants, not only now, but also in the future.

Water can also make brilliant generals. Water has an instinctive understanding of how an enemy's mind works, and this enables Water to outmanoeuvre the opposition on the battlefield. Examples of watery generals include Montgomery and Rommel (both Scorpios), as well as Alexander the Great (Cancer). So, if you find yourself in a confrontation with Water, don't be fooled by appearances. Water will be second-guessing your every move, and if you make one slip, you'll be finished.

COMPATIBILITY BETWEEN THE ELEMENTS

In Chapter Four we saw how a comparison of two people's Sun signs could give valuable information on how they get on with each other. The Elements can also be used as a further test for compatibility. So, if Fire is your strongest element,

Table 14 **Compatibility Table Between Elements**

	Fire	Air	Water	Earth	
Fire	4	4	3	2	4 = excellent combination
Air		3	2	1	3 = very compatible
Water			3	4	2 = needs working on
Earth				4	1 = exciting but difficult

while your partner's is Earth, you can look up the compatibility between Fire and Earth.

Fire and Fire

This is one of the best possible elemental combinations. It is a very harmonious and long-lasting match, which is helped by the fact that neither partner will ever get bored by the other. There are, nonetheless, things which need to be guarded against: both partners are likely to have pretty big egos and as a result there could be ego clashes. Under these circumstances, it is vital that the two Fire signs learn how to compromise.

Fire and Earth

This combination can indicate a considerable amount of conflict. Earth dislikes Fire's impulsiveness, while Fire gets extremely impatient with Earth's obsession with practicality. To make this relationship work, a good deal of tolerance is required. Fire needs to understand Earth's concerns, while Earth should make a real effort to respect Fire's desire for freedom and space.

Fire and Air

Air and Fire signs are compatible and on the whole they stimulate each other's creativity. Air has big ideas, which Fire's energy and vision can stimulate into action. On the downside, there may be times when Air gets annoyed with Fire's big ego and general selfishness, and other times when Fire gets jealous of Air's independence and detachment. However, this shouldn't get in the way of an otherwise healthy relationship.

Fire and Water

It is important to be aware of some of the problem areas in this relationship. Water's tendency to brood and sulk can irritate Fire. Fire's irritation may eventually turn to anger, which could lead to serious arguments and misunderstandings. However, the union between Fire and Water generates a lot of love and steamy passion, which could be used to heal old wounds.

Earth and Earth

There can be no doubt that this is a most stable elemental relationship. Both partners know exactly what they want from each other and they will have similar goals and expectations. On a physical level this relationship is very powerful and the two Earth lovers should find it easy to satisfy each other's sexual needs. Overall, Earth and Earth are able to make a solid commitment to the relationship, which ensures that it can survive almost any crisis.

Earth and Air

Earth and Air is not an easy mix. Air needs plenty of room in which to circulate and finds it difficult to stay in one place for too long. Earth doesn't appreciate this volatility and will often attempt to restrict Air's movement. As a result, there could be a battle of wills. On a more positive note, Air can inspire Earth to take life more lightly, while Earth can help Air to be more realistic and practical.

Earth and Water

This is an excellent combination, which often manifests itself in a sympathetic and emotionally secure relationship. Earth is looking for a partner who can provide stability and it is likely that this is something which Water's sensitivity can provide. The only problem with Earth – Water matches is that they can be slightly too easy. Nothing out of the ordinary will happen to rock the romantic boat and as a result the relationship may be a little boring.

Air and Air

When Air and Air get together there is an explosion of ideas and conversation. They always have something to say to each other and their powerful intellects tend to spark each other off. So there is no reason why two Air people can't be the very best of friends. However, from the point of view of emotion and passion this relationship can be a non-starter. This is because feelings are likely to be drowned by a sea of words.

Air and Water

There is no doubt that Air and Water fascinate each other, and this fascination can lead to the beginnings of a close relationship. Air is hypnotized by Water's depth and complexity, while Water admires Air's detachment and objectivity. However, it should be appreciated that Air and Water are very different elements. If Air and Water get too close to each other, they may find that they are fundamentally incompatible.

Water and Water

This can be an ideal combination. Both the Water signs are sensitive and emotional. They quickly pick up on each other's feelings and worries, so there is a great deal of mutual sympathy and understanding. However, it is vital that Water people don't rely on their feelings completely. There are likely to be certain issues which need to be confronted and discussed in a calm and rational way. If these issues are avoided, the relationship could run into serious trouble.

....

YOUR ASCENDANT SIGN

14. YOUR ASCENDANT AND ITS MEANING

The Ascendant is of crucial importance. Without it, astrologers cannot draw up a full horoscope, which means that they are limited in what they can predict for their clients. The Ascendant is also very useful for describing people's characters and, in particular, the way they express themselves in public.

In this chapter you are going to find out about the Ascendant. We start off by telling you what the Ascendant is and why it is different from the planets. We then give step by step instructions for calculating the Ascendant. Having done that, we will describe the ways in which the Ascendant influences our characters and destinies. Among other things, we will tell you about your ruling planet, which has a special connection with the Ascendant.

Finally, at the end of this chapter, you will find detailed descriptions of the Ascendant when it falls in each sign of the zodiac, which we hope you will find fascinating.

WHAT IS THE ASCENDANT?

Before you start reading this section, relax. Take the phone off the hook, and put a Do Not Disturb sign on your door. Breathe deeply and rhythmically until you feel comfortable. Once you feel completely relaxed, we would like you to use your imagination.

Imagine the Earth spinning round and round on its axis, like a merry-go-round. Every twenty-four hours the Earth turns round once. In order to prove this to yourself, imagine that you are sitting on a hill, with open countryside all around you. You and this hill are all part of the Earth, which is constantly spinning around. At dawn, you see the Sun on the eastern horizon. As the Earth moves around, the Sun starts to rise above the horizon. For a brief moment, you think it is the Sun that is moving, not the Earth. You are rather like a child on a merry-go-round. As the merry-go-round gathers speed, the child may get the impression that neither he nor his horse is moving. Instead, it looks as if the fairground and his waiting parents are spinning *around him*.

So, the Sun itself does not move over the horizon. It is the spinning Earth that makes the Sun appear to move in this way. As time elapses, while sitting on your hill, you see the Sun rising higher and higher. At noon, the Sun is due south of you. It can get no higher in the sky, and from then on it starts to set. As the Earth spins round even more, you can see the Sun appearing to move slowly down towards the west. Then, at dusk, it disappears, and darkness quickly falls.

As you sit on the hill in the dark, the Earth continues to move, although you can no longer see the Sun. On this particular night, there is a Full Moon, so as the Sun sets, you start to see the Moon edge its way over the eastern horizon. Like the Sun before it, the Moon rises up towards the south. At around midnight, it reaches its highest point, and then it starts to set towards the west. As it disappears below the western horizon, you see the eastern horizon light up. The light gets stronger and stronger, until the Sun finally emerges to greet the new day.

You have now seen an entire twenty-four-hour cycle. The Earth has spun around once during this time and, because of this spinning, the Sun and the Moon have risen in the east and set in the west. You can now climb down off the hill and have a well-deserved rest.

Like the Sun and the Moon, the signs of the zodiac rise and set. The best way to imagine this happening is to picture the twelve signs of the zodiac joined together in a ring, which surrounds the earth. Unlike looking at the Sun and the Moon, it is not possible to physically see this ring, so you'll have to make a real effort to use your imagination.

The zodiacal ring does not move; it remains fixed in space. However, as the Earth moves round, this ring *appears* to move (see diagram, p. 204). In twenty-four hours, each of the twelve signs of the zodiac on this ring will rise, reach the highest point in the south and set, just like the Sun and the Moon. There will always be one sign which is rising over the eastern horizon. Each sign takes between one and three hours to rise over this horizon. This rising is a bit like a long snake crossing a road. The snake starts to cross the road when its head touches the tarmac. As it moves forward, more and more of its body is on the road. Then, as it moves to the other side, it starts to move into the undergrowth. Finally, when the end of the snake's tail has cleared the other side, you can say that it has finished crossing the road. Like the snake, a sign finishes rising when it has cleared the horizon. It then starts moving towards the south, and the following sign starts to rise.

Let's take an example of a sign moving across the horizon: in England, at about 6.00 p.m. in the evening on 21 March, the sign Libra starts to rise. Libra carries on rising until about 8.50 p.m. At this time, it finishes rising and the sign Scorpio moves on to the horizon in its place.

The sign that is rising on the eastern horizon is known by most astrologers as the Ascendant. Some astrologers call it the 'rising sign'.

In our example, if a baby had been born at any time between 6.00 p.m. and 8.50 p.m., he would be described as having a Libra Ascendant. If the birth had been at 9.00 p.m. Libra

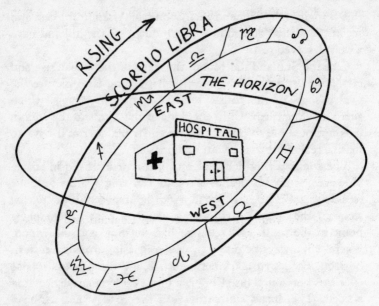

The rising and setting of the signs of the zodiac.

would have finished rising and his Ascendant would be Scorpio.

If you look at the illustration above, you can see the situation at 9.00 p.m. when our baby is born. You can see the hospital in the middle of the picture. The ring containing the signs of the zodiac surrounds the Earth. At this particular place on Earth, you can see that the part of the ring which has Libra on it has just cleared the eastern horizon, and that the beginning of the sign Scorpio has moved on to it.

Before we move on to the next section, let us remind ourselves about the main features of the Ascendant. The Ascendant is not a planet, but a sign of the zodiac which has special significance. A person's Ascendant is the sign which was rising over their eastern horizon at the time of their birth.

Because signs take no more than three hours to rise, you can see why it is so important to have a time of birth as well as a date of birth. Without a time of birth you cannot know what someone's Ascendant is.

WORKING OUT YOUR ASCENDANT

You'll be pleased to know that it is really easy to find your Ascendant. All you have to do is follow our simple to follow, step by step method. However, before you start, it is vital that you know, not just your date of birth, but also your time of birth. If you don't know your birth time, then you'll have to find it out. There are a number of ways of doing this:

a   Look at your birth certificate. In England and Wales the birth certificate will not have a time on it, unless you are a twin. However, in Scotland and many other countries of the world, the time of birth is written on the certificate.

b   Ask your mother.

c   Ask other relatives who might have been around at the time of your birth, like your father, or your brothers or sisters.

d   Look at family records, such as diaries and family Bibles.

e   Write to the hospital where you were born. Many hospitals keep records of births, going back many years.

f   Consult a psychic or a medium. This is an absolute last resort. Sometimes these people will claim to be able to tell you things about the past, including the time of your birth. We are only mentioning this course of action; we are certainly not recommending it.

If you can discover only an approximate time, don't worry. Very few people know their time of birth to the minute, and if you know it to within an hour or two either side, it should be okay. For example, your mother might tell you that she was under anaesthetic at the time you were born, and all she knows is that you were born some time between 2.00 p.m. and 6.00 p.m. No problem. If you can't get a more accurate time, then choose a time which is halfway between the two. In other words, go for 4.00 p.m.

Whatever route you have taken, we hope that you have managed to find a birth time for yourself. In which case, you are now ready to discover your Ascendant.

Step One

Firstly, in calculating the Ascendant, we always use Greenwich Mean Time (GMT). To find this we need to eliminate any movement of the clocks. For example, if you were born in a country that puts its clocks forward during the summer, and you were born during the summer, then you will probably have to take an hour off your birth time to account for summer time (this is sometimes called 'daylight saving time').

For example, if you were born at 2.23 a.m. on 1 August, which is during the summer in places north of the equator, you will probably have to take one hour off. So you count your birth time as 1.23 a.m.

Below we give a table for summer time in Great Britain and Northern Ireland (table 15). You can see that certain dates are in bold print. These dates are especially important. If your birthday falls between any of the pairs of dates listed (*except* those in bold print) or between the last weekend of March and the last weekend of October in years since 1980, you should deduct one hour off your birth time. If your birthday falls in between the pairs of dates which are in bold print, then deduct two hours from your birth time. If your birthday doesn't fall anywhere in this list, then do nothing. Leave your birth time just as it is.

For example, if you were born in Great Britain on 1 April 1965 at 4.00 p.m., you should deduct one hour from your birth time. This is because 1 April 1965 falls between the two dates

21 March and 24 October 1965 and, therefore, requires you to deduct one hour, making your correct birth time 3.00 p.m. If, however, you were born on 10 March 1965 at 4.00 p.m., you would leave your birth time just as it is, since this birthday doesn't fall between the pair of dates listed for that year.

If your birthday was on 1 May 1945, you'll notice that the pair of dates which it lies between are 2 April and 15 July, and that these are in bold print. So, you should deduct two hours from your birth time. If your birth time was 4.00 p.m., it now becomes 2.00 p.m.

This is very easy – just look at our special conversion table and find out what GMT was when you were born.

Step Two

You now have to find the Ascendant finder appropriate to the place where you were born. At the back of this book (pp 446–51) we give Ascendant finders for the following locations:

- table 26: Southern England, France, Germany and Southern Canada.
- table 27: Northern England, Scotland and Southern Scandinavia.
- table 28: Southern Europe, Northern United States and the Great Lakes.
- table 29: Southern United States.
- table 30: New Zealand, Southern Australia and Cape Province.
- table 31: Northern Australia and South Africa.

Select the area that matches your place of birth. If you are not sure which one to go for, don't get too worried. For example, if you were born in Lincolnshire, and you are not sure whether it comes under Northern or Southern England, just choose the one you feel happiest with. It is unlikely to make much difference to your final Ascendant.

Table 15 **Convert Your Birth Time to GMT**

★ If your birthday falls between any one of the pairs of dates listed below, deduct one hour from your birth time.

★ If your birthday falls between one of the pairs of dates in bold print, deduct *two* hours from your birth time.

★ If your birthday does not fall between any one of the pairs listed below, do nothing — leave your birth time as it is.

1927	10 Apr	2 Oct	1951	15 Apr	21 Oct
1928	22 Apr	7 Oct	1952	20 Apr	26 Oct
1929	25 Apr	6 Oct	1953	19 Apr	4 Oct
1930	13 Apr	5 Oct	1954	11 Apr	3 Oct
1931	19 Apr	4 Oct	1955	17 Apr	2 Oct
1932	17 Apr	2 Oct	1956	22 Apr	7 Oct
1933	9 Apr	8 Oct	1957	14 Apr	6 Oct
1934	22 Apr	7 Oct	1958	20 Apr	5 Oct
1935	14 Apr	6 Oct	1959	19 Apr	4 Oct
1936	19 Apr	4 Oct	1960	10 Apr	2 Oct
1937	4 Apr	3 Oct	1961	26 Mar	29 Oct
1938	10 Apr	2 Oct	1962	25 Mar	28 Oct
1939	16 Apr	19 Nov	1963	31 Mar	27 Oct
1940	25 Feb	31 Dec	1964	22 Mar	25 Oct
1941	1 Jan	3 May	1965	21 Mar	24 Oct
1941	**4 May**	**10 Aug**	1966	20 Mar	23 Oct
1941	11 Aug	31 Dec	1967	19 Mar	29 Oct
1942	1 Jan	4 Apr	1968	18 Feb	31 Dec
1942	**5 Apr**	**9 Aug**	1969	1 Jan	31 Dec
1942	10 Aug	31 Dec	1970	1 Jan	31 Dec
1943	1 Jan	3 Apr	1971	1 Jan	31 Oct
1943	**4 Apr**	**15 Aug**	1972	19 Mar	29 Oct
1943	16 Aug	31 Dec	1973	18 Mar	28 Oct
1944	1 Jan	1 Apr	1974	17 Mar	27 Oct
1944	**2 Apr**	**17 Sept**	1975	16 Mar	26 Oct
1944	18 Sept	31 Dec	1976	21 Mar	24 Oct
1945	1 Jan	1 Apr	1977	20 Mar	23 Oct
1945	**2 Apr**	**15 July**	1978	19 Mar	22 Oct
1945	16 July	7 Oct	1979	18 Mar	26 Oct
1946	14 Apr	6 Oct	1980*	16 Mar	26 Oct
1947	16 Mar	12 Apr			
1947	**13 Apr**	**10 Aug**			
1947	11 Aug	2 Nov			
1948	14 Mar	31 Oct			
1949	3 Apr	30 Oct			
1950	16 Apr	22 Oct			

* After 1980, the clocks changed in the last weekend of March and the last weekend of October.

Step Three

Turn to the Ascendant finder for your birth location. You will notice that the months of the year run along the bottom of this table, starting with January and going through to December. Run your eyes along the months of the year until you find the month in which you were born. Don't worry about the year of your birth – when it comes to finding the Ascendant, that is not needed, only the summer time corrections done in Step One.

You will see that each month has five notches on it; the first notch is shared with the previous month, and the last notch is shared with the following month.

Now choose a notch, depending on your birth date. This is your birth date notch: If you were born between the 1st and the 6th of the month, choose the first notch. If you were born between the 7th and the 12th of the month, choose the second notch. If you were born between the 13th and 18th of the month, choose the middle notch. If you were born between the 19th and 25th of the month, choose the fourth notch. If you were born on the 26th of the month or after, choose the last notch.

Let's give an example of this: below, we show an enlargement of the month of August, as found on all of our Ascendant finders, with the months July and September on either side. You can see which notch to go for, depending on what part of the month someone was born in. You will notice that someone born on 29 July would share the same notch with someone born on 1 August. Madonna was born on 16 August (see diagram i), so her birth date notch is the middle notch of this month.

Now that you have found the month you were born in, plus the appropriate notch for your birth date, make a note of it. You might like to put a faint pencil mark next to your birth date notch.

Diagram i

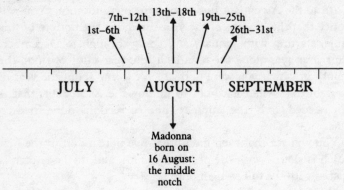

Madonna
born on
16 August:
the middle
notch

Step Four

Now that you have found your birth date notch, you must find
the birth time notch.

On the left and right sides of the Ascendant finder you can
see the twenty-four hours of the day. At the bottom, you can see
midnight. Above that is 1.00 a.m., then 2.00 a.m., up until
12.00, which is noon. Then it is 1.00 p.m., after that 2.00
p.m., until, right at the top, we get back to midnight.

What you have to do is find the time of your birth. Each
hour is divided into four, as can be seen on the diagram, and
each notch represents a quarter of an hour. For example, look
at the notch marked 7.00 a.m. Between the 7.00 a.m. notch and
the 8.00 a.m. notch, there are three unmarked notches, which
represent 7.15 a.m, 7.30 a.m, and 7.45 a.m. What we have to
do is find the notch which is closest to the birth time.

Madonna was born at 7.00 a.m., so the closest notch to this
time is the exact 7.00 a.m. notch. (See diagram ii.) If she had
been born at 6.55 a.m., we would still have gone for this notch,
because 6.55 a.m. is so close to 7.00 a.m.

Diagram ii

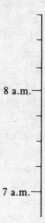

8 a.m. —

7 a.m. —

Now find the nearest notch to your birth time. If you want, mark it with a pencil.

Step Five

You will see that the Ascendant finders have lots of stripes on them. Within each stripe is the name of a sign of the zodiac. If you look at the stripe on the extreme bottom left, you can see that it is marked 'Libra'. The next one up is marked 'Scorpio', the next one is 'Sagittarius', and so on. Astrologers call these stripes 'Ascendant stripes'.

Now take a piece of paper and line up the right-hand edge with your birth date notch and the top edge with the birth time notch, just as we have done in the illustration below (diagram iii). Look at the top right-hand corner of this piece of paper. You will see that it is inside one of the Ascendant stripes. The sign written on this stripe is your Ascendant.

Just so that you are quite sure how this is done, diagram iii uses the example of Madonna. She was born in Bay City, Michigan, which is in the Northern United States. So we select the Ascendant finder for Southern Europe, Northern United States and the Great Lakes, on p. 448. She was born on 16 August, so we put a small pencil mark on the middle notch for August. This is the birth date notch.

She was born at 7.00 a.m., so we put the birth time notch here. Then we take a piece of paper and put the right-hand edge on the birth date notch (16 August) and the top edge against the birth time notch (7.00 a.m.). We can see that the right-hand corner of the piece of paper is within the Virgo stripe, so we now know that Madonna has a Virgo Ascendant.

You may have one last question: what if the right-hand corner of the paper is exactly on a boundary between two Ascendant stripes? For example, say that you were looking up your Ascendant, and the paper was exactly on the line between the Libra and Scorpio stripes.

In this case you would look up the meanings for Libra *and* Scorpio Ascendants. These Ascendants have very different character traits: one is friendly and compromising, while the other is intense and brooding. You should therefore be able to tell which one you are. Alternatively, you could ask someone else for their opinion – preferably a partner, spouse or lover. They probably have a pretty good idea of which description fits you best!

THE MEANING OF THE ASCENDANT

Many astrologers regard the Ascendant, or Rising sign, as just as important as the Sun sign. So, when you are using astrology to analyse someone's character, make sure that you look at this crucial part of the horoscope. In order to understand the meaning of the Ascendant, it is useful to compare it with your Sun sign and your Moon sign.

The Sun sign represents a person's core self, and it is symbolic of the creative energy that a person is able to direct at the achievement of his or her goals. The Moon Sign, on the

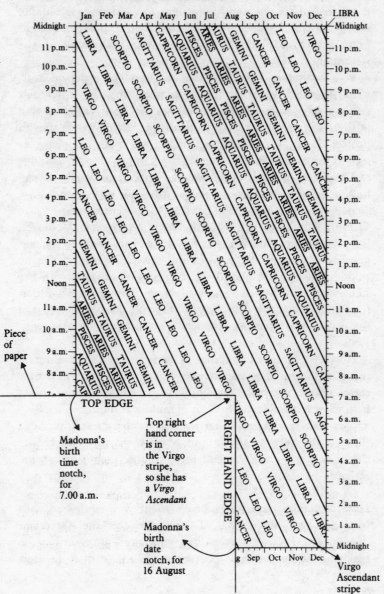

Diagram iii **Ascendant Finder Showing Madonna's Ascendant**
The Northern United States

other hand, is more passive, and indicates a person's feelings and emotional responses. Very often, an individual may choose not to reveal his Sun and Moon signs to the outside world. He may be unsure about how other people will respond and might find it safer to hide behind a mask. This mask is the Ascendant.

The Ascendant represents the way in which a person deals with the world, and it also says a lot about the way individuals relate to friends, family and colleagues. Another way of looking at the Ascendant is to see it as the image that a person tries to project. It can, therefore, describe the way a person speaks, as well as the clothes that he chooses to wear.

To give an example of the way the Ascendant works, we can look at Marilyn Monroe: She had the Sun in Gemini and a Leo Ascendant. Marilyn's inner self was represented by her Gemini Sun. She was versatile and talkative, and enjoyed having plenty of variety in her life. Like every Gemini, she was curious, interested in new ideas and new philosophies. Yet the public image she projected was far more in keeping with her Leo Ascendant. Marilyn was a superstar who had the world at her feet. In public, she played this role and exhibited the temperamental arrogance which is so often associated with Leos.

However, recent biographies have shown that she was much more intelligent than her 'bimbo' image suggested. This may mean that her larger-than-life Leo Ascendant was a mask, behind which her versatile Gemini mind was hiding.

Now that you know what the Ascendant means, you can turn to the section at the end of this chapter, which lists the meaning of the Ascendants through each sign of the zodiac.

How well does your Ascending sign fit you, compared with your Sun and Moon signs? Do you feel that the Ascendant describes your outer personality, while the Sun describes the real you? When we meet people who don't seem to fit their

Sun signs, it is very often because their Ascending Sign describes them better.

At this stage, there is one final question to answer. What if you were born around dawn, and your Sun sign is the same as your Ascending sign?

Well, this means that you have a very powerful personality. Your outer personality is working in the same way as your inner self, so you have no problems when it comes to expressing your feelings and your needs. You probably feel that you have nothing to hide and that what people see is what they get. It is likely that you have strong will power and an almost magical ability to make things happen in the external environment. Astrologers often call people with the same Sun and Ascending signs 'doubles'. So, someone with the Sun and the Ascendant in Gemini would be described as a 'double Gemini'. If the Moon was in Gemini as well, they would be a 'triple Gemini'.

THE RULING PLANET

If you read Sun sign columns in newspapers and magazines, you will see frequent references to 'ruling planets'. Before describing what a ruling planet really is, we will briefly describe what Sun sign columnists mean by the term.

Sun sign columnists only know one thing about the people they are writing for: their Sun sign. In order to make predictions and forecasts, columnists pay close attention to the planets which rule the different signs of the zodiac. If, for example, a columnist was making a prediction for Taurus, he would look carefully at the movement of the planet Venus. This is because Venus 'rules' Taurus. What astrologers mean by this is that Venus has a special connection with Taurus. If Venus is in a good position on a particular day, columnists would predict that Taurus would have a good time.

On p. 216 we give you a table, showing the planets which rule

the various signs. You will notice that some planets rule two
signs; for example, Venus rules both Taurus and Libra. You
will also notice that Uranus, Neptune and Pluto do not rule
any signs.

Some astrologers claim that Uranus rules Aquarius, Neptune
rules Pisces and Pluto rules Scorpio. However, we have found
that these rulerships do not work in practical astrology, and
there is certainly no historical justification for using them. So,
please stick to the list below:

Ascending Sign	Ruler
Aries	Mars
Taurus	Venus
Gemini	Mercury
Cancer	The Moon
Leo	The Sun
Virgo	Mercury
Libra	Venus
Scorpio	Mars
Sagittarius	Jupiter
Capricorn	Saturn
Aquarius	Saturn
Pisces	Jupiter

The ruling planet which Sun sign columnists write about has
only a very general connection to the personality. If you don't
know someone's time of birth, however, then it may be worth
looking at it.

The real ruling planet, which most professional astrologers
use in their work, is the planet which rules the Ascending sign.
In Marilyn Monroe's case, this is Leo; the Sun rules Leo, so
her ruling planet is the Sun. If someone has an Aquarius
Ascendant, his ruling planet would be Saturn, because Saturn
rules Aquarius. Simple, isn't it?

SO, WHAT DOES THE RULING PLANET MEAN?

The ruling planet can tell us about our real selves and about the environment in which we feel happiest. For example, if you have a Taurus Ascendant, you can see that your ruling planet is Venus, because Venus rules the sign of Taurus. Look in Chapter Eight to find out in which sign of the zodiac Venus fell when you were born.

If Venus fell in the sign of Libra, then the description of Venus in Libra will be especially important for you. When you read the description of Venus in Libra, try to remember it and think about it carefully, because it may be one of the most important planets in your whole horoscope.

So – check on the sign position of the planets right now, by looking back through Chapters Six to Twelve, as well as Chapter Two.

To go back to the example of Venus in Libra: this person may be very concerned with relationships, with physical appearances and with socializing. Because Venus is the ruling planet, it assumes a great deal of importance in this person's life.

To elaborate on this: if a person has the Sun in Aries (see the description in Chapter Two), we might expect him or her to be a bit aggressive, assertive and generally to steam ahead with little thought for the consequences. However, suppose the *same* person has a Pisces Ascendant, and suppose Jupiter (the ruler of Pisces) is placed in Libra. Well, Jupiter in Libra people are into compromise, diplomacy and usually think before they act (see Chapter Ten).

Now because, in this case, Jupiter is the planet ruling the Ascendant, Jupiter (the ruling planet) will probably have more importance than the Sun in Aries. So this person would *not* be particularly aggressive or assertive, but more into compromise and harmony than would normally be the case. So we can see how the ruling planet usually takes precedence over other planets when it comes to describing someone's personality.

In the above case, we can see how fortunate it can be to have a ruling planet, such as Jupiter, moderating the effects of other more aggressive and impulsive planets. Let's take an opposite example: suppose a person has the Sun in Libra (see Chapter Two). He or she would be expected to be very diplomatic and easy-going. But suppose he or she has a Scorpio Ascendant (Mars rules Scorpio), and suppose Mars is positioned in the sign of Aries (see the description of Mars in Aries in Chapter Nine). Well, straight away, we know that this person will *not* be as charming or tactful as we might expect, because their ruling planet is Mars, and Mars is positioned in dynamic, impulsive Aries. And, of course, we already know that the ruling planet is usually more important than the Sun sign.

This is another reason why so many people do not seem to fit the description of their Sun signs and, therefore, the predictions made for them in the media. It is why, for example, many people who should be down-to-earth Capricorns are punk poets and amateur revolutionaries (their ruling planet may be Mercury positioned in rebellious Aquarius – see Chapter Seven for a description of Mercury in Aquarius).

It should now be becoming clear why the Ascendant and the ruling planet can be so important when looking at your horoscope.

If we continue with the example of Marilyn Monroe, we notice that her ruling planet is the Sun. When she was born, the Sun fell in the sign of Gemini. This means that her Sun in Gemini was very important. To remind yourself of what it means to have your Sun in Gemini, have a quick look at the description of this placing in Chapter Two.

Let's take another example, this time of Princess Diana: she has a Sagittarius Ascendant, so her ruling planet is Jupiter. If you look at Chapter Ten, you will see that Jupiter is an optimistic planet which is often connected with a higher vision or purpose. So whatever obstacles Diana may have to deal with, it is vital that she looks on the bright side of life. Somehow her faith and her optimism will see her through.

Diana's Jupiter is positioned in the sign of Aquarius. This gives us further information about how her ruling planet is working. If you look at the description of Jupiter in Aquarius, you'll see that this is an idealistic and humanitarian sign for Jupiter to be placed. So, in order for Diana to be really happy, it is important that she is doing things which are for the greater good of society. For although she has the Sun in Cancer (see Chapter Two for a description), which emphasizes her maternal and domestic nature, her ruling planet, Jupiter, will give her many other, very important interests *outside* the home.

Of course, sometimes the ruling planet will simply emphasize the qualities of the Sun sign. For example, suppose we have a person with the Sun in Cancer, who also has a Cancer Ascendant (this Ascendant is ruled by the Moon), and suppose the Moon is also positioned in Cancer. Here we have an example of a *very* Cancer sort of person, with the Sun, Moon and Ascendant in Cancer! This would signify a home-loving individual, with a great love of children and the family.

THE MEANING OF THE ASCENDANT IN EACH SIGN OF THE ZODIAC

Aries Ascendant

Aries rising gives an enormous amount of energy and enthusiasm. Sometimes there is a desperation to succeed and the individual usually expects immediate results for his efforts. To maximize the chances of success, it is important that the emphasis is on dynamic action, rather than on logical analysis of the facts. On the whole, this Ascendant is much better at starting new projects than finishing them, and tends to abandon tasks the moment their novelty has worn off. Aries is the first sign of the zodiac, and this makes for a highly competitive person who wants to win every race and is never content with second-best.

Taurus Ascendant

It is very important for the Taurus Ascendant to achieve some form of solid success in life. As a result of this ambition, such a person is likely to move through life with care and caution, always looking out for ways of improving material and economic circumstances. Taurus enjoys the good things of life and has an efficient and practical method of attaining them. Once people with this Ascendant are secure, both emotionally and financially, there is a determination that nothing and no one should take away their gains. Individuals with Taurus rising often have great physical magnetism and good looks, especially if the ruling planet (Venus) is placed in Libra or Taurus.

Gemini Ascendant

Gemini wants to experience as many different areas of life as possible and, as a result, people with this Ascendant frequently change their interests, their appearance and even their friends. A thirst for knowledge and an eagerness to study make natural scholars, whilst an active imagination often makes brilliant writers or journalists. However, it is important that the Gemini Ascendant doesn't chop and change too much, because otherwise life could easily end up being shallow, superficial and a bit meaningless. So it's a good idea to have one special talent that these people can stick to, come hell or high water.

Cancer Ascendant

Self-preservation is very important to people with Cancer rising. People with Cancer Ascendants are quick to defend their vital interests, as well as those of their loved ones and family. Other people are often daunted by this hard front, as symbolized by the crab's protective armour. However, under it all there is a sympathetic and sensitive approach to life, and these individuals genuinely care about the feelings of other people. On balance, Cancer rising probably takes many things far too personally, lacking the degree of objectivity and logic of other less vulnerable signs. This means that they are sometimes over-emotional in the way they express themselves.

Leo Ascendant

The Leo Ascendant usually signifies a person who projects a grandiose image, which is often combined with a tendency to dramatize and exaggerate. At the same time, Leo rising has tremendous creative and organizational abilities, as well as a very generous disposition. This frequently brings tremendous popularity and a great deal of love from partners and friends. However, people with a Leo Ascendant demand respect, adore flattery and get extremely angry if others fail to give them the attention and respect they deserve. Those who have Leo rising love stylish clothes, beautiful surroundings and expensive ornaments.

Virgo Ascendant

A highly resourceful placement which also gives a good eye for detail. Virgo rising signifies a person who is efficient, practical and eager to help others. This makes for a person in much demand. However, people with Virgo rising need to guard against some of their more negative attributes. These include a narrow outlook on life and a tendency to get bogged down in details. When dealing with other people, they should avoid being overly critical and make sure that they focus on other people's good points as well as their bad ones. Health and hygiene matter a great deal and there is usually an insistence that food, clothes and living conditions are spotlessly clean.

Libra Ascendant

To people with Libra rising, other people are very important. As the Libra Ascendant goes through life, there is an awareness of the need to accommodate these other people, even if this means sacrificing one's own interests. There is undoubtedly a great talent for bringing harmony and tranquillity into the social environment, and anger or bad temper is hardly ever expressed. The ability to detach oneself from the environment means that, when it comes to dealing with other people, Libra is brilliant at analysing their actions and motivations. With intelligence, this Ascendant can give the talent for using this skill as a means of getting the better of rivals.

Scorpio Ascendant

This placement makes for an emotionally intense person who is able to demonstrate a high degree of self-control. People with Scorpio rising are not very trusting and don't confide in people unless they are certain that they won't be let down. Scorpio rising has a razor-sharp sense of perception, and there is very little that escapes their notice. They immediately know if someone is hiding the truth, so the people around them are advised to behave with scrupulous honesty. The Scorpio Ascendant gives enormous emotional force, and once something is started it is invariably seen through to the very end.

Sagittarius Ascendant

Sagittarius rising is characterized by an open and optimistic approach to life. People with this Ascendant like to speak their mind and as a result have a certain (justified?) reputation for tactlessness. Travel is very important and they love the thrill of visiting new, exciting and even dangerous places. A breadth of vision and adventurousness make Sagittarius rising a fascinating person to have as a friend. However, they hate it when their freedom of action is interfered with, and will avoid making commitments at all costs. There are some people who find these aspects of Sagittarius rising rather hard to handle.

Capricorn Ascendant

Capricorn rising usually signifies a fairly restrained person, who is not prone to impulsive or frivolous behaviour. In social situations these people keep their distance until they are sure that they are totally accepted. However, once they realize that others have accepted them, they will quickly establish their presence, and it isn't long before they are the centre of attention. It should be appreciated that, unlike those with Leo rising, Capricorn rising doesn't make a show of actively seeking the limelight. Instead, they allow it to come to them naturally and quietly. This apparent modesty makes Capricorn rising seem very trustworthy and, as a result, they are able to progress rapidly up the social ladder.

Aquarius Ascendant

People with this Ascendant need to express themselves in original ways which often conflict with the established way of doing things. In a group, the inspiration and creativity of the Aquarius Ascendant makes these people stand out as very special – people who always have something interesting to say. However, there is a stubborn streak, and on occasion self-willed obstinacy can lead to long-running power struggles with friends and colleagues. On the plus side, these people are real humanitarians and the suffering of others is something that they can never ignore. Indeed, they can always be counted on to come up with brilliantly original solutions to other people's problems.

Pisces Ascendant

An impressionable person, who is extremely sensitive to other people's thoughts and feelings. A Pisces Ascendant gives a natural ability to listen to others, although these people have to be careful that they don't allow themselves to be swamped by their emotions and their worries. On the whole, people with Pisces Ascendant dislike confrontation, although indecisiveness can often lead to the very confrontations which they are trying to avoid. From a creative point of view they are part of a very talented group of people: many musicians, painters and singers have the Ascendant, Sun or Moon in Pisces.

....

YOUR INDIVIDUAL HOROSCOPE

15. CASTING YOUR PERSONAL HOROSCOPE

Every time an astrologer sees a client, he casts a horoscope. The horoscope is a special diagram which contains all the necessary astrological information needed to describe some-one's character and future. It shows the positions of the planets and the Ascendant at the time of birth, and also gives details of things like the elements and the ruling planet.

In this vital chapter, you are going to learn how to draw up your own horoscope. You will soon find that this is an easy and enjoyable task. All you have to do is follow our step by step method.

Our method is very simple. We will be casting Madonna's horoscope in stages. When we have been through the first stage of casting Madonna's horoscope, we want you to go through the first stage of casting your own horoscope. Then we can move on together to the second stage, and so on, until we have a complete horoscope.

As we go through the stages, you can fill in the blank diagrams provided with your own astrological details. We strongly advise you to use a pencil, just in case you make a mistake. If you don't want to mark the book, then you might want to draw up your own diagrams as you go along. As you can see, these diagrams are very simple and should be easy to copy.

Before we get down to business, we do need to briefly discuss the symbols of the horoscope. When astrologers write down the name of a planet or sign, they often use a symbol rather than the actual word. So, instead of writing 'Venus' or 'Mars' they will draw a ♀ or a ♂. As you will soon see, symbols, rather than words, are used when filling in the horoscope circle. So you must know what the symbols for the planets and signs are. Below we give a table listing them all. You don't have to learn this off by heart, but as you go through the chapter you should constantly refer back to it.

Sun	☉	Aries	♈
Moon	☽	Taurus	♉
Mercury	☿	Gemini	♊
Venus	♀	Cancer	♋
Mars	♂	Leo	♌
Jupiter	♃	Virgo	♍
Saturn	♄	Libra	♎
Uranus	♅	Scorpio	♏
Neptune	♆	Sagittarius	♐
Pluto	♇	Capricorn	♑
		Aquarius	♒
		Pisces	♓

CASTING YOUR HOROSCOPE IN FIVE EASY STAGES

Stage One: Sorting Out the Raw Details

So far, you have learnt about the planets, the signs and the Ascendant. You know what signs all your planets are in, and, if you know what time you were born, you will know what your Ascending sign is. This is all the information you need to cast your horoscope. If you don't know what time you were born, it is possible to draw up a simplified horoscope, as we will explain in Stage Two.

The first thing that an astrologer does when casting a horoscope is to draw up a simple table, which contains the raw details of the sign placements of the planets and the Ascendant. If we take the example of Madonna, we know that her details are as follows:

Sun in Leo	☉	♌
Moon in Virgo	☽	♍
Mercury in Virgo	☿	♍
Venus in Leo	♀	♌
Mars in Taurus	♂	♉
Jupiter in Libra	♃	♎
Saturn in Sagittarius	♄	♐
Uranus in Leo	♅	♌
Neptune in Scorpio	♆	♏
Pluto in Virgo	♇	♍
Ascendant is Virgo	ASC	♍

If you look at diagram iv for Stage One, you will see a table listing the positions of Madonna's planets and Ascendant. We

Diagram iv **Stage One**

The sign positions of the planets and the Ascendant for Madonna.

The Sun (☉) is in Leo (♌)
The Moon (☽) is in Virgo (♍)
Mercury (☿) is in Virgo (♍)
Venus (♀) is in Leo (♌)
Mars (♂) is in Taurus (♉)
Jupiter (♃) is in Libra (♎)
Saturn (♄) is in Sagittarius (♐)
Uranus (♅) is in Leo (♌)
Neptune (♆) is in Scorpio (♏)
Pluto (♇) is in Virgo (♍)
The Ascendant is Virgo ♍

have used both words and symbols for the planets and signs. This is to help you get used to using symbols.

We now want you to do exactly the same thing for your own planets and Ascendant, using diagram v. Start by filling in your name, and then write out the sign positions for each planet. Don't forget to draw the symbol for each sign, as well. If you don't know your time of birth, you won't know your Ascendant, and you will have to leave this blank for now.

Diagram v　**Stage One**

The sign positions of the planets and the
Ascendant for ....

The Sun (☉) is in
The Moon (☽) is in
Mercury (☿) is in
Venus (♀) is in
Mars (♂) is in
Jupiter (♃) is in
Saturn (♄) is in
Uranus (♅) is in
Neptune (♆) is in
Pluto (♇) is in
The Ascendant is ....

Stage Two

The actual horoscope is a circle, in which the signs and the planets are written. The diagrams for Stage Two show you what horoscope circles look like (diagrams vi and vii). You can see that they are like cakes, divided into twelve slices. The slice on the left of the horoscope has the number '1' written on it and as you go anti-clockwise you can see that the slices are numbered up to '12'. When you eventually draw up your own horoscope circles, it is important that you number the slices in this same way, and that you make sure that your numbering starts with the slice on the left.

228

Diagram vi **Stage Two**
Horoscope for ....

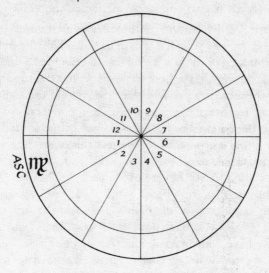

Diagram vii **Stage Two**
Horoscope for ....

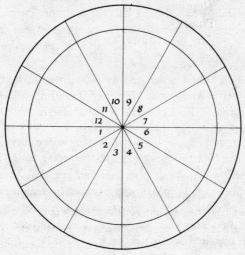

It's nice to be able to describe the horoscope as being like a cake cut up into twelve slices. However, astrologers don't use the word 'slice'. Instead they use the term 'house'. So, from now on, we will be describing these slices as 'houses'. In the next chapter we tell you all about houses, but, for the moment, carry on thinking of them as being just like slices of a cake.

Around the edge of the horoscope circle you can see an outer ring, and this is where you will place the signs of the zodiac. On diagram vi, for Stage Two, you will see the symbol for Virgo entered on the outer edge of the first house. Virgo is Madonna's Ascendant, and astrologers always put the Ascending sign in the first house. To make this absolutely clear, we have written the abbreviation 'ASC' next to Madonna's first house.

Now, turn to diagram vii, for Stage Two. Fill in your name, and on the outer edge of the first house fill in the sign of your ascendant. When you have done this, write 'ASC' next to it, just like we have done in Madonna's horoscope circle.

Before we move on to Stage Three, we have to tell you what to do if you don't know your time of birth, and therefore don't know what your Ascendant is. In this case, you should put the Sun sign in the outer edge of the first house. So, if you are a Taurus, write in the symbol for Taurus and the word ASC next to the first house, using Taurus as the ascending sign. Astrologers call this kind of horoscope a 'solar horoscope'.

On p. 231 we show what we would do if we had no birth time, only a date for Madonna. However, it is important that you remember that this horoscope is *only* used when there is no time of birth.

Stage Three

This stage is very simple. Now that you have filled in the sign of the first house, go round the horoscope circle, filling in all the other signs in the same way. Remember to go anti-clockwise, moving from the first house to the second house.

Diagram viii **Stage Two**
Horoscope for Madonna

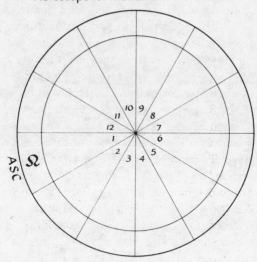

(with no birth time)
The solar horoscope

Start with the sign of the Ascendant (first house) and then proceed in the order shown on page 226 of this Chapter. If you have an Aries Ascendant, start with Aries (first house), then draw in Taurus (second house), then Gemini (third house), and so on. If your Ascendant is Sagittarius (first house), start by drawing in Sagittarius for the first house, then Capricorn (second house), Aquarius (third house), and so on, through the signs.

So, let's see what Madonna's horoscope looks like at Stage Three (diagram ix). If you have a quick glance at the list of signs at the beginning of this chapter, you will notice that Virgo is the sign of her first house, since she has a Virgo Ascendant. Therefore, Libra is associated with her second house, since the sign of Libra follows Virgo. This means that in the outer ring of the second house we draw in the symbol for

Diagram ix **Stage Three**
Horoscope for Madonnna

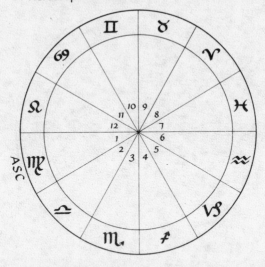

Libra. Having done that, we move to the third house and draw in the Scorpio symbol, because Scorpio follows Libra, and so on, round the circle.

Now, draw in the signs around your own Stage Three horoscope, using diagram x. You have already filled in the sign of the first house, which will be the same as your Ascendant, (or your Sun sign, if you don't know your time of birth). Now move to the second house, and fill in the sign which follows. When doing this, remember that the sign after Pisces is Aries. So if you had Pisces in the first house, you would put Aries in the second house and Taurus in the third house.

Diagram x **Stage Three**
Horoscope for ....

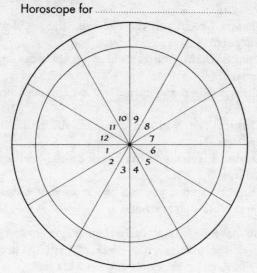

Stage Four

This is a very important stage, because now you are going to
fit the planets into the horoscope circle. When you have finished, you will have in front of you an exact replica of the
astrological situation at the time of your birth. This is the
horoscope, and in the years to come you will look back at it
again and again for guidance and inspiration.

Drawing the Planets into the Horoscope: First, you should look
back at Chapters Two, Six, Seven, Eight, Nine, Ten, Eleven,
and Twelve, in order to refresh your memory and to check on
the positions of each planet in each sign for the moment of
your birth.

*   In Chapter Two you can check on the position of your Sun
    sign.

* In Chapter Six, you can check on the position of your Moon sign.
* In Chapter Seven, you can check on the position of your Mercury sign.
* In Chapter Eight, you can check on the position of your Venus sign.
* In Chapter Nine, you can check on the position of your Mars sign.
* In Chapter Ten, you can check on the position of your Jupiter sign.
* In Chapter Eleven, you can check on the position of your Saturn sign.
* In Chapter Twelve, you can check on your Uranus, Neptune and Pluto sign positions.

Once you have looked at each chapter, write down all the positions of the planets on a piece of paper. Then look at Chapter Fourteen, to check once again what sign your Ascendant falls in. You are now equipped with all the information you need to set up your horoscope properly.

When you draw the planets into the horoscope, you will be drawing in their symbols, as you did with the signs. Refer back to the table at the beginning of the chapter, to find out what the planetary symbols are.

Before drawing in the planets, astrologers sort them into signs. So, the distribution of Madonna's planets over the signs is as follows:

Aries:	no planets
Taurus:	Mars
Gemini:	no planets
Cancer:	no planets
Leo:	Sun, Venus, Uranus
Virgo:	Moon, Mercury, Pluto
Libra:	Jupiter
Scorpio:	Neptune
Sagittarius:	Saturn

Capricorn: no planets
Aquarius: no planets
Pisces: no planets

The reason astrologers do this sorting is to find out if there are any signs which have a lot of planets in them. If this happens, they will have to draw them into the horoscope circle carefully, so that they will all be able to fit into one house.

When adding the planets into the horoscope, you should be as neat as possible. The planets should be placed on the outer edge of the inner circle and, if possible, spaced out evenly along this edge.

Now, let's draw Madonna's planets on to the horoscope circle (diagram xi), starting with Aries. Aries covers the eighth

Diagram xi   **Stage Four**
Horoscope for Madonna

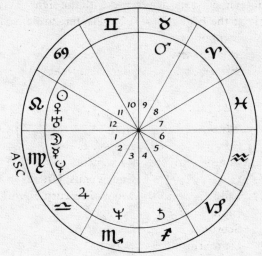

house, but there are no planets here, so we leave this house blank, and move on to Taurus. Mars is the only planet in this sign, so we fill it in, on the outer edge of the horoscope's inner circle. Madonna has no planets in Gemini or Cancer, so we leave the tenth and eleventh houses blank. She has three planets in Leo, which covers the twelfth house. When drawing these planets in, it is important not to make them too big, because we have got to be able to fit them all in along the outer edge. Likewise with the Virgo planets. When we have finished with these (Moon, Mercury and Pluto), it is just a question of drawing in Jupiter, Neptune and Saturn. Jupiter is in Libra in the second house, Neptune is in Scorpio in the third house and Saturn is in Sagittarius in the fourth house.

Now that you see how the planets in Madonna's chart are filled in, you can start drawing in your own planets, using diagram xii. However, before you start, remember to sort your planets

Diagram xii   **Stage Four**
Horoscope for ....

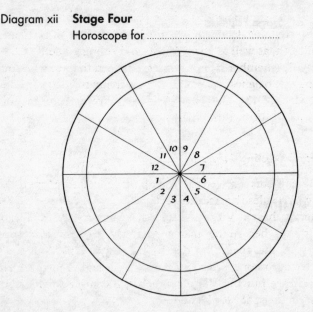

into the signs, just in case you have a large grouping. You may be interested to know that astrologers have a piece of jargon for three or more planets in the same sign. They call this a 'stellium'. So Madonna has two stelliums, one in Leo, and one in Virgo.

Remember, too, to take your time when putting your planets into the horoscope circle. It is particularly important that the end result is tidy and, above all, accurate. What you must avoid is accidentally putting a planet into the wrong house.

So, now you've done it! You've got your own horoscope in front of you. All we have to do now is fill in a few extra details.

Stage Five

Now that you have gone through every stage of casting a horoscope, it is time to put all the information on one piece of paper.

As you can see on Stage Five diagram xiii, we have a completed horoscope form for Madonna. As well as the horoscope circle and the sign positions of the planets and the Ascendant, this form contains details of her time of birth, date of birth and place of birth, as well as her elements and ruling planet.

You will remember from Chapter Thirteen that, to work out the elemental balance, we count up how many planets someone has in each of the elements. (Although we do not include Uranus, Neptune or Pluto in this count.)

More about Ruling Planets

In Chapter Fourteen we told you about the ruling planet, the planet which rules the Ascending sign.

Madonna has a Virgo Ascendant. Mercury rules Virgo, which makes her ruling planet Mercury. We therefore put Mercury in the space for the ruling planet. In Madonna's particular horoscope, Mercury is in Virgo, and is in the First House. So we put the Virgo symbol in the space for its sign, and 'ist' in the space for its house.

Diagram xiii **Stage Five**
Horoscope for Madonna

Time of birth 7.00 a.m.
Date of birth 16 August 1958
Place of birth Bay City, Michigan

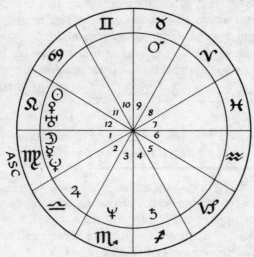

The Elements
Fire   3
Earth   3
Air   1
Water   0
Ruling Planet   ☿
Ruling
  Planet's sign   ♍
Ruling
  Planet's house 1st

The Sun (☉) is in Leo (♌)
The Moon (☽) is in Virgo (♍)
Mercury (☿) is in Virgo (♍)
Venus (♀) is in Leo (♌)
Mars (♂) is in Taurus (♉)
Jupiter (♃) is in Libra (♎)
Saturn (♄) is in Sagittarius (♐)
Uranus (♅) is in Leo (♌)
Neptune (♆) is in Scorpio (♏)
Pluto (♇) is in Virgo (♍)
The Ascendant is Virgo ♍

Diagram xiv **Stage Five**
Horoscope for

Time of birth ....
Date of birth ....
Place of birth ....

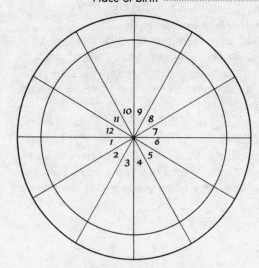

The Elements
Fire
Earth
Air
Water
Ruling Planet
Ruling
  Planet's sign
Ruling
  Planet's house

The Sun (☉) is in ....
The Moon (☽) is in ....
Mercury (☿) is in ....
Venus (♀) is in ....
Mars (♂) is in ....
Jupiter (♃) is in ....
Saturn (♄) is in ....
Uranus (♅) is in ....
Neptune (♆) is in ....
Pluto (♇) is in ....
The Ascendant is ....

If your Ascendant is in Libra, your ruling planet is Venus. Once you have checked this out and made a rough note on your piece of paper, then look to see in which house Venus will fall. If Venus is in the sign of Libra, then Venus will be in the first house. If Venus is in the sign of Aries, then Venus will be in the seventh house. If Venus falls in the sign of Virgo, then Venus will be in the twelfth house, and so on.

All you have to do now is fill in the blank Stage Five horoscope form (diagram xiv). In the previous stages you will have already filled in your horoscope circle and the sign positions of your planets and Ascendant. We hope you don't mind having to repeat yourself.

Having done that, fill in your time, date and place of birth, together with the details of your elements and ruling planet. If your mind needs refreshing on these last two, have a quick look back at Chapters Thirteen and Fourteen. After that, pat yourself on the back, because you are now well on the way to becoming a serious astrologer.

16. THE HOUSES

The houses have been used by countless generations of astrologers. Again and again, the houses have shown themselves to be the key to accurate astrology, both in terms of making predictions and in describing the personality. So if you yourself want to be an accurate astrologer, it is vital that you get a clear grasp of the houses. Fortunately, they are very simple to understand, and by the time you come to the end of this chapter you will have discovered their incredible power.

This chapter has three sections. In the first section we will tell you what the houses are. If you have read the previous chapter on casting your own horoscope, this part will be very familiar to you. In the second section you will find out how to use houses in your work as an astrologer. You will discover the practical differences between the signs and the houses, and how to blend the meanings of the two together. In the final section we give you an in-depth description of the twelve houses.

WHAT ARE THE HOUSES?

In the previous chapter we described how the circle of the horoscope is divided into segments, which astrologers call 'houses'. There are twelve of these, numbered from one to twelve. The names of these houses are ridiculously easy to remember, because astrologers call them 'first house', 'second house', and so on.

The first house is the same as the sign of the Ascendant. So, a person with a Virgo Ascendant has a Virgo first house. All planets positioned in the sign of Virgo in this horoscope are also in the first house.

Look back at Madonna's horoscope in the previous chapter. She has a Virgo Ascendant, so Virgo is her first house. Her Moon, Mercury and Pluto are all positioned in the sign of Virgo, so we can say that these planets are also in the first house.

The second house is the sign which follows the Ascending sign. Madonna has Virgo Ascending. Libra is the sign which follows Virgo, so Libra is her second house. She has Jupiter in Libra, so she also has Jupiter in the second house. As you noticed in the previous chapter, each segment, or house, of the horoscope circle is numbered. This number represents the house. When looking at Madonna's horoscope, you can tell immediately that Taurus is her ninth house, because the Taurus house is numbered '9'.

Just to make sure that you have really got the hang of houses, let's look at Margaret Thatcher's horoscope. Her planets and Ascendant are in the following sign positions:

Sun:	Libra
Moon:	Leo
Mercury:	Libra
Venus:	Sagittarius
Mars:	Libra
Jupiter:	Capricorn
Saturn:	Scorpio
Uranus:	Pisces
Neptune:	Leo
Pluto:	Cancer
Ascendant:	Scorpio

Margaret Thatcher has Scorpio as her Ascendant. We therefore make Scorpio the first house. Sagittarius, which is the following sign, is the second house, and so on. When we have entered all the signs around the horoscope circle, we find that the twelve houses are in the following signs:

First house:	Scorpio
Second house:	Sagittarius
Third house:	Capricorn
Fourth house:	Aquarius
Fifth house:	Pisces
Sixth house:	Aries
Seventh house:	Taurus
Eighth house:	Gemini
Ninth house:	Cancer
Tenth house:	Leo
Eleventh house:	Virgo
Twelfth house:	Libra

Once we know what sign is in each house, we can then tell what houses the planets are in. Margaret Thatcher has a Scorpio first house. She has Saturn in Scorpio, so her Saturn is in the first house. She has a Sagittarius second house. Her Venus is in Sagittarius, so her Venus is in the second house. Her Jupiter is in Capricorn, so her Jupiter is in the third house.

SIGNS AND HOUSES

From Chapter Five through to Chapter Twelve, we told you about the planets and the signs. Each of the planets represents principles which we all share. For example, everyone has Venus in their horoscope. Venus represents the capacity to relate to other people and, indeed, we all relate to each other in some way. Similarly, we all have Mercury in our horoscope; we all have a way of communicating.

However, the sign position of the planet tells us precisely *how* the principle works. For example, Margaret Thatcher has her Moon in Leo. The Moon concerns the emotions and the way people respond to the outside world. Everyone has emotions, but the sign position of the Moon tells us precisely how the emotions work for the individual. The Moon may also be about the overall personality, because very often in women's horoscopes the sign of the Moon can describe the personality just as well as the Sun sign.

With her Moon in Leo, Margaret Thatcher feels a need for attention. This is because Leo is a grand sign, which likes to be in the centre of things. When the attention is there, Margaret Thatcher should feel happy. However, if she is being ignored, she is likely to feel less content. If her Moon had been positioned in Cancer instead of Leo, it would have been less important for her to get loads of attention. It might have been enough to have been emotionally supported by her husband and immediate family. This is because Cancer is a sign which is often connected with the home and the family.

Although the signs give us a lot of information, they don't tell us precisely where a planet is going to act. When we say 'where', we mean *in what area of life*. Is Margaret Thatcher's Moon going to have a special influence on her home-life, on her children, or on her money?

In order to find out where a planet is going to act in the everyday world, we see what house it is in. At the end of this chapter we give detailed descriptions of each house, but for the moment, here are some brief descriptions:

First house:	personality, appearance
Second house:	money
Third house:	brothers and sisters
Fourth house:	the home, the family, the father
Fifth house:	children, enjoyment
Sixth house:	health, routine, diet, pets
Seventh house:	relationships
Eighth house:	other people's money, sex
Ninth house:	religion, travel
Tenth house:	career, the mother
Eleventh house:	friends, groups
Twelfth house:	institutions

Look carefully at this list. Can you see that it covers almost every aspect of your daily life? A planet placed in a particular house will have a special effect on it.

If we look at Margaret Thatcher's Moon, we can see that it is in the tenth house. This is because the Moon is in Leo and her tenth house is Leo. The tenth house is connected with the career. So the specific area of life which the Moon in Leo affects will be career. With the Moon in this house, it will be important for her to be successful and to be recognized in her working environment.

So that's Margaret Thatcher's horoscope. What about your horoscope? How would you look at the signs and houses in that?

The first thing to do is to get a feel for the meaning of the sign position of each of your planets. Then turn to Chapter Seventeen, and check out the meanings of each of their house positions. For example, if you have Mercury in Gemini in the second house, you should first look up in Chapter Seven to see what Mercury in Gemini means. This tells you that you have a quick and versatile mind. Next, look up Mercury in the second house. You are told that you are always thinking of new ways to make money. To begin with, you should keep these meanings separate: Mercury in Gemini means one thing, and Mercury in the second house means something else. As you become more experienced, you can merge these meanings together, so Mercury in Gemini *and* in the second house means someone who has a versatile mind who is good at thinking of many new and different ways of making money, perhaps by writing or by selling communications equipment.

At this stage you may have one final question: what if a house has no planets in it? If there are no planets in the tenth house, does this mean that there is no career? Don't worry! There are ten planets and twelve houses. So there aren't enough planets to go round. Everyone has twelve houses in their horoscope, even if some houses have no planets in them.

Everyone has a fourth house and everyone has, or had, a father. But if a house has no planets in it, it may simply mean

245

that this particular area of life is uncomplicated. There are indeed many people who have no planets in the tenth house, but who are still tremendously successful.

THE TWELVE HOUSES

The First House

This is the most important house, because it contains the Ascendant, from which all the other houses flow. The first house can describe our appearance and the way in which we come over in public. Planets in the first house are particularly noticeable. For example, people with Mars in the first house tend to be assertive, while people with Jupiter here are often optimistic and larger than life. The first house is the self. Therefore, people with three or more planets placed here are likely to be very dynamic and full of self-confidence. They may believe that they are in charge of their own destiny and that no power on earth can stop them from succeeding. However, a strong first house can have its disadvantages: it can signify arrogance, as well as a failure to appreciate other people's needs.

The Second House

The second house is the area of the horoscope which rules money. Planets in the second house tell us about people's attitude to money and how good they are at managing personal finances. When Mars, Saturn or Neptune are placed here, they need to be very careful about money. These people should avoid over-expenditure and get into financial agreements only if they really know what they are doing. The second house doesn't just rule money, but all of our possessions, as well as the things which we value most. So people with Mercury in the second house will place great value on their education and will regard their dearest possessions as being their academic qualifications. However, people with Mars placed here may regard their strength and physical power as the things which they treasure the most. Venus or Jupiter in this house usually indicates material good fortune.

The Third House

The third house is the house of communications, so both letters and telephones come under its rulership. Planets in the third house tell us about the way people communicate. So people with Venus here are often diplomatic and graceful, while Mars can signify a style which is aggressive and tactless. By looking at the planets in this house you can often get some idea of how a person gets on with his brothers and sisters. Venus or Jupiter can indicate a harmonious relationship, while Pluto suggests jealousy and rivalry. Indian astrologers connect the third house with dancing, acting and music. If you find that someone has a lot of planets here, this may suggest special talents in these fields. You should then encourage them to make a great effort to explore their showbiz potential.

The Fourth House

The fourth house covers the home and the family. Planets placed here can tell us about people's home-life and their parents. It has a particularly strong connection with the father. If you see Mars, Saturn or Pluto in the fourth house, this is a hint that you have to be careful. The person you are dealing with may be very defensive about the past, and may get angry if you ask too many personal questions. A planet in the fourth house may also describe the father. For example, Mercury in the fourth house may indicate a talkative father, while Saturn may indicate a father who believed in discipline and hard work. Four or more planets in the fourth house are an indication of people who are introverted, who prefer staying at home to mixing with other people. You should perhaps encourage them to be a little more sociable.

The Fifth House

In astrology the fifth house is very fortunate. Planets placed here tell us about the things which a person enjoys most. One form of pleasure which the fifth house covers is light-hearted romance, in particular the one-night stand. The fifth house also gives us information about the games we play, whether they be football, golf, or poker. Poker has a strong connection with the fifth house, because it is not only a game, but also a form of gambling. Gambling and all forms of speculation, like stock-market trading, are covered by this house. It also describes our creative abilities, like painting, art and sculpture. Finally, and most importantly, the fifth house tells us about children. By looking at planets in the fifth house we can discover information about someone's attitude to children, as well as the kind of children a person will have. Jupiter or Venus in this House usually make a woman fertile, especially if either planet is positioned in Pisces, Cancer or Scorpio.

The Sixth House

The sixth house is rather a difficult and unexciting house. It covers hard work, routine and a person's sense of duty. People with a strong sixth house often feel that it is important to organize their life according to a fixed plan. As a result, long lists are written of all the many tasks that need to be done over the course of a day. There is also a connection between this house and health, and people with a lot of planets in this house may be obsessed with body matters. Diet may be very important and they will usually be careful to eat all the right things. At the same time, they will be good at creating a regular exercise programme for themselves. One other thing that the sixth house rules is small animals, like dogs and cats. You will find that many animal lovers will have a couple of planets in this section of the horoscope.

The Seventh House

Astrologers are always being asked about relationships. It is, therefore, essential that they know about the seventh house. This house covers all kinds of relationships. Planets placed here give valuable information about the kind of partner that someone is attracted to. When Mars, Saturn, Uranus or Pluto are here, it can indicate people who frequently get into unstable relationships. They find themselves involved in heated arguments with their partners, which are hardly ever their fault. Venus or Jupiter here are particularly favourable for love relationships. The Moon in this house emphasizes the importance of relationships – and can indicate someone who has frequent relationships. The seventh house can tell us about other kinds of relationships, such as business partnerships and close friendships. It can also tell us about enemies. A person with many planets here may be good at making enemies. The astrologer should, therefore, advise him or her to be more pleasant and diplomatic in their dealings with other people.

The Eighth House

Sex is a subject which astrologers are often asked about. There are three houses which rule sex: the fifth, the seventh and the eighth. The fifth house rules sex for fun. The seventh house covers a more intimate and meaningful kind of sex, usually within a long-standing relationship. Modern astrologers believe that the eighth house covers the raw emotion and intensity that make up the sexual act. It is, therefore, a very private and hidden part of the horoscope, which the astrologer should handle with care. If you find the Sun or Moon placed here, this is an indication that someone is not prepared to talk about his real feelings. This house does have another, more material set of meanings: it can cover other people's money, as well as debt, legacies and alimony. Occasionally, strong eighth houses can indicate an interest in magic and the supernatural.

The Ninth House

Traditionally, the ninth house covers long journeys – travel, holidays, distant countries and things like aeroplanes and coaches. People with several planets placed here usually love travelling, and if the opportunity comes up they often choose to live or work abroad. The ninth house doesn't just refer to material travel; it is also connected to religion, philosophy and spirituality. People with strong ninth houses (that is – with many planets positioned in the ninth house) often have prophetic dreams, religious insights and out of body experiences. The ninth house also rules the law courts: planets placed here can indicate interest in legal matters. When it comes to career, you can safely suggest that someone with three or more planets in this house should be a lawyer, a priest or a travel agent.

The Tenth House

This is an important house, which describes career and ambition. Planets in the tenth house give indications about the career path, and the way a person relates to the working environment. This house is also connected with status and recognition. People who have four or more planets in the tenth house often want or need plenty of recognition and praise. They want to be seen by everyone and, as a result, lead active and high-profile social lives. The tenth house can also tell us about the mother. At first sight, this may sound odd – that the same house which rules the career also rules the mother – however, we should remember that most people have their first contact with the outside world through their mother. These first impressions can have a crucial influence on the grown adult's eventual career path.

The Eleventh House

The eleventh house covers friends and social activities. Those with a lot of planets in this house love people and like to have as many different friends as possible. Very often, planetary activity in this house makes people feel that they have to join something, like a political party or an environmental pressure group. They feel that by being a member of a group they can do something positive in order to change society. Astrologers sometimes call the eleventh house 'the house of hopes and wishes'. People with powerful eleventh houses have a strong vision of the things they most want out of life and, through the power of positive thinking, these people almost always get them. If you see anyone with two or three planets in the eleventh house, make sure that you tell them to have faith, because in the end they are bound to realize their dearest ambitions.

The Twelfth House

The final house is rather a lonely house. It is about solitude, isolation and quiet reflection. A person with several planets in this house often needs time to be alone, away from the noise and confusion of everyday life. This house does have a spiritual nature to it and if it is strong in someone's horoscope this person may be interested in religion, karma and reincarnation. In the material world, the twelfth house often refers to institutions, like schools, hospitals and prisons. People with planets here may work in such places, or else be concerned with things like the welfare of prisoners. Additionally, in the same way as the sixth house refers to small animals, the twelfth house refers to large ones, such as cows, elephants and whales. Don't laugh – it could be important if you are a farmer, a lion tamer, or an employee of a dolphinarium.

17. THE MEANING OF THE PLANETS IN EACH HOUSE OF THE HOROSCOPE

THE MEANING OF THE SUN IN EACH HOUSE

The Sun in the First House

People with the Sun placed here have enormous self-confidence. They know what they want and are not afraid of asking for it. First house Sun people are also very honest, because they find it impossible to hide their real intentions. This position is common in the horoscopes of people with strong psychic abilities. With practice, these people can not only read minds, but also move objects at a distance.

The Sun in the Second House

Second house Sun people tend to be materialistic. Whatever they do, they want to be paid for it – either now or later. These people are also concerned about their income, because it shows how much society values them. If they are not earning enough, they feel unappreciated and unloved ... So with this house position it really is the case that money can buy happiness.

The Sun in the Third House

These people are good communicators and can always be relied on to get a message across loudly and clearly. At the same time, third house Sun people are keen to know what is going on around them, and usually know about all the latest news and gossip. These people probably know their neighbourhood backwards and, as a result, would make excellent community police-men or local journalists.

The Sun in the Fourth House

If the Sun is in the fourth house, it means that a person is born close to midnight. These people are, therefore, often on peak form after dark. At an emotional level, they give the impression that they are holding something back. Somehow, Sun in the fourth people feel that they cannot risk expressing their entire personality. So perhaps the astrologer should persuade them to be more open and trusting.

The Sun in the Fifth House

The fifth house is a good place for the Sun to be. The Sun knows how to have a good time, and these are great people to invite to parties. The Sun in the fifth also enjoys playing games, and is particularly suited to competitive sports. However, they should be careful when it comes to playing games for money – they are not quite as lucky as they think they are!

The Sun in the Sixth House

These people most definitely need a structured life. If every-thing around them isn't in exactly the right place, they feel that they cannot express their potential to the full. So it is important that both sixth house Sun people and those around them are tidy and organized. Once they have managed to assert full control over their environment, there is very little that they cannot achieve.

The Sun in the Seventh House

People with this Sun position believe that relationships are essential. If they are single, they probably feel that something is missing from their life. Sun in the seventh house will then do everything in their power to remedy the situation. They are usually very good listeners. If they can learn to be more self-reliant they would make excellent counsellors or psychotherapists.

The Sun in the Eighth House

When you see the Sun in the eighth house you should be alert to the possibility that you are dealing with someone who is very intense. This person takes life very seriously and is fond of talking about topics such as sex and death. People with the Sun in this position do find it difficult to express themselves, and as a result you will often find that they don't appear to fit the description of their Sun sign very well.

The Sun in the Ninth House

The ninth house is probably the best place for the Sun. People with the Sun here have a sense of adventure and are not afraid of novel experiences. They definitely believe that travel broadens the mind, and will go abroad at every opportunity. At the same time, Sun in the ninth people understand the value of learning, and are always prepared to study new and exotic subjects.

The Sun in the Tenth House

People with the Sun in the tenth house are often extremely ambitious. They want to get to the top of their chosen career, regardless of the consequences. It is also important for them to be praised and recognized. Sometimes, tenth house Sun people are a little too anxious to succeed: they cut corners and forget about the needs of other people. In the process, they could make one enemy too many.

The Sun in the Eleventh House

Eleventh house Sun people have to learn to work in a team. Their immediate inclination may be to ignore other people's advice and to go their own way. However, experience eventually tells them that this is the wrong approach. As soon as the Sun in the eleventh house starts to co-operate with others and to share any knowledge and expertise, things start to move very rapidly in their favour.

The Sun in the Twelfth House

The twelfth house is not the easiest house for the Sun to be in. At times it may be difficult for these people to assert themselves and they may have to make a real effort in order to be noticed. On the plus side, this house position can give a profound spirituality. The Sun may benefit from meditation and from occasional retreats to isolated places in the middle of nowhere.

THE MEANING OF THE MOON IN EACH HOUSE

The Moon in the First House

People with the Moon in the first house often have a sensitive streak. They are quick to pick up on other people's feelings and their moods can change quickly. The Moon in this house can also result in rapid weight changes. A few days of overeating can lead to a few burst seams, although, on the plus side, first house Moon is very responsive to crash diets.

The Moon in the Second House

This can signify continual changes in financial fortune. One moment the money's pouring in, and the next it has completely dried up. To protect themselves from the bad times, these people should avoid extravagance, and save as much money as possible. Some second house Moons are good at smelling out money, and quick to take advantage of unexpected financial opportunities.

The Moon in the Third House

These people enjoy conversation, especially with close friends. They love telephones and have an easy and natural telephone manner. The third house is, in fact, the best house for the Moon to be in, and can bring some very special talents. Third house Moon people are often superb writers. As an astrologer, you should encourage them to write more and perhaps to get published.

The Moon in the Fourth House

The fourth house Moon feels that there are always things going on at home and in the family which need constant attention. As a result, these people find it difficult to relax when they are far away from the domestic base. At the very deepest level, fourth house Moon people are trying to rediscover a lost childhood. However, it is unlikely that they will admit it.

The Moon in the Fifth House

People with the Moon placed here want to direct all their emotional energy into the expression of their talents, whether they be artistic or social. At the same time, it is always important for fifth house Moon people to enjoy expressing themselves. They are, also, very good with children. They know how to respond to them, how to keep them amused and how to get them to sleep.

The Moon in the Sixth House

The sixth house Moon is concerned with health and routine. People with the Moon here feel that it is necessary to have a high degree of organization in their life, and when routines are disrupted they often feel lost. So it is important that the sixth house Moon makes a real effort to stick to schedules, particularly when it comes to work, exercise and diet.

The Moon in the Seventh House

One-to-one relationships are going to be an area of concern to a seventh house Moon. While these people feel that it is important to be in a close relationship, they are only too aware of how other people's behaviour and moods affect them. Very often, the Moon in the seventh gets involved with partners who are extremely emotional and who find it difficult to control their feelings.

The Moon in the Eighth House

Astrologers have to be careful when seeing clients with eighth house Moons. There are a lot of things which these people don't like talking about, probably because they take their emotions very seriously. These people tend to have strong passions and their sex life is always very important. This is because sex is the one sure way in which they can express their pent-up emotions.

The Moon in the Ninth House

If people with the Moon in the ninth house get stuck in one place for too long, they first become bored, then irritable and then unstable. So the moment these Moon people feel the call of the wild, it is vital that they do something adventurous to satisfy the craving. Running a marathon may be enough, but very often it is necessary to skateboard blindfolded down Everest.

The Moon in the ninth house likes to skateboard blindfolded down Everest.

The Moon in the Tenth House

Tenth house Moons thrive on recognition and success, and will do all in their power to push themselves into the public eye. However, to save themselves unnecessary worry, the Moon in the tenth house does need patience. These people often cannot choose when they will succeed, but have to wait for external factors to thrust success upon them.

The Moon in the Eleventh House

An active social life is very important to eleventh house Moons. They get a lot of pleasure and emotional support from friends, and in social situations, like parties, they are often star performers. The eleventh house is the house of hopes and wishes, and so people with the Moon here are often amazing optimists, who believe that everything will be all right in the end.

The Moon in the Twelfth House

This is the most introspective position for the Moon. Twelfth house Moons often spend a lot of time on their own, and when forced to be in a group can be isolated and withdrawn. The Moon in the twelfth house tends to be very sensitive and these people are often excellent judges of character. These are great people to consult if you want to know whether or not to trust someone.

THE MEANING OF MERCURY IN EACH HOUSE

Mercury in the First House

This is an extremely communicative place for Mercury to be in. These people find it easy to get their message across, and often make excellent salesmen or politicians. The only possible problem with Mercury in the first house is that they talk too much. Once they have put their message across, they should make a real effort to shut up. That way, their audience won't get bored with them!

Mercury in the Second House

People with Mercury in this house spend a lot of time thinking about new ways of boosting their income and avoiding the taxman. As far as actual ways of earning money are concerned, anything to do with writing and communications should work out very well for Mercury in the second house. This could include telephone sales, selling satellite television dishes, or even writing novels.

Mercury in the Third House

The third house is a good place for Mercury to be. These people are highly versatile and able to talk about any subject under the sun. With a bit of discipline and training, they are capable of being excellent teachers or educators. Very often, third house Mercury can indicate mechanical skill, so they might be good at both fixing and driving cars.

Mercury in the Fourth House

The fourth house Mercury tends to have a very long memory, particularly for places and events. While this is a useful skill, these people should avoid the temptation to live in the past. It is also worth noting that Mercury in this position often makes natural electricians. People with this Mercury should, therefore, take evening classes in order to unlock this potential.

Mercury in the Fifth House

People with Mercury in the fifth house are extremely creative. Mercury is full of ideas and makes an excellent poet, artist or writer. Mercury in the fifth people like nothing better than to share their creativity with children, perhaps by inventing games for them or else by telling them stories. These people often have children who are themselves very talented.

Mercury in the Sixth House

Mercury in this house gives superb organizational abilities. These people very rarely lose things and are never late for an appointment. They usually have an elaborate filing system, both at home and at work, and have their schedule planned months in advance. However, working with them can be quite exhausting – they like bombarding you with impossible deadlines.

Mercury in the Seventh House

When Mercury is in the seventh house it can indicate people who are constantly looking for partners – partners who are not only loveable, but also intelligent and able to provide good conversation. Indeed, people with a seventh house Mercury love having deep and meaningful conversations with their friends and loved ones. As a result, their telephone bills are often astronomical.

Mercury in the Eighth House

People with Mercury in this house position are usually fairly secretive. They don't like talking about their plans and it can be difficult to keep track of their movements. As a result, this placing is good for spying and undercover police work. Mercury in the eighth house gives excellent intuition, and these people are frequently able to anticipate their opponents' actions.

Mercury in the Ninth House

A head in the clouds can result from a ninth house Mercury: people who are forever thinking about ways of rising above everyday reality. This may be through travel to far-off places, or else through spiritual enlightenment. On balance, people with this Mercury need to be more realistic. Before they fly off to the Himalayas to meet their guardian angels, they should at least pay the gas bill.

Mercury in the Tenth House

These people are ambitious, and want to make the most out of their talents. As a result, they will usually choose a career which is both rewarding and challenging. Mercury in this position gives superb interviewing skills and these people often get the job they go for. Ideal careers for this house placing include the law, publishing and being a tri-lingual secretary.

Mercury in the Eleventh House

People with Mercury in this house find it easy to make friends, and enjoy being in group situations. They have fairly strong political opinions, so it might be a good idea for them to join a pressure group or a political party. Mercury in this position is ideal for public speaking. These people are likely to find that their easy and articulate style attracts considerable praise and attention.

Mercury in the Twelfth House

This is not the best house for Mercury to be in. The twelfth house placement makes it difficult for individuals to be direct and to the point, and as a result their words are often misunderstood. On the plus side, this placing is very imaginative. If these people can find somewhere where they can be quiet and undisturbed, there is no reason why they could not translate their imaginings into an amazing painting or poem.

THE MEANING OF VENUS IN EACH HOUSE

Venus in the First House

Venus in the first house is charming and attractive. These people make those around them feel at ease, and Venus in this position tends to be very popular. This house placement bestows a natural understanding of how to behave in social situations, so they hardly ever embarrass themselves (or anybody else, for that matter!). When it comes to finding a love partner, the only problem is being spoilt for choice.

Venus in the Second House

When Venus is in this house it gives the opportunity to make money out of the fashion and beauty industry. Possible careers might then be clothes designer, beauty therapist, or jeweller. Money is something which Venus in the second house people certainly need, because they have extravagant tastes. When it comes to food, wine and clothes, Venus only buys the best, even if this means personal bankruptcy.

Venus in the Third House

These people enjoy the company of close friends, particularly in an intimate environment. Large parties are not to their taste: they are too impersonal. Venus in the third house often makes for very good teachers. This is because Venus is able to sympathize with the learning needs of the students. One final point to make about this placing is that it gives good relationships with brother and sisters.

Venus in the Fourth House

Venus in this house is definitely happiest at home. These people don't like going out too much, and prefer to do their socializing either in their own house or over the telephone. Harmony is important to Venus in the fourth house people, so wherever possible they live in tastefully decorated homes, situated in quiet neighbourhoods. If there is money to spare, they will collect paintings and antiques.

Venus in the Fifth House

Venus in the fifth house people are real pleasure-seekers. They are always on the look-out for fun and excitement, and are at their very best at parties and on the beach. The love life of Venus in the fifth house is active and varied. People with this Venus placement usually have a short attention-span and, if they are in a relationship for longer than a few weeks, their bodies and their passions start wandering.

Venus in the Sixth House

People with Venus in the sixth house are very aware of their responsibilities to others. In a relationship, they feel that it is up to them to make the thing work. As a result, Venus is often left clearing up the material and emotional mess that their partners leave behind. It is therefore important that these people find caring partners, who are prepared to share the household chores.

Venus in the Seventh House

A man with this house position is often looking for a perfect woman who is beautiful, responsive and sympathetic. Needless to say, he never finds her. A woman with Venus in the seventh house is often quite 'hard'. She doesn't have too much sympathy for other people's weaknesses and believes that it is important to be self-reliant. However, she often attracts men who are over-emotional.

Venus in the Eighth House

Venus in the eighth house people are extremely seductive and are very good at getting what they want out of other people. Venus in this house position takes relationships very seriously and has no interest in frivolous encounters. Indeed, these people are looking for an emotionally charged relationship which will catapult them into a new dimension of sexual experience.

Venus in the Ninth House

Venus in the ninth house people tend to find their own country rather boring. They feel that they have to go abroad to find real excitement and adventure. If travel is impossible, these people tend to surround themselves with friends who are unusual and who have strange philosophical and religious beliefs. When it comes to romance, Venus in the ninth house is likely to be attracted to foreigners.

Venus in the Tenth House

People with a tenth house Venus often find that their charm (or looks) are useful in their careers. These individuals quickly get noticed, and are good at talking the boss into giving them promotion and pay-rises. Frequently, Venus in the tenth house meets lovers and future marriage partners through work. If this placement has any faults, it is vanity and an obsession with appearance.

Venus in the Eleventh House

Eleventh house Venus people love parties and group activities and, as a result, they lead busy social lives. Venus usually has hundreds of friends, although few of these friends can be regarded as close. This is because Venus in the eleventh house finds it difficult to devote too much time to any one person. As far as career is concerned, they are very good at publicity work and organizing conferences.

Venus in the Twelfth House

The twelfth house is not the most sociable place for Venus. These people certainly enjoy their own company and shy away from parties and other large-scale gatherings. In the area of relationships, Venus in the twelfth house is extremely secretive. They don't like talking about their private lives, and if they are in a relationship, you'll be the last person to know about it.

THE MEANING OF MARS IN EACH HOUSE

Mars in the First House

People with a first house Mars believe strongly in themselves, and find it difficult to take into account the opinions of others. Very often, this position gives an aggressive streak, which leads to arguments and fights. So Mars in the first should make an effort to be more diplomatic. This is particularly the case in relationships, which can turn into war zones if precautions aren't taken.

Mars in the Second House

People with Mars in the second house are careful to safeguard their money and property. Their cars are full of the latest anti-theft devices and their homes resemble Fort Knox. When they go shopping, they always count the change, and if it is a penny short they complain loudly. As far as a career is concerned, these people would make good bank managers or pawnbrokers.

Mars in the Third House

In astrology, the third house rules short journeys and, as a result, people with this placement are always on the move. However, when Mars is in this position there is a great need to be careful when driving, since their impatience can lead to traffic violations and accidents. Mars in the third house people frequently argue with their neighbours. Once an argument starts, it usually goes on until one party dies or moves.

Mars in the Fourth House

Mars in this position puts a lot of energy into home and domestic life. The family unit is particularly important to these people, and anyone that threatens their security or happiness is likely to get killed. People with Mars in the fourth need to be on their guard against household accidents. They shouldn't rush domestic tasks and, in case of mishaps, should have a first-aid kit close at hand.

Mars in the Fifth House

This is an energetic placement for Mars. These people want to make the most out of life and always live for the present. They enjoy all kinds of sport, although they are particularly partial to those which involve personal risk. Individuals with this house position tend to lead dangerous love lives. Their belief that anyone is fair game for their romantic attentions often has fatal consequences.

Mars in the Sixth House

These people are very disciplined, and are able to work extremely hard. As a result, they always achieve their ambitions. Health matters are usually important for Mars in the sixth house and they tend to put a lot of effort into keeping fit. It is particularly important that people with this placement keep regular hours and that they get as much exercise as possible.

Mars in the Seventh House

The seventh house is not one of the easier places for Mars to be. It can cause arguments and misunderstandings in close relationships, which may be difficult to resolve. Part of the reason for this problem is that these people attract partners who like picking fights. The best way for Mars in the seventh house people to deal with this situation is to assert themselves with tact and grace.

Mars in the Eighth House

An eighth house Mars often gives individuals a lot of hidden anger, which they find difficult to express. In order to avoid undue tension, it might be a good idea for them to take up a martial art, like karate or judo. This position is also connected with a powerful sexuality, which needs to be expressed in an emotionally honest relationship.

Mars in the Ninth House

Mars in the ninth house people need to put their energy into broadening their horizons. This could be through religious or spiritual pursuits, or, alternatively, it could be through travelling. However, they should make sure, before going abroad, that their documentation really is in order. This is because these people often have arguments with foreign officials about passports and visas.

Mars in the Tenth House

These people are extremely ambitious and will do practically anything to succeed. They are able to throw everything they've got at their career, and very often get to the top. Mars in the

Mars in the eleventh house people have a tyrannical streak, and if their comrades don't watch out, they could turn out to be real Stalins.

tenth house could guarantee success, if only these people were a little more sensitive. Sometimes they are so keen for results that they forget about the needs of their colleagues, and this in turn leads to bad feeling.

Mars in the Eleventh House

Mars in the eleventh house believes that groups are important and these people will often be members of half a dozen different clubs and societies. They can be very good at motivating other people and are excellent organizers of demonstrations, strikes and sit-ins. On the down side, Mars in the eleventh people have a tyrannical streak and if their comrades don't watch out, they could turn out to be real Stalins.

Mars in the Twelfth House

This is not one of the most assertive places for Mars. It is difficult for people with this Mars to take the initiative, and they find it almost impossible to express their real feelings. So it is important that Mars in the twelfth house is able to work off excess frustrations through something like yoga or meditation. They might also consider sport, because many brilliant athletes have this placing.

THE MEANING OF JUPITER IN EACH HOUSE

Jupiter in the First House

The first house is a great position for Jupiter. These people are optimistic and full of fun and have a reputation for being lucky. They find it difficult to take things seriously, and do their best to treat life as one long laugh. Jupiter in the first house is rather an indulgent placing. It can lead to bouts of over-eating, which can in turn lead to overweight.

Jupiter in the Second House

Jupiter in this house can be a two-edged sword. On one hand, these people have definite money-making abilities. They are quick to spot good deals and their hunches usually pay off. On the other hand, people with Jupiter in this house need a lot of money to be able to afford their desire for champagne, fast cars, boats, holidays in the Caribbean and any other extravagance you care to mention.

Jupiter in the Third House

Third house Jupiter people often have a great interest in the arts. They enjoy going to the theatre and to the opera, and are very knowledgeable about paintings and the history of art. Jupiter in the third house usually indicates better than average writing abilities, and these people should at least make an effort to write a few short stories.

Jupiter in the Fourth House

This placing is very good for home life. It creates domestic security, and indicates that the family is an unending source of happiness. These people are often lucky when it comes to buying property and have natural talents for redecoration and interior design. When it comes to career, Jupiter in the fourth house makes good estate agents, builders and landscape gardeners.

Jupiter in the Fifth House

Jupiter in the fifth house is a very creative placement. These people excel in the performing arts and are good at encouraging the talents of others. They are particularly good with children, and their own children are invariably happy and well-adjusted. For a woman, Jupiter in the fifth is usually a very fertile place, especially if Jupiter is in the sign of Cancer, Pisces or Scorpio. The only problem with this house placement is that it can occasionally lead to an addiction to gambling and speculation.

Jupiter in the Sixth House

These people enjoy organizing things. They are not too bothered by what they are actually organizing, as long as they are doing it. So, if you are planning a village fête, or the next world war, get their help. On a more constructive level, Jupiter in the sixth house people are often skilled at the healing arts. They are very good at things like massage, acupuncture and aromatherapy. If you're feeling under the weather, give Jupiter a call.

Jupiter in the Seventh House

This is a very good placement for relationships. Jupiter in the seventh house is able to benefit substantially from lovers, both materially and emotionally. From a business point of view, this position indicates that it should be relatively easy to find partners who are trustworthy and competent. The main disadvantage of having Jupiter in this house is that it can lead to laziness and complacency.

Jupiter in the Eighth House

In astrology, the eighth house can rule other people's money. When Jupiter is placed here, this gives a natural ability to make other people part with their money. So people with this placing could make excellent thieves or con men. Jupiter in the eighth house people often claim to have had unusual occult experiences. However, you shouldn't believe everything they say, because they are prone to exaggeration.

Jupiter in the Ninth House

People with Jupiter in the ninth house have immense faith. They believe that no matter how bad things may seem on the surface, they will eventually sort themselves out. Jupiter in the ninth house is often an indicator of a profound spirituality. So much so, that individuals with this placement are frequently able to get in touch with that part of themselves which is eternal and immortal.

Jupiter in the Tenth House

This house position enables individuals to be successful in their career. While hard work and ambition play a part in their success, these are not the only ingredients. Jupiter in this house gives a generosity of spirit which ensures the good will of both workmates and employers. Indeed, no one feels threatened by Jupiter in the tenth house people, which is why their career paths run into so few obstacles.

Jupiter in the Eleventh House

This is an excellent place for Jupiter. Jupiter in the eleventh house people are very idealistic. They like to think that they can join up with other people in order to create a better world and, as a result, often make a valuable contribution to the work of pressure groups and charities. All in all, people with Jupiter in this house have inspirational qualities which can move nations with their shining vision of the future.

Jupiter in the Twelfth House

Jupiter in the twelfth people can be rather pessimistic, and frequently complain that they never get any lucky breaks. The reality of the situation is rather different. People with this Jupiter position hardly ever come to too much harm, because they are surrounded by an aura of protection. So, if they have any ambitions, they should not be afraid of going out into the world and achieving them.

THE MEANING OF SATURN IN EACH HOUSE

Saturn in the First House

People with Saturn in the first house or the Ascendant believe in the value of hard work, and often find it difficult to relax. In their careers, these people tend to do either very well or very badly. This is because they frequently choose a single life goal, which they pursue to the very end. If it is the right goal, they get to the top. If it is the wrong one, they may not realize it until it's too late.

Saturn in the Second House

These people feel that their financial security can never be taken for granted and are often terrified of being out on the street without a penny. As a result, Saturn in the second house people are very careful with their money, and avoid getting into debt. Although they are never quite satisfied with their financial position, their caution ensures that their worst fears never happen.

Saturn in the Third House

When you see Saturn in the third house in a horoscope, this is an indication that you are dealing with people who may have bad memories of school. Perhaps they felt pressurized to keep up with a successful brother or sister. In other ways, this is not a bad position for Saturn. These people are able to express themselves with great precision and often have excellent writing skills.

Saturn in the Fourth House

The fourth house can be a fairly difficult placement for Saturn. These people may often feel that family life is a burden from which they cannot escape. At the same time, they may not find it easy to discuss their inner feelings. To discover real peace of mind, it is important that Saturn in the fourth house people create a special place for themselves, where they can be free from interruption and disturbance.

Saturn in the Fifth House

It is important for these people to be recognized as creative and talented. As a result, they push themselves hard and are not satisfied until they have created a masterpiece. This masterpiece could be a painting, a knitted jersey, or a perfectly installed central heating system. It should also be noted that Saturn in the fifth house people have high expectations of their children.

Saturn in the Sixth House

Anyone with Saturn in the sixth house needs to make sure that they lead a disciplined and organized life. If they are sloppy, or forget to look after their health, they will quickly pay the price. So people with this house position should give up unhealthy habits, like smoking and over-eating. It is also very important that they take regular aerobic exercise.

Saturn in the Seventh House

In a relationship, Saturn in the seventh house people are prepared to take their share of the responsibility, and will go to great lengths to safeguard their loved one's interests. However, it is very important that they find the time to look after themselves. This is because their partners or lovers sometimes have a selfish streak, and tend to take advantage of Saturn in the seventh's good nature.

Saturn in the Eighth House

These people may have emotions which they are afraid of and which they don't want others to know about. It is nonetheless vital that Saturn is able to get in touch with these feelings, perhaps through the right kind of relationship. At another level, Saturn in this house has to be careful about financial dealings, and in particular, these people should never sign contracts without having first read the small print.

Saturn in the Ninth House

Saturn in the ninth house people feel that their lives are not as exciting as they should be. As a result, they are frequently obsessed with travel and adventure. However, the moment they find their paradise, they get bored with it. Sometimes Saturn in the ninth eventually realizes the limitations of physical travel. They then get involved with weird cults which offer short-cuts to heaven.

Saturn in the Tenth House

These people are very ambitious and usually get what they want out of life, especially if Saturn is positioned in Capricorn, Aquarius or Libra. However, they should realize that there is a price to pay for success. Saturn in the tenth house people often pay insufficient attention to their social and family life and when not at work often feel lonely and isolated. They should make a greater effort to relax and to socialize.

Saturn in the Eleventh House

People with Saturn in the eleventh house have a rather odd attitude to groups. On one hand, they find group situations difficult and tend to be shy and withdrawn. On the other hand, they regard group activities as very important, however painful they may be. These people often bite the bullet, therefore, and force themselves into the limelight.

Saturn in the Twelfth House

The twelfth house is one of the better places for Saturn. These people often have unusual interests and like to have plenty of time and space in which to study. They are fairly secretive and very few people know exactly what they are doing with their lives. People with this position can work very well in institutions, and make very good prison warders, doctors, nurses or teachers.

THE MEANING OF URANUS IN EACH HOUSE

Uranus in the First House

First house Uranus people are real individuals. They don't believe in conforming to society's norms, and often wear unusual clothes. In group situations they really stand out. Anyone that is prepared to approach them will be staggered by their brilliant originality. However, in relationships the independent-mindedness of Uranus in the first house can be difficult to deal with.

Uranus in the Second House

These people are always having new ideas for making money. A few of these ideas are worth pursuing, but most of them are no-hopers. If there is a way for them to become rich, it may be through the sale of communications equipment and computers. Sometimes Uranus in the second may be prepared to throw all scruples to the wind, in which case they can make a killing out of the arms trade.

Uranus in the Third House

People with Uranus in the third house are very interested in science and technology. They like reading books about these subjects, and are good at building and repairing electronic gadgetry. Very often Uranus in the third house people are attracted to unusual methods of transport and, if possible, would love to travel to work by hovercraft or by spaceship.

Uranus in the Fourth House

There are always unexpected things happening in the domestic environment of people with Uranus in the fourth house. And as a result it is difficult for them to plan things in advance. Uranus in the fourth house must be particularly careful with household appliances, because they often break down. On the plus side, these people have an exciting family, who always keep them amused with their eccentric sense of fun.

Uranus in the Fifth House

These people think that they are totally different from the rest of humanity. They usually realize this in the first years of life, and from then on do their best to develop unique skills and unusual beliefs. Very often, Uranus in the fifth people have children who are even more independent-minded than they are, so they probably won't have to lecture their children on how to rebel.

Uranus in the third house would love to travel to work by hovercraft or spaceship.

Uranus in the Sixth House

Uranus in this house dislikes routine and often leads a life which is hopelessly disorganized. This approach is not very sensible. While it is important that these people express their individuality, they should recognize that their lives need some kind of a structure if they are to be healthy and successful. Once Uranus in the sixth people have got themselves together, they make excellent practitioners of alternative medicine.

Uranus in the Seventh House

This position of Uranus often indicates unstable relationships. This is because these people are attracted to strongly independent partners, whose moves can rarely be predicted. Uranus in the seventh people also have to be careful about their choice of business partners, because if they get hooked up to the wrong person, their reputation and credibility could plummet.

Uranus in the Eighth House

When Uranus is placed here it is often an indicator of people with some very bizarre interests. They are frequently attracted to magic and the occult, and are often avid readers of science fiction. When it comes to financial matters, Uranus in the eighth house has a certain amount of luck. In particular, they are good at benefiting from other people's death and misfortune.

Uranus in the Ninth House

These people adore travelling, but hate tourists. So you are more likely to find them touring the steel mills of Pittsburgh than lounging around on a Malibu beach. Uranus in the ninth house is also interested in religion and has frequent conversions: today an atheist, yesterday a Buddhist and tomorrow a Baptist.

Uranus in the Tenth House

These people need great independence in their career. They don't like their superiors telling them what to do, and often prefer to work freelance. The career path of Uranus in the tenth people is often rather erratic, partly because they frequently change jobs. Suitable careers include television and radio presenters, astronauts and rocket scientists.

Uranus in the Eleventh House

Individuals with this house position are frequently interested in radical politics, and tend to be good at winning over people's hearts and minds. They strongly believe that if enough people unite behind a common goal, the world really can be changed. So the security services should keep tabs on them, in case they start a revolution – or maybe they shouldn't, depending on your point of view.

Uranus in the Twelfth House

This position indicates people who, on the surface, like to blend in. Uranus in the twelfth house people don't want others to see them doing anything unusual, and their tastes appear to be very conservative. However, underneath it all they have a desperate need to rebel and do something wild. As an astrologer, it is your role to tell these people that it's okay to be outrageous, and that it really doesn't matter if the tabloids get their story.

THE MEANING OF NEPTUNE IN EACH HOUSE

Neptune in the First House

People with this house position are quick to tune into other people's emotions, and usually know when those around them are unhappy or angry. There are times when such sensitivity can be overwhelming, and people with this placement are advised to avoid heavy emotional scenes. When it comes to their general well-being, they should live by the sea, or at least go swimming regularly.

Neptune in the Second House

These people are often a bit vague about their finances. They find it difficult to keep track of expenditure and frequently forget what their income is. Usually, they manage to muddle through without going bankrupt, but they still need to make a greater effort to put their financial affairs in order. When it comes to careers, Neptune in the second house makes good chemists and bartenders.

Neptune in the Third House

People with Neptune in this house have colourful imaginations which can stimulate their creativity. They are often able to use music and literature to express their inner fantasies to a wider audience, so it is important that they are encouraged to explore this potential. Very often, Neptune in the third house has unusual contacts with brothers and sisters, which have an almost telepathic quality.

Neptune in the Fourth House

Neptune in the fourth house in someone's horoscope suggests that the individual's father may have been rather distant –

there may even have been a mystery around him. However, this is a very delicate area and we advise you not to pursue the matter unless you really know what you are doing. On a more mundane level, people with this placement should check carefully for subsidence before buying property.

Neptune in the Fifth House

These people enjoy nightclubs and bright lights, and actively seek out the company of exciting and exotic people. When it comes to romance, Neptune in the fifth house is looking for someone who is out of this world. As a result, they tend to fall in love with ghosts and vampires! The one thing these people should avoid at all costs is gambling. Once they start, they find it impossible to stop.

Neptune in the Sixth House

People with Neptune in the sixth house need to look after their health and diet. It is important that they eat good quality food which is free of chemicals and additives. They should also stay well clear of cigarettes and drugs, and never drink more than two glasses of wine a day. On the plus side, Neptune in the sixth people often have amazing gifts as faith healers.

Neptune in the Seventh House

Neptune in the seventh house is an indication that relationships are something of a weak spot. Such people find it very difficult to stand up to their partners, and in extreme cases are prepared to sacrifice everything for love. This is a great shame, which is made worse by the fact that their partners often turn out to be untalented frauds.

Neptune in the Eighth House

These people are extremely seductive and are able to attract practically anyone. In relationships, the sexual element tends to be very important and Neptune in the eighth's idea of bliss is abandoning themselves to an intensely passionate coupling. However, Neptune in the eighth people should try not to get too carried away, because otherwise they may lose touch with their core identity.

Neptune in the Ninth House

Individuals with Neptune in this position are often looking for amazing experiences which will completely transform their lives. Sometimes they fantasize about being kidnapped by aliens, while at other times they believe that enlightenment can be found in a supermarket car park. If these people are looking for a real experience, they should take up sailing. After a few years' practice, they'll be able to circumnavigate the globe!

Neptune in the Tenth House

These people frequently find it difficult to choose a career. They often change their minds about what they want to do, and it can take many years to find their real vocation. Nonetheless, there are careers at which Neptune in the tenth house can excel. These include photography, music management and film work. Other possibilities are make-up artist and fish breeding.

Neptune in the Eleventh House

When you see Neptune in the eleventh, you will instantly know that these people have plenty of friends and enjoy parties and other group activities. However, some of these friends are not only unusual, but also a bad influence. Neptune in the eleventh people are usually idealistic, and would love to alleviate other people's suffering, but they find it difficult to translate compassion into positive action.

Neptune in the Twelfth House

People with this placement need to be careful if they work in a large organization. They can quickly lose their individuality and end up as mere numbers. Occasionally, Neptune in the twelfth people may actually want to sacrifice their identity to a higher cause, in which case they should enter a monastery or the civil service. When Neptune in the twelfth house people get stressed, they should go swimming, preferably with dolphins.

THE MEANING OF PLUTO IN EACH HOUSE

Pluto in the First House

This is a fairly defensive house position. These people are wary of the outside world and are careful to reveal as little about themselves as possible. At the same time, Pluto in the first house people have a powerful charisma and usually get what they want out of others. This placement is also very unforgiving and will go to great lengths to settle old scores.

Pluto in the Second House

People with Pluto in this house feel that money is vital and if they see a financial opportunity, they throw everything they've got at it. However, they do need to be careful that they don't cut too many corners in their rush to be rich – or they may end up in prison! Possible money-making schemes for Pluto in the second house include counterfeiting and selling plutonium to banana republics.

Pluto in the Third House

Pluto in the third people find it difficult to let go of childhood injustices. They still blame their teacher for unfairly accusing them of cheating – even though the event happened in early 1911! When it comes to relationships with brothers and sisters, old rivalries are never far from the surface. In addition, these people frequently get on appallingly with their neighbours.

Pluto in the Fourth House

If you see anyone with this position, just forget about it, unless you are a trained psychotherapist. It represents some heavy emotional issues which these people may find difficult to discuss. Instead of trying to talk about these areas, make up something harmless to tell them. For example: 'in your previous incarnation you lived in Ancient Egypt, where you were a very successful tarot card reader'!

Pluto in the Fifth House

These individuals are obsessed with the idea of having fun. They will go to great lengths to plan their leisure time, and at parties are often so busy enjoying themselves that they don't have time to laugh or smile. The love life of people with this house position is often intense. They tend to get drawn into passionate affairs, which can take years to run their course.

Pluto in the Sixth House

Pluto in the sixth house people are often very concerned about their health. They are terrified of catching dangerous diseases and will often go to elaborate lengths to avoid possible contamination. Pluto in the sixth is also worried about radiation and chemical pollution of the water supply. The best advice that

Pluto in the sixth can be given is to relax and have another cigarette.

Pluto in the Seventh House

People with this house position are often attracted to people who are powerful and manipulative. They know that such attractions are dangerous and should perhaps be avoided. However, they find it very difficult to hold back from them. When it comes to business, Pluto in the seventh house people should avoid partnerships at all costs. Otherwise, they could become involved in unwinnable power struggles.

Pluto in the Eighth House

This position of Pluto is common in the horoscopes of those who are attracted by power. These people want to be in total control of their environment and, at worst, they are inclined to see other people as pawns. Pluto in the eighth people tend to have a sexual magnetism which they are able to utilize in their many power games. This placement can also lead to interests in hypnotism and psychic phenomena.

Pluto in the Ninth House

Individuals with Pluto in the ninth are fascinated by mysteries, and often spend a lifetime trying to uncover hidden knowledge. As a result, they are at their happiest in libraries and in ancient ruins. However, when they do find the lost secret to the universe, they tell no one and take their secret to the grave. Ideal careers for this position include private investigator and horror story writer.

Pluto in the tenth house is desperate to succeed and will do anything to be recognized.

288

Pluto in the Tenth House

Career matters are very important to these people. They are desperate to succeed and will do anything to be recognized. When Pluto in the tenth house does get promoted, it is usually not through talent, but through an acute understanding of office politics. So it doesn't really matter what career they choose, provided that there is a coherent power structure to exploit.

Pluto in the Eleventh House

People with Pluto in the eleventh house are very sensitive to what is going on in society, and tend to be the first ones to adopt a new fashion or style. They don't do it deliberately; it just happens. So if you want to be trendy, all you have to do is imitate Pluto in the eleventh's clothes, haircut and speech. These people make excellent dress designers and rock stars.

Pluto in the Twelfth House

The twelfth house is probably the most spiritual placement for Pluto. These people value contemplation and solitude, and are not particularly interested in material wealth. Through meditation they sometimes get in touch with a higher power, which completely transforms their life and goals. Whatever their career, they would ideally make brilliant poets, philosophers or visionaries.

....

HOW TO INTERPRET YOUR HOROSCOPE

18. THE ASPECTS: WHAT THEY ARE

In this chapter you are going to learn about the aspects, what they are, how to find them and what effect they have on your character and destiny.

You will be pleased to know that they are really easy to find and that, in no time at all, you will be able to experience their full power and intensity. However, before we look at the aspects in detail, we are going to refresh your memory about planets, signs and houses.

THE PLANETS, SIGNS AND HOUSES REVISITED

In Sections One and Two of this book, we described the ten planets. As you now know, each planet represents a different part of the human character. For example, the position of Venus in the horoscope tells us about how someone relates to other people, and the position of Saturn gives us information about people's capacity to control and discipline their lives. We all have ten planets in our horoscope. So, no matter how difficult it is for us to get on with others or to discipline our lives, we all have a Venus and a Saturn.

What makes the ten planets individual to a person's character is their *sign* and *house* position. The sign tells us about the way a planet works for an individual, and the house tells us about the specific area of life in which this planet manifests itself.

To take an example, let's look at a person with Mars in Taurus, in the eleventh house: Mars is the planet of assertion, so these sign and house positions describe the way this person asserts himself.

The position of Mars in the sign of Taurus (see Chapter Nine) tells us that this person is stubborn and that he never gives up on a project once he has started it. However, he may find it difficult to get fast results. Mars is also in the eleventh house. This house has a lot of connections and associations to group activities and groups of people (see Chapter Sixteen). So a lot of this stubborn assertiveness may be directed into group activities (see Chapter Seventeen).

Because there are ten planets, one way of describing a person's character is to look at each planet in turn. In the case of Madonna, we could look at the following:

★ Her Sun in Leo in the twelfth house to describe her core personality.
★ Her Moon in Virgo in the first house to describe her emotions.
★ Her Mercury in Virgo in the first house to describe the way she communicates.
★ Her Venus in Leo in the twelfth house to describe her love life and the way she relates to other people.
★ Her Mars in Taurus in the ninth house to describe the way she asserts herself.
★ Her Jupiter in Libra in the second house to describe the areas of life in which she wants to expand.
★ Her Saturn in Sagittarius in the fourth house to describe her approach to self-discipline.

* Her Uranus in Leo in the twelfth house to describe the way she wants to be different from other people.
* Her Neptune in Scorpio in the third house to describe her spirituality.
* Her Pluto in Virgo in the first house to describe the things that she is obsessed about.

Is that it? Can a person's character really be divided into ten neat boxes, which are completely separate from each other? Surely different parts of the character influence one another? For example, people who are looking for love (Venus) may have to be assertive (Mars) in order to win over the object of their desires. Other people may be very reserved and disciplined in their love lives. You would, therefore, expect Saturn to influence Venus in this case.

The planets in a person's horoscope can indeed influence each other. They do this through 'aspects'. In the next section you will learn what an aspect is, and find out about the three main types of aspect and what they mean. After that you will learn about the ways in which the aspects can be put to practical use.

WHAT ARE ASPECTS?

Aspects are rather like communication lines. It is through these communication lines that planets influence each other. Aspects always run between pairs of planets. So, the Sun might be in aspect to the Moon, or Mars might be in aspect to Pluto. When you find that two planets are in aspect, it means that they have an effect on each other.

In order to understand the effect that planets in aspect have on one another, it is necessary to look at the type of aspect they are in. In other words – what kind of relationship the two planets have. Is it a harmonious sort of relationship, a challenging type of relationship or a relationship requiring lots of work and perseverance?

There are three main kinds of aspect: the conjunction, the opposition and the trine. If you haven't come across these astrological terms before, don't worry. We will tell you all about them very soon. In general terms, however, two planets in conjunction aspect have a varied influence on each other and, therefore, a varied influence on the horoscope in question. Two planets in opposition have a stressful influence on each other and, therefore, a stressful influence on the horoscope in question. And two planets in trine have a beneficial influence on each other and, therefore, a beneficial influence on the horoscope in question.

If two planets are not aspected (that is, they have no relationship to each other), then this simply means that they have no influence on each other.

The next three sections cover the conjunction, the opposition and the trine. Each section will first of all tell you how to find the aspect, and then what it means. Although we will be using the example of Madonna's horoscope, we want you to apply our instructions and descriptions to your own horoscope.

Before you start, we need to say one more thing: most people will have a mixture of conjunctions, oppositions and trines in their horoscope. However, sometimes you will find that one type of aspect is missing. This is quite common and you shouldn't worry about it.

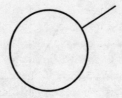

Finding the Conjunctions: The conjunction aspects are extremely easy to find: two planets are in conjunction when they are in the same sign as each other (see diagram xv). If you want to find all the conjunctions in a horoscope, follow these steps:

Step One

List all the signs which have two or more planets positioned in them and make a note of which planets they are and, of course, which sign they are positioned in.

In Madonna's horoscope, we notice that both Leo and Virgo have three planets in each of them (see diagram xv). We can list this as follows:

> Leo: Sun, Venus, Uranus
> Virgo: Moon, Mercury, Pluto

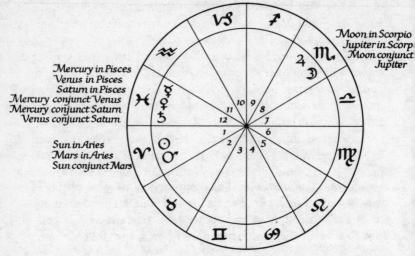

Diagram xv **Example Horoscope Showing Various Conjunctions**

Moon in Scorpio
Jupiter in Scorp
Moon conjunct
Jupiter

Mercury in Pisces
Venus in Pisces
Saturn in Pisces
Mercury conjunct Venus
Mercury conjunct Saturn
Venus conjunct Saturn

Sun in Aries
Mars in Aries
Sun conjunct Mars

CONJUNCTION TABLE			
Sign	Conjunction sign	Sign	Conjunction sign
Aries	Aries	Libra	Libra
Taurus	Taurus	Scorpio	Scorpio
Gemini	Gemini	Sagittarius	Sagittarius
Cancer	Cancer	Capricorn	Capricorn
Leo	Leo	Aquarius	Aquarius
Virgo	Virgo	Pisces	Pisces

Step Two

So, in Madonna's case, we first look at the planets she has in Leo, which are the Sun, Venus and Uranus. Remember that planets which are in the same sign as each other are in conjunction aspect to each other. This means that she has three conjunction aspects in Leo. They are the Sun conjunct Venus, the Sun conjunct Uranus and Venus conjunct Uranus.

Now we turn to her Virgo planets, which are the Moon,

296

Mercury and Pluto. These will all be in conjunction with each other. She will have the following conjunctions in Virgo: the Moon conjunct Mercury, the Moon conjunct Pluto, and Mercury conjunct Pluto.

To use an example – it is as if you are sitting in a waiting room. The people on either side of you are in conjunction with you. If your name is Mary and on one side of you is Peter and on the other side Paul, we would say that Mary is conjunct Peter, Mary is conjunct Paul and Peter is conjunct Paul.

Before you move on to Step Three, make sure that you have found all the conjunctions in your horoscope. Most people have conjunctions, but if all your planets are spread evenly through the signs you might not have any. If this is the case, don't worry.

Step Three

Once you have found all the conjunctions in someone's horoscope, you can enter them on to the horoscope form. On p. 298, you will see a complete horoscope form for Madonna (diagram xvi). At the bottom of the form you will see three columns, where you write in the aspects. The first column is headed 'Conjunctions', the second 'Oppositions', the third 'Trines'.

In the column headed 'Conjunctions' we have written in all the conjunction aspects in her horoscope. They are as follows:

> Sun conjunct Venus
> Sun conjunct Uranus
> Venus conjunct Uranus
> Moon conjunct Mercury
> Moon conjunct Pluto
> Mercury conjunct Pluto

Diagram xvi **Horoscope for Madonna**

Time of birth 7.00 a.m.
Date of birth 16th August 1958
Place of birth Bay City, Michigan

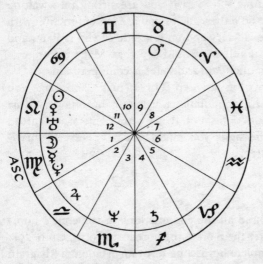

The Elements
Fire   3
Earth   3
Air   1
Water   0
Ruling Planet   ☿
Ruling
   Planet's sign   ♍
Ruling
   Planet's house 1st
Superstar Aspect
   Moon conjunct
   Mercury

The Sun (☉) is in Leo
The Moon (☽) is in Virgo
Mercury (☿) is in Virgo
Venus (♀) is in Leo
Mars (♂) is in Taurus

Jupiter (♃) is in Libra
Saturn (♄) is in Sagittarius
Uranus (♅) is in Leo
Neptune (♆) is in Scorpio
Pluto (♇) is in Virgo

The Ascendant is Virgo

ASPECTS

Conjunctions	Oppositions	Trines
Sun conjunct Venus	Mars opposition Neptune	Sun trine Saturn
Sun conjunct Uranus		Moon trine Mars
Venus conjunct Uranus		Mercury trine Mars
Moon conjunct Mercury		Venus trine Saturn
Moon conjunct Pluto		Mars trine Pluto
Mercury conjunct Pluto		Saturn trine Uranus

Diagram xvii **Horoscope for** ....

Time of birth ....
Date of birth ....
Place of birth ....

The Elements
Fire
Earth
Air
Water
Ruling Planet
Ruling
  Planet's sign
Ruling
  Planet's house
Superstar Aspect

ASPECTS		
Conjunctions	Oppositions	Trines

We have included a blank chart form (diagram xvii). Fill in
the horoscope wheel, as you did in Chapter Fifteen and write
down all your conjunctions in the conjunction column.

WHAT DO CONJUNCTIONS MEAN?

Of all the aspects, the conjunctions are the most powerful. When two planets are in conjunction their meanings try to blend in with each other. This may sound a bit confusing. After all, aren't the planets separate from each other? Yes, they are, but they can still influence each other, in the same way that independent people can influence each other. The conjunction aspect can best be compared to a marriage. In the same way that two very different individuals attempt to share their lives, so two very different planets attempt to share a sign.

To show you how a conjunction might work, let's look at Madonna's Venus conjunct Uranus. Venus rules love and relationships, while Uranus rules independence, originality and unexpected events. What happens if these two planets are in conjunction and, therefore, have meanings which blend into each other? You get a person who wants independence in relationships, but who is also drawn towards people whose behaviour can be unpredictable.

People who have a lot of conjunctions in their horoscopes are often very independent-minded. They don't like other people interfering with their lives, and it is difficult to get them to change their minds. So it is not surprising that conjunctions can give immense will-power, which is capable of moving mountains.

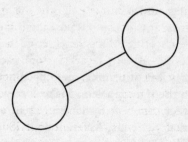

Finding the Oppositions: Two planets are in opposition when they are in opposite signs to each other. It is as if you are sitting in a waiting room and any people sitting opposite you in that room are said to be making an 'opposition' aspect to you. For example, if Mary is sitting opposite both Peter and Paul in the waiting room, she is said to be in opposition to Peter and in opposition to Paul. She is in opposition to both of them. However, Peter is only in opposition to Mary, and Paul is only in opposition to Mary. Of course, as we have just discovered, because Peter and Paul are sitting next to each other, they are in conjunction with each other!

As astrologers, we describe signs as being opposite when they are opposite each other on the zodiac circle. Have a look at the zodiac circle and the opposition table on page 303 (diagram xviii). Notice that we have put a line through every pair of opposite signs. You can see that Aries and Libra are joined up, as are all the other pairs, like Taurus and Scorpio and Gemini and Sagittarius. In the table we have listed all the signs of the zodiac, and next to each one we indicate its opposite. An example of two planets in opposition aspect is Venus in Aries and Mars in Libra, because Aries and Libra are opposite each other.

Finding the opposition aspects in the horoscope is so easy that you only have to go through two steps. We don't expect you to have any difficulties.

Step One

Look through your list of planets, and check to see if there is another planet in the sign opposite. Make sure you go through the planets in order. Start with the Sun, then move on to the Moon, then Mercury, Venus, Mars, Jupiter, Saturn, Uranus, Neptune and finally Pluto.

To take the example of Madonna: we start by looking at the Sun. Her Sun is in Leo. We look at the opposition table and see that the opposite sign to Leo is Aquarius. There are no planets in Aquarius, so there are no opposition aspects involving the Sun. We then turn to the Moon. It is in Virgo. The opposite sign to Virgo is Pisces. There are no planets in Pisces, so the Moon has no oppositions. We then go to Mercury, and then Venus, neither of which has any oppositions. When we get to her Mars in Taurus, we notice that Neptune is in the opposite sign of Scorpio. Therefore, Madonna has an opposition aspect between Mars and Neptune. Jupiter, Saturn and Uranus have no oppositions.

When we come to Neptune in Scorpio, we see that Mars is in the opposite sign of Taurus. So there is an opposition aspect between Neptune and Mars. However, we have already noted this aspect, because Mars opposition Neptune is the same as Neptune opposition Mars. There is, therefore, no need to write down the same aspect twice.

Diagram xviii   **Zodiac Circle, with Lines Drawn between Each Pair of Opposite Signs**

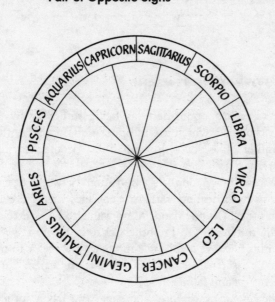

OPPOSITION TABLE			
Sign	Opposite sign	Sign	Opposite sign
Aries	Libra	Libra	Aries
Taurus	Scorpio	Scorpio	Taurus
Gemini	Sagittarius	Sagittarius	Gemini
Cancer	Capricorn	Capricorn	Cancer
Leo	Aquarius	Aquarius	Leo
Virgo	Pisces	Pisces	Virgo

Step Two

We now know that Madonna has a single opposition, Mars opposition Neptune. We can now write it in the column of her horoscope form headed 'Oppositions' (see diagram xvi, p. 298).

Before you read all about the meaning of the opposition aspect, make sure that you have discovered your own oppositions and that you have written them down on your personal horoscope form.

WHAT DO OPPOSITIONS MEAN?

Astrologers regard oppositions as being rather awkward aspects. Two planets which are in opposition conflict with each other, rather like two incompatible people having an argument.

In the case of Madonna's opposition between Mars and Neptune, we are dealing with two energies that are clashing with each other. On one hand, Mars wants to be assertive, and to take the initiative. On the other, chaotic Neptune wants to drift off into fantasy. Neptune's influence may seek to undermine Mars's assertiveness and, as a result, this aspect can often lead to delusion and failure.

Madonna is an example of someone who has a sufficiently strong character to stand up to the difficulties of the opposition between Mars and Neptune. However, it may still have an effect on her life. Perhaps she is aware of two needs, which conflict with each other. One part of her may want to be assertive and to achieve great things in the world, while another part may want to pursue unusual fantasies. Somehow she has to lead a life which acknowledges both sides of her character.

People who have a lot of oppositions in their horoscope often feel that they have to struggle for everything, and that nothing can be taken for granted. On the plus side, they are rarely lazy, and are capable of working incredibly hard. If they can find a way of dealing with the many conflicts in their lives, there is no reason why they cannot be very successful.

THE TRINE ASPECT

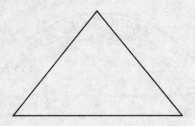

Finding the Trines: It is slightly more difficult to find the trines than it is to find the conjunctions and oppositions. However, these aspects are not going to present you with any great problem. Two planets are in trine with each other when their signs are different, but their elements are identical.

So Jupiter in Scorpio is trine Saturn in Pisces. This is because Scorpio and Pisces are signs which share the same element: namely, Water. If you need to remind yourself about the elements, have a look back at Chapter Thirteen.

To help you find the trines, we have provided a diagram of the zodiac circle, with the signs of the same element connected up (diagram xix). Can you see how signs of the same element are joined up in a triangle? Now you know why trines are called trines. If you had a planet in Aries and you wanted to know whether other planets were making a trine to this planet, you would follow the lines coming out of Aries and you would see that they led to its fellow Fire signs of Leo and Sagittarius. You might also find it useful to consult our trine table, which takes you through each of the twelve signs, and tells you which two signs make trines to it.

Now that you know what trines are, you can find out in two easy steps how many of them both you and Madonna have.

Diagram xix   Zodiac Circle with Signs in Trine Linked Up

TRINE TABLE

Sign	Trine signs	Sign	Trine signs
Aries	Leo, Sagittarius	Libra	Aquarius, Gemini
Taurus	Virgo, Capricorn	Scorpio	Pisces, Cancer
Gemini	Libra, Aquarius	Sagittarius	Aries, Leo
Cancer	Scorpio, Pisces	Capricorn	Taurus, Virgo
Leo	Sagittarius, Aries	Aquarius	Gemini, Libra
Virgo	Capricorn, Taurus	Pisces	Cancer, Scorpio

Step One

All you do is look through the sign of every planet in your horoscope and see what other planets are making trines to it. This is made very easy with the trine table. Make sure that you go through the planets in order: Sun, Moon, Mercury, Venus, Mars, Jupiter, Saturn, Uranus, Neptune and Pluto last of all.

In the case of Madonna, you can see that her Sun is in Leo. If you look at the trine table, you will see that Sagittarius and Aries are both trine to Leo. Madonna has Saturn in Sagittarius, so her Sun is trine Saturn.

We now move to the Moon. Her Moon is in Virgo. The table tells us that both Capricorn and Taurus are Virgo's trine signs. Madonna has nothing in Capricorn, but she has Mars in Taurus. So she has a trine between the Moon and Mars. Madonna's Mercury is also in Virgo, so her Mercury trines Mars as well. Madonna's Venus is in Leo, which trines Saturn in Sagittarius.

Her Mars is in Taurus, which trines the Moon, Mercury and Pluto. We don't need to write down Mars's first two aspects, because they have already been counted. Her Jupiter receives no trines.

Her Saturn trines the Sun, Venus and Uranus. We spotted the first two of these aspects earlier, so we are only concerned about Saturn's trine with Uranus. Having looked at Saturn's trines, we move on to Uranus. We know about Uranus's trine to Saturn, so we can move on to Neptune, which makes no trines. Finally, there is Pluto, whose trine with Mars we already know about.

Step Two

It is now simply a question of entering the trines we have found into the column headed 'Trines'. We would enter the following trines on to Madonna's horoscope form, diagram xvi:

> Sun trine Saturn
> Moon trine Mars
> Mercury trine Mars
> Venus trine Saturn
> Mars trine Pluto
> Saturn trine Uranus

WHAT DO TRINES MEAN?

Astrologers regard trines as being wonderful aspects, which can make people's lives easy and stress-free. Planets that are in trine aspect work very well together and often indicate natural talents, which don't need any effort to be developed. The only problem with trines is that they can be slightly too easy and can, therefore, encourage a person to be lazy.

Let's have a look at a trine in Madonna's horoscope. She has Mercury trine Mars. Mercury is the planet of communication and Mars is the planet of energy and assertion. This means that Madonna finds it easy to communicate in an assertive way. It may also mean that she is good at arguing, and that she knows how to be rude when she wants to be.

People who have a lot of trines in their horoscopes are very lucky. Things usually go their way and opportunities seem to land in their lap from nowhere. However, if they want to be successful, it is important that they are not complacent. Their good fortune sometimes needs to be supported with discipline and hard work.

Madonna is a good example of someone with plenty of trines. She is very talented and has luck on her side, so, even if she had spent her life watching the clouds go by, she would probably have been a moderate success. Fortunately for her, she also knew how important it was to work hard, and was therefore able to make the very most out of the trines in her horoscope.

HOW TO LOOK UP THE MEANINGS OF THE ASPECTS

When you have found all the aspects and written them all into the horoscope form, it is time for you to interpret them. This is really easy, because in the following chapters we give a detailed description of each aspect:

In Chapter Nineteen we describe all the conjunctions, in Chapter Twenty, the oppositions and in Chapter Twenty-one the trines. So if you have a conjunction between the Moon and Pluto, just turn to Chapter Nineteen, and look it up.

Each chapter contains around forty aspects. This is quite a lot of aspects to search through, so, to help you find a particular aspect, we have created a special system. All you have to do is go through the following steps:

Step One

Decide what aspect you are looking for. If it is a conjunction, go to Chapter Nineteen, if it is an opposition, go to Chapter Twenty and if it is a trine, go to Chapter Twenty-one.

Step Two

At the beginning of each chapter there is a list of all the aspects contained within it. Each aspect has a number. So, at the beginning of Chapter Nineteen you will see a list of 42 conjunctions. You will see that they are numbered: Sun conjunct Moon is number 1, and Saturn conjunct Pluto is number 42. For example, if you want to find Moon conjunct Pluto, you look through the list, and find that it is number 17.

Step Three

Now look through the chapter, until you find the paragraph which matches the number you have just looked up. This will be your aspect. In the case of Moon conjunct Pluto, look through the chapter until you find a paragraph headed: 17. Moon Conjunct Pluto

It's really simple. Chapters Nineteen, Twenty and Twenty-one will give you complete descriptions of all the aspects, which you can immediately apply to your personal horoscope.

One thing to note is that no descriptions are given for aspects between Uranus and Neptune, Uranus and Pluto, and Neptune and Pluto. These aspects stay in place for many years and you cannot apply their meaning to an individual's horoscope. However, there is nothing wrong with noting these aspects on the horoscope form, even if you are not interpreting them.

Something else you may notice is that no trines or oppositions are listed for the Sun and Mercury, the Sun and Venus, and Mercury and Venus. For some strange scientific reason, these aspects never occur and you will therefore never find them in a horoscope.

THE STAR RATING SYSTEM

When interpreting a horoscope, it is quite acceptable to list the aspects and then look up their meanings in Chapters Nineteen, Twenty and Twenty-one.

However, if you want to be more sophisticated, you should make some effort to weigh up the aspects, because in practice some aspects are more important than others. This is particularly the case when you have aspects which have conflicting meanings. For example, what would you do if you found someone who had Moon opposition Saturn and Venus conjunct Jupiter? Look closely at the different meanings we give for each aspect:

The Moon Opposition Saturn: The oppositions find it hard to express their feelings and in social situations are often withdrawn and reserved. These problems won't get better of their own accord and if these people want to have a fuller life they need to make a greater effort to meet people. It is particularly important in relationships that the Moon opposition Saturn finds a partner who is gentle, sympathetic and caring.
Star rating: ★★★

Venus Conjunct Jupiter: These people are liked by everyone and are never short of friends. They have an enormous amount of warmth and affection to give out and make perfect marriage partners. This aspect is very generous – some would say too generous. They always pay for other people's drinks, and are often suckers for a sob story. However, at the end of the day it doesn't matter, because people with this aspect always go to heaven.

Star rating: *****

You can see that these meanings are a little bit contradictory. If you have ever had your horoscope interpreted by a computer, you may have come across contradictions like this. The computer finds all the aspects in a horoscope, then lists their meanings, even if they contradict one another.

Fortunately, proper astrologers are not computers. We are able to weigh things up. If a person has both the Moon opposition Saturn and Venus conjunct Jupiter, they may well display both characteristics. In certain circumstances, they will be cold and withdrawn, and, in other circumstances, they will be loving and friendly. However, that's not quite good enough. We have to say which aspect is strongest and most likely to have a strong influence on the personality. In order to decide which one to emphasize, astrologers sometimes use a star rating system.

The star rating system is very simple. Every aspect is given a star rating, and the more stars it has, the more important it is. In the above example, we would put more emphasis on Venus's conjunction with Jupiter, because it has five stars, compared with the Moon opposition Saturn's three stars.

So when you look up the aspects in a horoscope, it would improve your interpretation if you noted the star rating of each aspect. This would help you deal with any conflicting messages.

Star ratings also give you information about the overall

importance of an aspect. They tell you how much weighting you should give it when you look at a horoscope. This ensures that you spend a lot of time considering the most important aspects and that you don't get side-tracked on minor ones.

The meaning of each star rating is as follows:

Five-star aspects ★★★★★   These are extremely important aspects, which always have a crucial effect on the personality.

Four-star aspects ★★★★   Four-star aspects are nearly as important as five-star ones. Their effects are usually very noticeable.

Three-star aspects ★★★   These aspects are worth looking at, but don't place too much emphasis on them.

Two-star aspects ★★   You should probably only mention these aspects if their message is repeated elsewhere in the horoscope.

One-star aspects ★   These aspects usually have no impact on the personality. Don't talk about them unless you are very sure of yourself.

The Superstar Aspect: The superstar aspect is the strongest aspect in the horoscope. It always has a powerful influence and must never be ignored. Finding the superstar aspect is easy, because it is very simply the aspect in someone's horoscope which has the highest star rating. So any five-star aspects are automatically regarded as superstar aspects. If someone doesn't have any five-star aspects, look for four-star aspects instead.

Sometimes people can have more than one superstar aspect. For example, if a person has Venus conjunct Jupiter and the Sun trine Mars, these would both be superstar aspects, because they both have five-star ratings. Alternatively, if someone has no five-star aspects, but two four-star aspects, these would both have superstar status. This is because they both have an equally high star-rating.

In Madonna's case, she has just one five-star aspect, which is the Moon conjunct Mercury. Look up its meaning in Chapter Nineteen. The aspect tells us all about her personality and her talents, and it also gives us a clue about the fact that she is indeed a superstar.

19. THE MEANING OF THE CONJUNCTIONS

AN EASY REFERENCE LIST FOR YOUR CONJUNCTION ASPECTS

1. Sun conjunct Moon
2. Sun conjunct Mercury
3. Sun conjunct Venus
4. Sun conjunct Mars
5. Sun conjunct Jupiter
6. Sun conjunct Saturn
7. Sun conjunct Uranus
8. Sun conjunct Neptune
9. Sun conjunct Pluto
10. Moon conjunct Mercury
11. Moon conjunct Venus
12. Moon conjunct Mars
13. Moon conjunct Jupiter
14. Moon conjunct Saturn
15. Moon conjunct Uranus
16. Moon conjunct Neptune
17. Moon conjunct Pluto
18. Mercury conjunct Venus
19. Mercury conjunct Mars
20. Mercury conjunct Jupiter
21. Mercury conjunct Saturn
22. Mercury conjunct Uranus
23. Mercury conjunct Neptune
24. Mercury conjunct Pluto
25. Venus conjunct Mars
26. Venus conjunct Jupiter

27. Venus conjunct Saturn
28. Venus conjunct Uranus
29. Venus conjunct Neptune
30. Venus conjunct Pluto
31. Mars conjunct Jupiter
32. Mars conjunct Saturn
33. Mars conjunct Uranus
34. Mars conjunct Neptune
35. Mars conjunct Pluto
36. Jupiter conjunct Saturn
37. Jupiter conjunct Uranus
38. Jupiter conjunct Neptune
39. Jupiter conjunct Pluto
40. Saturn conjunct Uranus
41. Saturn conjunct Neptune
42. Saturn conjunct Pluto

1. Sun Conjunct Moon

A conjunction between the Sun and the Moon is also known as a New Moon. People born on a New Moon see life as a mission, which must be accomplished at all costs. The aim of this mission may be to feed the starving, to make vast amounts of money, or to achieve spiritual salvation. However, people with a New Moon in their horoscope are also very secretive and avoid discussing their life's mission with other people.
Star rating: *****

2. Sun Conjunct Mercury

This aspect is extremely common and when you find it in someone's horoscope you shouldn't make too big a deal about it. However, the conjunction is sometimes an important factor, particularly if the Sun and Mercury are in Sagittarius or Pisces. People with this configuration may be so concerned about themselves and their egos that they find it difficult to make balanced and reasonable decisions.

Star rating: ★★

3. Sun Conjunct Venus

Like the Sun conjunct Mercury, this aspect is common and it is unlikely to be an important factor unless the planets are placed in Virgo or Scorpio. If you do decide to interpret this aspect, then it may sometimes describe people who find it difficult to form close relationships. Although men with this aspect may not take women seriously, they do, however, get numerous opportunities for love and romance. Women with this aspect may be attracted to men who try to dominate them.

Star rating: ★★

4. Sun Conjunct Mars

This aspect can be fairly accident prone, so people with this combination need to watch how they go. If they try to do everything in a hurry, then they may be asking for trouble. Sun conjunct Mars may end up walking into lamp-posts and nailing their fingers into walls. Cooking is a particularly danger-ous activity for these people, and it is better that they get someone else to do it rather than risk burning the house down.

Star rating: ★★★★

5. Sun Conjunct Jupiter

The Sun's conjunction with Jupiter is an optimistic combina-tion. It gives a bubbly personality which is able to project good humour and spontaneous enthusiasm. Everything that these people do is larger than life and they are particularly good at entertaining and buying expensive presents. While there is nothing wrong with generosity, people with this combination should make a greater effort to curb overspending.

Star rating: ★★★★★

Cooking is a particularly dangerous activity, and people with the Sun conjunct Mars risk
burning the house down.

6. Sun Conjunct Saturn

This is a serious aspect, which can be inclined towards pessimism. The root cause of this may be that one or both parents had a terribly negative attitude to life. As an astrologer, your role is to tell anybody with this aspect to lighten up and to start having fun. Tell them to forget about their responsibilities and do something really wild, like running away to the circus or becoming a game-show host.

Star rating: ★★★

7. Sun Conjunct Uranus

The Sun conjunct Uranus finds it very difficult to relax and quickly gets bored. As a result, behaviour can be erratic and unpredictable. A woman with this configuration often finds herself drawn towards men who are unusual and who have strange ideas. There is nothing wrong with this, provided that she doesn't find herself hitched up to Rasputin.

Star rating: ★★★★

8. Sun Conjunct Neptune

People with this aspect live in a world of their own. They have a powerful imagination and are often able to dream up all sorts of fantasies and illusions. As a result, the Sun conjunct Neptune often has exceptional artistic talents. However they do need to be a little more down to earth. They should, therefore, consider taking courses in personal finance and car maintenance.

Star rating: ★★★★

9. Sun Conjunct Pluto

If you meet a person who has the Sun conjunct Pluto, you need to be careful. This aspect needs to be treated with great respect and you should avoid prying into his or her private life. These people keep their feelings hidden and will only confide in people in whom they have absolute trust. Women with this conjunction are frequently attracted to men who are of the silent, brooding type.

Star rating: ★★★★

10. Moon Conjunct Mercury

The conjunction between the Moon and Mercury gives excellent communication skills and a good intellect. These people are able to express their desires and feelings without having to think and there is frequently a connection with writing. In the horoscope of a man, it can mean that he is looking for a partner who is not only intelligent and witty, but who can also hold her own in an argument.

Star rating: ★★★★★

11. Moon Conjunct Venus

The Moon's conjunction with Venus gives a natural ability to get on with other people, as well as good taste. People with this aspect are experts at matching colours and materials, so if you are planning on buying new clothes or redecorating your home, get their advice. A man with this aspect expects his partner to be a traditional woman. He wants her to stay at home, cook his meals and bear his children.

Star rating: ★★★★★

12. Moon Conjunct Mars

A few hundred years ago, a French astrologer said: 'A woman that has Mars with the Moon is right; I'll warrant her.' What this means is that a woman with the Moon conjunct Mars always believes that she is right, and there is no point in arguing with her, even if she's completely wrong. A man with this aspect will often find himself dominated by an aggressive woman, who believes that a man's place is in the home.

Star rating: ★★★★

13. Moon Conjunct Jupiter

The Moon's conjunction with Jupiter is a really nice aspect. It brings both luck and generosity, as well as an optimistic and carefree nature. Usually, these people are very popular and have no trouble making friends. At the same time, they love children, and women with this aspect will want to have as many as possible. Men with this configuration are attracted to extrovert women with a wild sense of humour.

Star rating: ★★★★★

14. Moon Conjunct Saturn

People with the Moon conjunct Saturn keep their emotions under tight control. They don't want others to know what their real feelings are, and they hardly ever cry. While people with this aspect are usually able to keep their head during a crisis, there are times when they should make an effort to confide their feelings to a friend or a partner. Men with this conjunction often marry women who are a little cold and distant.

Star rating: ★★★★

15. Moon Conjunct Uranus

This aspect can be very disruptive, so if you take these people out anywhere, make sure they wear a gag and a straitjacket. Otherwise, their offensive behaviour will turn you both into social outcasts. A man with this aspect may find that the sultry brunette he married last week is a well-known international

320

terrorist with a reputation for blowing up her husbands with Semtex.

Star rating: ★★★

16. Moon Conjunct Neptune

Aspects between the Moon and Neptune are often connected with the emotions and with sensitivity. The conjunction represents someone who finds it impossible not to tune into other people's feelings, even in the most unlikely places. While queuing at the supermarket, these people may suddenly become aware of the overwhelming tragedy and despair that is etched into the checkout girl's aura!

Star rating: ★★★★

17. Moon Conjunct Pluto

This is a heavy-duty aspect which the astrologer should treat with extreme caution. There is a lot that these people are keeping secret, and if you want to gain their trust it is essential that you don't ask too many questions. Women with this configuration are obsessed with power and will do their best to be in control of their lives. Men, on the other hand, will often seek out domineering partners.

Star rating: ★★★

18. Mercury Conjunct Venus

The conjunction between Mercury and Venus is an amazing aspect. It signifies people who are confident and friendly and who find it easy to gain other people's trust. Astrologers frequently connect this aspect with art and culture, so these people may be accomplished artists, or, at the very least, art lovers. They may also have a good singing voice, particularly if the conjunction is in Taurus.

Star rating: ★★★★★

19. Mercury Conjunct Mars

Communication is very important to Mercury conjunct Mars people. They want other people to hear them loud and clear and if they feel that their message isn't getting through, they will spice it up with an insult or two. Therefore, it is not surprising that these people often find themselves being sued for libel and defamation of character. People with this aspect are ideally suited for careers in either politics or journalism.
Star rating: *****

20. Mercury Conjunct Jupiter

Mercury's conjunction with Jupiter makes people full of big ideas, and they refuse to allow things like reality to get in the way of their vision of the future. These people can put ideas into practice and be successful. However, to protect themselves from making mistakes, they should get regular advice from someone who is practical and down to earth. Perhaps from an accountant who has the Sun in Taurus or Capricorn.
Star rating: *****

21. Mercury Conjunct Saturn

People with a conjunction between Mercury and Saturn don't say things unless they are sure of their facts, and they never rush into decisions. As a result, they make very few mistakes. If these people do make a mistake, it is usually because they are too cautious. They may spend ages weighing up the pros and cons of a genuine business opportunity. By the time they've made up their mind, it is too late to take advantage of it.
Star rating: *****

22. Mercury Conjunct Uranus

People with Mercury conjunct Uranus are full of original

ideas, and if they put some of them into practice they can make themselves very rich. It may be that these people can invent some wonderful labour-saving devices, which everyone will want to buy. Alternatively, they may be able to find a new use for existing technology. Perhaps they can buy up a few space-shuttles and organize package holidays to Mars.

Star rating: ****

23. Mercury Conjunct Neptune

Mercury's conjunction with Neptune is an aspect to watch out for. These people find lying easy and make brilliant swindlers. So avoid lending them any money, unless you know them very well. However, you shouldn't believe that everyone with Mercury conjunct Neptune is dishonest. It is just that a few bad apples have spoilt this aspect's reputation.

Star rating: ***

24. Mercury Conjunct Pluto

The conjunction between Mercury and Pluto signifies people who want to get to the bottom of life's mysteries. They enjoy finding out new things and are frequently interested in psychology and the supernatural. At the same time, people with this aspect have a strong will and are very difficult to control. They like being in positions of power and often get a thrill out of ordering other people around.

Star rating: ****

25. Venus Conjunct Mars

All aspects between Venus and Mars are connected with sex and with sex appeal. The conjunction is particularly powerful. It gives a magnetic personality and a natural seductiveness. This aspect tends to evoke strong feelings. People with this aspect may find that for every person that loves them, there is another who hates them. Politicians frequently have this aspect, examples including Adolf Hitler and Bill Clinton.

Star rating: *****

26. Venus Conjunct Jupiter

These people are liked by everyone and are never short of friends. They have an enormous amount of warmth and affection to give out and make perfect marriage partners. This aspect is very generous – some would say too generous. They always pay for other people's drinks and are often suckers for a sob story. However, at the end of the day it doesn't matter, because people with this aspect always go to heaven.

Star rating: *****

27. Venus Conjunct Saturn

People with a conjunction between Venus and Saturn find other people a strain and tend to prefer their own company. In relationships these people can be a little cold, although on the bright side they are almost always faithful to their partners. They are careful with their money and only buy things which they know they can afford. This is reflected in their frugal lifestyle and modest dress-sense. But they have great organizational abilities and can go a long way in terms of their career or profession.

Star rating: *****

28. Venus Conjunct Uranus

Venus conjunct Uranus people enjoy being in a relationship, provided that their partners are wild and exciting and are able to keep up with their frantic pace. However, these people do find it difficult to stay in one relationship for too long and are always on the look out for new romantic interest. People with this aspect are, however, often very artistic and are able to shock the world with their outrageous daring.

Star rating: ★★

29. Venus Conjunct Neptune

Relationships are extremely important to these people. They are always thinking about love, and have powerful fantasies about the ultimate relationship to end all relationships. There is certainly no reason why they can't find the right match, provided that they make some effort to be realistic. In particular, they must appreciate that no one is perfect, not even their dream lover.

Star rating: ★★★

30. Venus Conjunct Pluto

This is an intense and passionate aspect and people who have it in their horoscopes take love and sex very seriously. They want an all-embracing relationship with someone who they can possess and control. So don't get involved with them unless you really know what you are doing. Venus conjunct Pluto can also be quite an unforgiving aspect and if someone lets these people down, they'll make sure that they get their pound of flesh.

Star rating: ★★★

31. Mars Conjunct Jupiter

This is an action-packed aspect, which has an almost limitless supply of energy. In the space of one day, these people not only do two full-time jobs, but also take the children to and from school, feed them, feed the cat, feed the husband or wife, do some gardening and replace the cylinder head on the family car. At the end of the day, these people unwind with a bit of gentle weight-training. In love, they exhibit an enormous amount of courage and daring, but also get more than their fair share of good luck.

Star rating: ★★★★★

32. Mars Conjunct Saturn

The conjunction is a very controlled aspect. These people don't do anything unless they've thought about it first, and find spontaneity quite difficult. Nonetheless, they do have a lot of inner anger, which needs to be expressed. They need to find a violent activity which forces them to unleash their true feelings, so they should get involved in either evangelical preaching, or heavy metal guitaring . . . or perhaps both.

Star rating: ★★★

33. Mars Conjunct Uranus

The conjunction enjoys risk and adventure, and people with this aspect find it impossible to get worried about their own safety. When they go on holiday to the latest war-zone, they always forget to pack their sun cream and their flak jackets. As far as hobbies are concerned, they enjoy collecting and using weapons of mass destruction. Indeed, one of their greatest joys is demolishing their neighbour's house with an ex-Stalingrad T-34 tank!

Star rating: ★★

34. Mars Conjunct Neptune

People with a conjunction between Mars and Neptune love glamour and bright lights, and are addicted to nightclubs and rock concerts. At the same time, they have many beautiful and fashionable friends, who include musicians, actors and models. These people do have a dark side to their character, however.

They find the concept of evil fascinating, and are often drawn into the company of gangsters and Satanists.
Star rating: ★★

35. Mars Conjunct Pluto

People who have this aspect will stop at nothing to achieve their aims and won't care who gets destroyed in the process. So don't argue with them, unless your life, health, home and job are comprehensively insured. This combination of planets also gives immense physical stamina and these people are able to complete incredible feats of endurance, like cycling to the South Pole, or swimming across the Pacific Ocean.
Star rating: ★★★

36. Jupiter Conjunct Saturn

People with this aspect swing between extremes of optimism and pessimism. One moment, these people think that they're on the verge of a fortune, and the next, they are consigning their lives to the scrap-heap. However, to avoid going mad they must stop worrying about success and failure. Instead, they should work hard at a career they love. If they are sincere, their career will eventually come up trumps.
Star rating: ★★★

37. Jupiter Conjunct Uranus

This aspect is positive and enthusiastic, and people who have it in their horoscopes have an aura of sparkling excitement. So if you want to throw great parties, invite plenty of guests who have Jupiter conjunct Uranus. On a more serious note, those with this aspect make exceptional therapists and counsellors. This is because they know how to make people feel good about themselves.
Star rating: ★★★

38. Jupiter Conjunct Neptune

People who have this aspect in their horoscopes often believe that they are protected by a divine force. As a result, they enjoy activities like gambling, flying and rock climbing. They are also very imaginative, and they can turn ordinary objects into fantastic masterpieces. If you give them a battered watering-can, they will take it to their studios and within days it will be hailed as the next Mona Lisa.

Star rating: ★★

39. Jupiter Conjunct Pluto

These individuals always want to improve themselves, and work hard to gain promotion and further qualifications. They frequently study for a degree or a diploma while doing their full-time job. People with this aspect are also very concerned about their children's education. They will move heaven and earth to get them into a good school and, once there, will expect them to be top of the class.

Star rating: ★★

40. Saturn Conjunct Uranus

On the surface, people with this aspect are respected pillars of the establishment, who are good at organizing garden parties and other society events. However, under the surface there is a wild creativity, which is desperate to get out. It is essential that these people find an outlet for this hidden energy, because otherwise their behaviour may become dangerous and self-destructive.

Star rating: ★

41. Saturn Conjunct Neptune

Saturn's conjunction with Neptune is an aspect which tries hard to lead a disciplined and organized life. These people do their best to get up early and do a proper day's work. They even make some effort to do the washing up. Unfortunately, their good intentions are often wrecked by unforeseen events. Like burst pipes, malfunctioning alarm clocks and getting lost on the way to the front door.

Star rating: *

42. Saturn Conjunct Pluto

Those with this aspect push themselves to the limits. They work long hours and they sleep as little as possible. They hate relaxing and if they have some spare time, they will perform some useless task, like breaking rocks with their bare heads. It is certainly difficult to understand their excessive behaviour. Perhaps these people enjoy pain. Alternatively, they may enjoy making their family and work-mates feel guilty.

Star rating: *

20. THE MEANING OF THE OPPOSITIONS

AN EASY REFERENCE LIST FOR YOUR OPPOSITION ASPECTS

1. Sun opposition Moon
2. Sun opposition Mars
3. Sun opposition Jupiter
4. Sun opposition Saturn
5. Sun opposition Uranus
6. Sun opposition Neptune
7. Sun opposition Pluto
8. Moon opposition Mercury
9. Moon opposition Venus
10. Moon opposition Mars
11. Moon opposition Jupiter
12. Moon opposition Saturn
13. Moon opposition Uranus
14. Moon opposition Neptune
15. Moon opposition Pluto
16. Mercury opposition Mars
17. Mercury opposition Jupiter
18. Mercury opposition Saturn
19. Mercury opposition Uranus
20. Mercury opposition Neptune
21. Mercury opposition Pluto
22. Venus opposition Mars
23. Venus opposition Jupiter
24. Venus opposition Saturn
25. Venus opposition Uranus
26. Venus opposition Neptune

1. Sun Opposition Moon

Oppositions between the Sun and the Moon can be a bit difficult. If people have oppositions, they often see their parents as being opposed to each other in some way. Relationships can be an area of difficulty, unless a special effort is made to find exactly the right partner. On the plus side, this aspect can give a natural ability to understand other people's emotional problems.

Star rating: ★★★

2. Sun Opposition Mars

This is not an easy aspect. When the Sun is opposition Mars, everything is seen as a battle, which can only be lost or won. As a result, people with this configuration are likely to be extremely competitive. At work they will always want to get better results than all their colleagues put together. This is fine, provided they don't get caught up with petty rivalries, which could ultimately damage their reputation.

Star rating: ★★

3. Sun Opposition Jupiter

The opposition seldom knows when to stop, particularly when it comes to partying and having fun. People with this aspect are usually up all night, destroying their ear-drums with ridiculously loud music and straining every muscle with non-stop break-dancing. However, occasionally you find people with this aspect who get pleasure from overeating, rather than over-partying.

Star rating: ★★★

4. Sun Opposition Saturn

The opposition between the Sun and Saturn can be heavy-going. People with this aspect often think that there is something weighing them down, preventing them from expressing their feelings and their creativity. It is, therefore, vital that they take up activities which free their blocked energy. Amateur dramatics or graffiti art (the law permitting) are both possibilities.

Star rating: ★★★

5. Sun Opposition Uranus

The Sun opposition Uranus can make life a little complicated. Weird and wonderful events are always cropping up, which can make it very difficult to plan ahead, so it is always a good idea to prepare for the unexpected. If, for example, Sun opposition Uranus people are going to a vital business meeting, they should leave home two hours early, just in case there's an earthquake or they get kidnapped by aliens!

Star rating: ★★★

6. Sun Opposition Neptune

People with this aspect find it difficult to decide what to do with their life. They have many different ideas, but are unsure

which one to go for. They also tend to have a low opinion of themselves and will only see a plan through if they get plenty of praise and support. If they want to be successful, they must stop listening to other people and start being more decisive.
Star rating: ★★★

7. Sun Opposition Pluto

The Sun opposition Pluto enjoys being in control and can often be very manipulative. People with this aspect get a real kick out of the idea that other people are relying on them. As a result, they are attracted to professions such as psychotherapy, plumbing, selling heroin and the priesthood. Whether they are good at any of these jobs is a matter for debate.
Star rating: ★★

8. Moon Opposition Mercury

People with the Moon opposition Mercury should be careful what they say. While they find it easy to communicate, they often blurt things out which they later regret. Sometimes it can be difficult for them to think rationally and, instead of looking at the reality of a situation, they allow their feelings and prejudices to get in the way. As a result, they can make terrible errors of judgement.
Star rating: ★★★

9. Moon Opposition Venus

The way this aspect works depends on whether you are dealing with a male or a female horoscope. In a woman's horoscope, it can mean that she finds it difficult to get on with other women, particularly if they are younger than her; she is likely to prefer the company of men. In the case of a man with the Moon opposite Venus, he is unsure whether he wants his partner to be a lover or a mother.

Star rating: ★★★

10. Moon Opposition Mars

People with this aspect tend to believe that they are unfairly treated by everyone. As a result, they are very sensitive to criticism. If, for example, they are told that their tie isn't straight, they are likely to let off a couple of intercontinental ballistic missiles without a moment's hesitation. Under these circumstances, it is important that people with this aspect are banned from running superpowers.

Star rating: ★★★★

11. Moon Opposition Jupiter

This aspect can be a little too emotional. People with this aspect find it difficult to control their feelings and will often give perfect strangers tearful accounts of their traumatic childhood. However, don't feel too sorry for Moon opposition Jupiter, because they are rather prone to exaggeration. These people can also be prone to overweight, so they should be careful to watch their diet and take plenty of exercise.

Star rating: ★★★

12. Moon Opposition Saturn

These oppositions find it hard to express their feelings, and in social situations are often withdrawn and reserved. These problems won't get better of their own accord and if these people want to have a fuller life they need to make a greater effort to meet people. It is particularly important that in relationships the Moon opposition Saturn finds a partner who is gentle, sympathetic and caring.

Star rating: ★★★

13. Moon Opposition Uranus

These people may find that life is chaotic. There are always unusual things going on and it may be difficult to find peace and quiet. This instability usually started in childhood and perhaps centred around an eccentric and erratic mother. If people with this aspect want to find lasting stability, they must create a routine for themselves. This may involve setting aside fixed times every day to relax and to meditate.

Star rating: ★★

14. Moon Opposition Neptune

These people soak up other people's feelings like a sponge and, as a result, experience massive emotional swings. If people with the Moon opposition Neptune talk to someone who is happy, they will likewise feel happy. If, five minutes later, they talk to a depressive, they will immediately become depressed. People with this aspect should avoid charity work, alcohol and drugs.

Star rating: ★★★

15. Moon Opposition Pluto

People with the Moon in opposition to Pluto find it difficult to release their emotions in everyday life and instead allow them to build up over a long period of time. People with this aspect don't bat an eyelid when their car is stolen, when their business goes bust, when their wife runs off with the postman . . . then one day the kitchen light fuses and their emotional dams burst in a torrent of anger, hatred and rage.

Star rating: ★★★

16. Mercury Opposition Mars

This can be quite a nervous aspect. These people often seem to be on edge and find it difficult to keep still. When dealing with other people they can be insensitive and frequently cause offence with their hasty remarks. It is important that these people find some way to physically let off steam, because otherwise both their health and their friendships may suffer. They should consider taking up either aikido or fencing.

Star rating: ★★★

17. Mercury Opposition Jupiter

Mercury opposition Jupiter finds it difficult to be realistic. In particular, these people are full of schemes for making money which are usually complete non-starters. One week they are excited about their latest plans to sell crude oil to Saudi Arabia and the next week they are talking about investing on the stock market, using astrological guidance. Fortunately, these people very rarely put their money where their mouth is.

Star rating: ★★

18. Mercury Opposition Saturn

The opposition has an excellent mind, and these people are good at activities which involve study and concentration. However, they are also very pessimistic and tend to expect the worst. If they see a police car outside their house, they assume that they are about to be arrested for murder. If these people ever come to you for advice, you must put their many fears to rest and assure them that everything will turn out just fine.

Star rating: ★★★

19. Mercury Opposition Uranus

This can be a rather stressful aspect. These people always have something on their minds and often suffer from insomnia. If you look at these people closely, you may notice that they move their hands a lot, particularly if they are non-smokers. This is a sure sign that they are a bundle of nervous energy.

The best way for them to calm themselves down is to either paint pictures or play musical instruments.
Star rating: ★★★

20. Mercury Opposition Neptune

Mercury opposition Neptune people find it difficult to be logical and they are often strongly influenced by their feelings. People with this aspect can also be too trusting and as a result they are vulnerable to con men and insurance salesmen. They should be particularly careful not to buy financial products, like insurance schemes or pension plans, without first getting independent advice.
Star rating: ★★★

21. Mercury Opposition Pluto

People with this opposition are worried about how the world will respond to their ideas and are often afraid of making a fool of themselves. As a result, this can be a very secretive aspect, and people with this aspect in their horoscopes find it difficult to express their creativity in public. However, there is no need for them to be so reserved. Their friends and colleagues find them fascinating, and will always respect their ideas and opinions.
Star rating: ★★

22. Venus Opposition Mars

This aspect is something of a contradiction. These people are desperately looking for someone special with whom they can have an intense physical relationship. However, they are also terrified of being dominated by another person. As a result, these people give their partners mixed messages, such as 'hold me closer, but make damn sure you stay on your side of the barbed wire'.
Star rating: ★★★

23. Venus Opposition Jupiter

This is a rather excessive aspect. These people want to have as much fun as possible and are addicted to parties. Their love life is usually very active and they frequently find that one relationship is not enough. However, sex and parties are not the only extravagances of this aspect. These people also enjoy food and chocolate and, if they are not careful, increasing weight can become a problem. However, the combination of these two planets is fortunate and many good things in life will come to these people, especially of the material kind.

Star rating: **

24. Venus Opposition Saturn

People with this opposition don't trust people, particularly on an emotional level. This can make relationships very difficult. They believe that if they rely on any one person, they will be let down and rejected. So they frequently walk out on their partners, before they have a chance to walk out on them. Your job as an astrologer is to tell these people that if they are patient enough, they are certain to find true and lasting love.

Star rating: **

25. Venus Opposition Uranus

The opposition between Venus and Uranus can be a bit tricky. These people nearly always get involved in unusual relationships and their partners are often unstable and unreliable. Things are made worse by the fact that they fall in love very quickly. They will meet a psychotic beach-bum one day and marry him the next. By the time they realize they've made a mistake, one of them will already be ten months pregnant. On a more positive note, these people can be brilliantly intelligent, very broad-minded and very tolerant.

Star rating: **

Venus opposition Uranus people nearly always get involved in unusual relationships. They will meet a psychotic beach-bum one day and marry him the next!

26. Venus Opposition Neptune

The opposition is a difficult aspect, which is desperately looking for love. These people tend to be let down by their partners and sometimes things get so bad that they retire to a monastery or convent – which is a pity, unless they have a genuine religious calling. The truth of the matter is that these people can find a fulfilling relationship, provided that they check out their partners' characters before dating them.

Star rating: **

27. Venus Opposition Pluto

People with this aspect often find themselves involved with amazingly attractive partners, who have the deadly allure of a black widow spider. At first, as they start to enter their complicated web, they enjoy the thrill and the excitement that such relationships can bring. However, by the time they reach the web's poisonous centre, they realize that they are trapped in a nightmare of twisted emotion and frustrated desire.

Star rating: **

28. Mars Opposition Jupiter

These people don't know what to do with all their energy, and often direct it into self-destructive activities. This may mean that they overeat, over-drink or over-smoke. Alternatively, they may decide to take up dangerous sports, like drag-racing or skydiving. What they really need is a satisfying career. They might consider the armed forces, provided that they are able to experience active combat.

Star rating: **

29. Mars Opposition Saturn

People with this aspect feel that the whole world is against them and that the only way to make progress is to fight, fight and fight again. However, their aggressive attitude does them no favours. Other people regard them as menacing bullies who need to be stopped at all costs. As a result, they deliberately frustrate their plans. These people are advised to calm down and start making friends rather than enemies.

Star rating: **

30. Mars Opposition Uranus

This is an accident-prone aspect, with a nose for trouble. People who have this aspect in their horoscopes have a habit of saying and doing the wrong things at the wrong time and, as a result, they are frequently involved in fights and arguments. They also find that cars and machinery break down the moment they touch them. So, if they are buying anything mechanical, they should make sure that all the guarantees are well in order.

Star rating: *

31. Mars Opposition Neptune

People with this aspect believe that one day they will be transported into a glittering fairyland of excitement, opportunity and wealth. Those that can back their faith up with grit, determination and ruthless ambition might well find what they're looking for. Unfortunately, most people with this aspect are hopelessly unrealistic and end up by sacrificing their potential on altars of fantasy.

Star rating: *

32. Mars Opposition Pluto

Those that have Mars opposition Pluto in their horoscopes

frequently find themselves in control of other people. This means that in relationships they tend to be the ones pulling the strings, usually because their partners enjoy being dominated. In their careers, people with this aspect quickly rise to positions of authority. Unfortunately, they frequently abuse this authority and, as a result, make a lot of enemies.

Star rating: *

33. Jupiter Opposition Saturn

People born with this aspect find that circumstances beyond their control sometimes interfere with their progress. It takes them ages to get anything done and they are often unable to get recognition for their achievements. These people shouldn't blame themselves, but instead they should turn their anger on their country, their employers and their family. If this means rebellion, then so be it.

Star rating: *

34. Jupiter Opposition Uranus

The opposition is well-meaning and is always trying to help other people. Unfortunately, this help tends to be useless: if a beggar stops them on the street, they will give him a one-hour presentation on the advantages of buying commercial property shares on the Hong Kong stock market. However, people with this aspect would never buy these shares themselves, because they are terrified of taking risks.

Star rating: *

35. Jupiter Opposition Neptune

This aspect is over-optimistic and, as a result of its influence, these people often chase unreal fantasies. They must, therefore, watch their life savings, because there is a real danger that they will invest them in schemes which are doomed to disaster.

They should also be wary of religious cults, particularly those which sell expensive season tickets to paradise.
Star rating: ★★

36. Jupiter Opposition Pluto

Those with Jupiter opposition Pluto in their horoscopes should never be underestimated. They are extraordinarily ambitious and will do practically anything to succeed. It should be born in mind that these people don't see success in purely financial terms. What matters most to them is that they have vast amounts of power when alive and that when dead they have a starring role in the history books.
Star rating: ★

37. Saturn Opposition Uranus

People who have Saturn opposition Uranus do their best to explain their ideas to others, but somehow the message never gets through. At first sight this seems terribly unfair, because the opposition is an aspect of genius, which deserves to be heard. However it should be borne in mind that these people are way ahead of their time and that it may take a few more decades before society can handle their brilliance.
Star rating: ★

38. Saturn Opposition Neptune

These people are great worriers and their basic philosophy is that if it can go wrong, it will go wrong. They are avid readers of medical dictionaries and are always diagnosing themselves as having the latest and most fashionable disease. Yesterday it was swamp fever, today cerebral malaria and tomorrow an electronically transmitted disease they caught over the telephone!
Star rating: ★

39. Saturn Opposition Pluto

People with Saturn opposition Pluto like to think that they are wonderfully modern and that they are on the cutting edge of technological and cultural progress. The reality is very different. They are terrified of change and the values which they pretend are so modern may actually be years out of date. It is, therefore, essential that these people get real and start facing up to the future.

Star rating: ★

21. THE MEANING OF THE TRINES

AN EASY REFERENCE LIST FOR YOUR TRINE ASPECTS

1. Sun trine Moon
2. Sun trine Mars
3. Sun trine Jupiter
4. Sun trine Saturn
5. Sun trine Uranus
6. Sun trine Neptune
7. Sun trine Pluto
8. Moon trine Mercury
9. Moon trine Venus
10. Moon trine Mars
11. Moon trine Jupiter
12. Moon trine Saturn
13. Moon trine Uranus
14. Moon trine Neptune
15. Moon trine Pluto
16. Mercury trine Mars
17. Mercury trine Jupiter
18. Mercury trine Saturn
19. Mercury trine Uranus
20. Mercury trine Neptune
21. Mercury trine Pluto
22. Venus trine Mars
23. Venus trine Jupiter
24. Venus trine Saturn
25. Venus trine Uranus
26. Venus trine Neptune

345

27. Venus trine Pluto
28. Mars trine Jupiter
29. Mars trine Saturn
30. Mars trine Uranus
31. Mars trine Neptune
32. Mars trine Pluto
33. Jupiter trine Saturn
34. Jupiter trine Uranus
35. Jupiter trine Neptune
36. Jupiter trine Pluto
37. Saturn trine Uranus
38. Saturn trine Neptune
39. Saturn trine Pluto

1. Sun Trine Moon

This configuration is usually very fortunate and creates a well-adjusted and well-balanced personality. Trines between the Sun and the Moon often mean that people's childhoods were fairly easy and that in later life they are able to form happy and healthy relationships. In everyday life, this aspect makes it easy to express emotions, particularly in public.

Star rating: *****

2. Sun Trine Mars

Trines between the Sun and Mars are very powerful. They give plenty of energy and strength and as a result these people often have marked sporting and athletic abilities. Trines between these two planets tend to be assertive and even aggressive. These people can look after themselves, even in extremely hostile conditions. If there is a fight or an argument, they usually come out the winner.

Star rating: ****

3. Sun Trine Jupiter

On the whole, this aspect brings good luck and the knack of being in the right place at the right time. People with this aspect have every chance of being successful in their career, and often have the potential to be very successful businessmen or businesswomen. On a different note, the trine is often connected with a deep spirituality and a belief in a caring God. These people will often donate as much of their income as possible to charitable causes.

Star rating: ★★★★

4. Sun Trine Saturn

This is a good aspect to have. These people are disciplined and hard-working, and able to see projects through to their completion. Anyone who has the trine is likely to do well in their job. After all, they know that genius on its own will get them nowhere and that the only sure way to the top is to work fourteen hours a day, seven days a week. However, they should try to get at least a week's holiday once a decade.

Star rating: ★★★★

5. Sun Trine Uranus

This is a good combination, which provides both originality and creativity. People with this aspect want to do something different which makes them stand out from the rest of humanity. When it comes to career, it is important that their job enables them to express their individuality. In an ideal world they should work freelance, because this is the only way they can guarantee their independence.

Star rating: ★★★

6. Sun Trine Neptune

The Sun trine Neptune tends to be a very intuitive combination. People with this aspect are good at predicting other people's next moves, as well as spotting their strong and weak points, so it is not surprising that they are often very good fortune-tellers. However, the trines should appreciate that their skills are there to help mankind, rather than to rip people off and take all their money.
Star rating: ★★★

7. Sun Trine Pluto

This is a great aspect to have, which gives power, charisma – and in male horoscopes, sex appeal. Nine times out of ten, the people with a trine get what they want, so if you see someone with this configuration, you should encourage them to make greater use of their natural assertiveness. Another point to bear in mind about this aspect is that these people are very resilient and capable of surviving practically any crisis or upheaval.
Star rating: ★★★

8. Moon Trine Mercury

This is a very fortunate aspect, which gives amazing creative abilities, as well as an excellent memory. Anyone with this trine should be encouraged to make the most of these gifts. It would certainly be a good idea to learn a new language, preferably French, Italian or Spanish. If Moon trine Mercury people feel really ambitious, they might consider taking up conjuring as a hobby, or even as a career.
Star rating: ★★★

9. Moon Trine Venus

The trine is warm and sympathetic and has a real understanding of people's needs and problems. If someone is in trouble

and wants a shoulder to cry on, they should seek out a Moon trine Venus person. This aspect is certainly well-suited to helping professions like nursing, social work and counselling. However, these people should avoid getting caught up in other people's suffering, unless they enjoy the pain of self-sacrifice.
Star rating: ★★★★

10. Moon Trine Mars

The Moon trine Mars is a fairly assertive aspect. These people are quick to defend themselves, although they should be careful not to get into unnecessary arguments and fights. They can be very athletic, and a person with the Moon trine Mars should try to do as much sport as possible. Running and cycling are obvious activities, although it might be worth considering something more unusual, like trampolining or hang-gliding.
Star rating: ★★★

11. Moon Trine Jupiter

The trines are in love with life and want other people to share in their happiness and spontaneity. People with this aspect are always telling people to 'cheer up', and if they see someone in trouble they will be the first to offer a helping hand. These people enjoy crowds and are often brilliant performers, so they can do very well as either singers or comedians.
Star rating: ★★★★

12. Moon Trine Saturn

The Moon's trine with Saturn can be very useful. It gives an ability to work hard and to ignore outside distractions. People with this aspect don't allow emotional considerations to get in the way of business needs, and find it easy to get rid of people who are not up to the job. In matters of love, they always know what is going on and will never allow their partners to play emotional power-games.

Star rating: ★★★★

13. Moon Trine Uranus

The trine between the Moon and Uranus is a wonderful aspect. It is interesting and unusual and hardly ever boring. People with this aspect refuse to accept other people's rules and always do things their own way. This means that they often clash with their family, employers and even the authorities. However, with a bit of hard work they should find that their creative genius eventually changes the world.

Star rating: ★★★

14. Moon Trine Neptune

The trine is very humanitarian and is easily upset by poverty and injustice. These people also care about animals, and will often rescue dogs with broken legs and birds with broken wings. They usually have healing abilities and their touch and their prayers have been known to work miracles. Occasionally these people have a prophetic quality and are able to predict the future.

Star rating: ★★★

15. Moon Trine Pluto

The trine between the Moon and Pluto is a good aspect to have, provided it is not misused. These people understand other people's emotions and know about their vulnerabilities. They can, therefore, play an important role in mending their psychological wounds. However, people with this aspect have a dark side. They can be very unforgiving, and can enjoy inflicting emotional pain on their loved ones.

Star rating: ★★★

16. Mercury Trine Mars

Mercury trine Mars people love to argue, and are usually able to batter their opponents to death with an endless volley of words. They often make good lawyers or used car salesmen, particularly if Mercury is in Taurus or Gemini. From a creative point of view, these people should consider taking up writing. Their razor-sharp wit is almost certain to get a publisher's attention.
Star rating: ★★★★

17. Mercury Trine Jupiter

This is an easy-going and friendly aspect. These people enjoy the company of others and are good at striking up conversations with strangers. If you are ever feeling bored or depressed, then have a quick chat with Mercury trine Jupiter people. They will soon cheer you up with a couple of terrible jokes. The only fault that they have, apart from their awful sense of humour, is that they sometimes talk too much.
Star rating: ★★★

18. Mercury Trine Saturn

If a company is having problems with cash-flow, or needs to reprogram its computers, then it should call in someone with Mercury trine Saturn. This is because these people are natural problem-solvers who can sort out practically anything. The only problem that they find difficult to solve is their own lack of confidence. They believe that they are completely useless, even though they are completely brilliant.
Star rating: ★★★

19. Mercury Trine Uranus

People with Mercury trine Uranus are usually fascinated by radio, television and electronic communications. Their homes are often stacked with video recorders, satellite dishes and listening devices. Their favourite hobbies are bugging their neighbour's phone calls and accessing the CIA's computer system. They can be very successful in the fields of espionage and counter-intelligence.

Star rating: **

20. Mercury Trine Neptune

This aspect gives appreciation of music and literature, and is often found in the horoscopes of actors and actresses. It is also connected with psychic abilities. So, with a bit of practice, these people should be able to read other people's thoughts and feelings. They can then use their telepathic skills to come to a better understanding of their loved ones and to outwit their business rivals.

Star rating: **

21. Mercury Trine Pluto

This aspect makes persuasive communicators. They know how to get their message across and are good at targeting the specific needs of their audience. The trine is particularly good at misleading the public. Their talents may, therefore, be of great use to advertising companies and the nuclear power industry. This aspect also has a streak of the macabre. These people feel at home in graveyards and love horror films.

Star rating: **

22. Venus Trine Mars

The trine is an attractive aspect, which other people find irresistible. As a result, these people tend to be followed around by a crowd of admirers. This is fine, provided that their flirtatious temperament doesn't make their partner jealous. They are not afraid of using their charm to get ahead in their careers, and their employers often find it difficult to refuse their gentle requests for pay rises and promotion.

Star rating: ★★★★

23. Venus Trine Jupiter

A lucky aspect, but people with a trine between these two planets tend to take each day as it comes and dislike making plans for the future. They are also a bit lazy and will do anything to avoid hard work. So, all in all, they are pretty good at wasting their talents. This is most noticeable in their careers, where sheer complacency can bring promotion prospects to a standstill. If they can ever be bothered to come to you for advice, you must tell them to get their act together *fast* and to take advantage of the great good fortune that this aspect naturally bestows.

Star rating: ★★★★

24. Venus Trine Saturn

People with this aspect keep control over their emotions, and rarely allow passion to interfere with their ambitions. In most cases, they only fall in love with someone after they have made a cost-benefit analysis of the situation. This often involves prior meetings with accountants and image consultants. From a creative point of view, these people are able to control their bodies as well as their emotions. As a result they make excellent dancers.

Star rating: ★★★★

25. Venus Trine Uranus

This is a great planetary combination. These people are friendly and tolerant and will always give others the benefit of the doubt. They seem to know people from many different walks of life and are just as comfortable with a homeless vagrant as with a Hollywood film-star. Their love lives are always full of surprises and their eventual marriage partners usually come out of a cake or a Christmas cracker!

Star rating: ***

26. Venus Trine Neptune

This is a very creative aspect. It gives a brilliant imagination, as well as powerful artistic and literary abilities. These people will be especially good at painting in water colours and composing love poems. As far as romance is concerned, they are gentle and sympathetic and will do everything possible to look after their partners. However, they should make sure that they are not being taken for granted.

Star rating: ****

27. Venus Trine Pluto

The trine between Venus and Pluto can be quite a magnetic combination. It is certainly attractive and – some would say – irresistible. Venus trine Pluto people are usually very successful in their love lives and are able to seduce and conquer practically anyone. Their skills are not just restricted to romance: they know how to make people feel guilty and, as a result, they are good at raising money for charity.

Star rating: **

28. Mars Trine Jupiter

Mars trine Jupiter people are eternal optimists. They believe that however bad things may seem on the surface, they will be okay in the end – so they are good people to have around if you are marooned on a slowly sinking life-raft, which is being circled by man-eating sharks. On the other hand, you wouldn't want Mars trine Jupiter to be your broker during a stock market crash, unless you enjoy personal bankruptcy.

Star rating: ★★★★

29. Mars Trine Saturn

The trine of Mars to Saturn makes people extremely disciplined. They work very hard and never allow themselves to be distracted from the task in hand. These people are perfectionists and when they want to get something right, they will practise for hours on end. As a result, they do particularly well in the performing arts. Ballet, dancing, ice skating and tightrope walking are all areas in which they can excel.

Star rating: ★★★

30. Mars Trine Uranus

People with this aspect are brilliant and original. They are not content to lead normal, nine to five lives, but instead they want to do something which makes them stand out from the crowd. These people might wear, or even design, clothes which are so shocking and outrageous that they launch a new fashion. Alternatively, they may start a political or cultural movement, which eventually shakes society to its foundations.

Star rating: ★★★

31. Mars Trine Neptune

People with this aspect like the water, and enjoy swimming and sailing. Possible careers include swimming instructor and deep-sea diver. However, these people may instead wish to tune into their clairvoyant abilities. They are experts at predicting other people's destinies and can be particularly good at reading palms. Perhaps they should move to a seaside town and set themselves up as fortune-tellers.

Star rating: ★

32. Mars Trine Pluto

This is an extremely dynamic aspect, which can move mountains. Once these people start a project they never give up on it, even when the odds are stacked up against them. Eventually, their hard work and grim determination get the better of the situation and by the time the project is finished they are super-rich. However, to maximize their successes, it is vital that they work alone, and avoid business partnerships.
Star rating: ★★

33. Jupiter Trine Saturn

The trine between Jupiter and Saturn is a sane and balanced aspect. Those who have it in their horoscopes are disciplined and responsible. They honour their commitments to others and are seldom late for appointments. At the same time, these people appreciate the good things of life. So once their working day is over, they enjoy music, films, restaurants and the company of friends and family.
Star rating: ★★★★

34. Jupiter Trine Uranus

Jupiter's trine with Uranus is free-thinking and original, and those who are born under its influence want to change everything around them. This means that if they are driving along and see a 40 mph speed restriction sign, they won't reduce their speed. Instead, they will increase the speed limit, by getting out a spray can and changing the '40' to a '90'!
Star rating: ★

35. Jupiter Trine Neptune

The trine between Jupiter and Neptune is an easy-going and sympathetic aspect, and those born with it are able to fit into

Jupiter's trine with Uranus is free-thinking and original, and those born under its influence want to change everything around them.

almost any social environment. At the same time, they are good at tuning into other people's feelings. If they are put into a crowded room, they will immediately spot someone who is miserable, or psychologically disturbed. They can then use their sensitivity to help this person out.

Star rating: ★★

36. Jupiter Trine Pluto

People with this aspect often experience radical transformations, which can happen in the space of a few seconds. For example, they may be walking down the street, quite content with their well-paid jobs in middle management, when they are struck by a thunderbolt of inspiration. They realize that their life so far has been a waste of time and that their true vocation is to be a chicken farmer in Ecuador!

Star rating: ★

37. Saturn Trine Uranus

People who have Saturn trine Uranus in their horoscopes do their best work when they are in a high pressure environment. This means that the more work they are given, the more they are able to do. These individuals are extremely difficult to work with, because they love tension. If the office is a little too quiet and laid back for their tastes, they will either start an argument, or set the fire alarms off.

Star rating: ★

38. Saturn Trine Neptune

This is a very spiritual aspect. Those that have it in their horoscopes can feel a divine presence, which they are able to get in touch with through prayer and meditation. These people tend to be sensitive, and are particularly concerned about other

people's suffering. As a result, they often give vast amounts of time, money and energy to charitable causes.
Star rating: *

39. Saturn Trine Pluto

Saturn's trine to Pluto can be a very powerful aspect which can really get things done. Once these people have decided that they want something, they are able to throw all their energy into getting it. They won't be put off by moral or ethical considerations and they won't care who gets hurt in the process. So, once these people are on the war-path, get out of their way.
Star rating: *

22. PUTTING IT ALL TOGETHER

Well done! You have made it to Chapter Twenty-two. Take a break, pat yourself on the back and open a bottle or two of champagne!

At this stage in the game, you have learnt a huge amount of astrology. After all, you know about the planets, the signs, the houses and the aspects. You can find your Ascendant and you can also draw up your personal horoscope. You can now describe yourself as a fully-fledged astrologer.

However, if you are a perfectionist, you will want to fine-tune your skills, so that you can judge every horoscope you see with stunning accuracy. Part of the skill of being an astrologer is being able to draw out the main points of a horoscope, without getting side-tracked by irrelevant detail. While we have already gone a long way towards showing you how to do this, we feel that it would help to include a chapter on putting it all together.

In this chapter we will tell you exactly what to look for when you read a horoscope. In particular, we will show you our eight steps to successful horoscope interpretation. There is nothing new in this chapter, but as we go through each of the eight steps, we will refer you back to earlier chapters, just in case you need to refresh your memory. To make the most of this chapter, make sure that you have your own horoscope to hand, so that you can apply the eight-step method to your own personality.

Once you have been through our eight steps, you will be able to look at your horoscope and give an accurate description of your personality. In most cases, this will be sufficient.

However, you will get clients who want in-depth information about specific areas, like their love life, their children and their career. The following four chapters show you exactly how to deal with these matters.

EIGHT STEPS TO SUCCESSFUL HOROSCOPE INTERPRETATION

In our experience as teachers of astrology, we have found that people are often frightened by their first attempts to interpret a horoscope. They see a lot of information in front of them and don't know where to start.

Well, there is no need to worry, provided that every time you read a horoscope, you follow our eight-step method. Make sure that you take one step at a time and that you follow the order we give. Start with Step One, which covers the elements, then move on to Step Two, which looks at the Sun sign. As you go through the steps, you will be creating an increasingly detailed picture of the person behind the horoscope and, by the time you have gone through Step Eight, you will be able to give an accurate character analysis.

As we describe each step, we will illustrate it, using the horoscope of Princess Diana (diagram xx). You will then be able to see how her personality profile is slowly being built up. Once we have been through all the eight steps, we will apply them to Madonna's horoscope.

Step One: The Elements

When you look at a horoscope, the first thing to look at is the elements. In Chapter Thirteen you found detailed descriptions of all the elements and you learnt how to count up how many planets were in each. If you see that one element contains a lot of planets, then this element is going to have a strong effect on someone's personality. You should also look at elements which

Diagram xx **Horoscope for Princess Diana**

Time of birth 7.45 p.m.
Date of birth 1 July 1961
Place of birth Sandringham (Southern England)

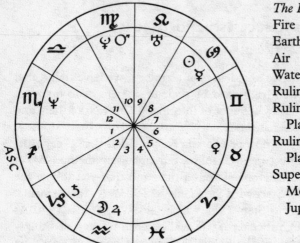

The Elements

Fire 0
Earth 3
Air 2
Water 2
Ruling Planet ♃
Ruling
   Planet's sign ♒
Ruling
   Planet's house 3rd
Superstar Aspect
   Moon conjunct
   Jupiter

The Sun (☉) is in Cancer
The Moon (☽) is in Aquarius
Mercury (☿) is in Cancer
Venus (♀) is in Taurus
Mars (♂) is in Virgo

Jupiter (♃) is in Aquarius
Saturn (♄) is in Capricorn
Uranus (♅) is in Leo
Neptune (♆) is in Scorpio
Pluto (♇) is in Virgo

The Ascendant is Sagittarius

ASPECTS		
Conjunction	Oppositions	Trines
Sun conjunct Mercury	Sun opposition Saturn	Sun trine Neptune
Moon conjunct Jupiter	Moon opposition Uranus	Venus trine Mars
Mars conjunct Pluto	Mercury opposition Saturn	Venus trine Saturn
	Venus opposition Neptune	Venus trine Pluto
	Jupiter opposition Uranus	Mars trine Saturn
		Saturn trine Pluto

are weak, in the sense that they have either one or no planets in them.

In the case of Princess Diana, her elemental break-down is as follows (remember, for elements we don't count Uranus, Neptune or Pluto):

Fire: –
Earth: Venus (Taurus), Mars (Virgo), Saturn
         (Capricorn)
Air: Moon (Aquarius), Jupiter (Aquarius)
Water: Sun (Cancer), Mercury (Cancer)

If we count the elements, we see that there are no Fire planets, 3 Earth planets, 2 in Air and 2 in Water. So the strongest element in Princess Diana's chart is Earth. This tells us that she is practical, and that she tends to judge things on the basis of their physical appearance.

It is also worth looking at the weakest element. Diana has no Fire, and this must be significant. If you remember from Chapter Thirteen, the element Fire is active and energetic. With this lack of Fire, she may at times lack an inner spark. It may then be difficult for her to take the initiative, unless she has the support of exciting, get-up-and-go people.

Before you move on to Step Two, look at your own elements. What's your strongest element? How does this element affect your everyday life?

Step Two: The Sun Sign

The Sun sign is crucial, because it describes the core personality. In Chapter Two we showed you what all the Sun signs meant, so have a quick look back at the description for your own Sun sign.

Diana's Sun is in Cancer, and this tells us about the real Diana. People with the Sun in Cancer can be quite emotional and are almost always warm and caring. This certainly fits Diana. She has put a lot of effort into supporting charitable causes, and she seems to really care about other people's suffering. The family is important to Cancerians, and we can see this in Diana's love for her two children. Cancer can also be quite a moody sign, and if we believe everything that the tabloid press tells us, this would seem to fit her too.

Step Three: The Moon Sign

The Moon describes the emotions and the way people respond to the outside world. In a female horoscope, the Moon has a special significance: from their late teens onwards, women become more like their Moon signs and less like their Sun signs. If you need to remind yourself about the Moon and its sign positions, turn back to Chapter Six.

The Moon in Aquarius: The Moon in Aquarius responds very well to group situations. People with the Moon in Aquarius like having lots of different people around and their open and gregarious behaviour ensures that they are always tremendously popular. One of the Moon's greatest virtues is a natural understanding of the plight of those less fortunate. As a result, these people can be very effective as charity workers. From a romantic point of view, they are logical and detached and want a partner to be as much a friend as a lover.

Princess Diana has her Moon in Aquarius. Aquarius is a freedom-loving sign, and it may be that in order to feel happy, she needs to be in an environment where she is able to do whatever she wants. Under these circumstances, the responsibilities of public life may cramp her style and prevent her from expressing herself in the way that the Moon in Aquarius would like.

Diana's Moon should perhaps be compared with her Sun in Cancer. We have seen how well the sign Cancer fits her, but we should also bear in mind that as she gets more mature, the Moon in Aquarius will have an increasingly powerful effect.

When she married Prince Charles, at the age of twenty, her

Moon was not very well developed. She found it difficult to express her real emotional needs. However, by the time she hit her thirties, this Moon started becoming an important part of her character. Diana probably became more independent-minded and detached and she may, by then, have found it easier to control the emotions of her Sun in Cancer. Nonetheless, the Sun in Cancer will always be a strong influence on Diana's life. She will always be caring and sympathetic, and family life will always be important to her.

When you are looking at a woman's horoscope, however mature she is, you can always put a lot of emphasis on the Sun sign. You must just make sure that you are aware that the Moon sign will be getting stronger and stronger with every passing year.

Step Four: The Sign of the Ascendant

The sign of the Ascendant is extremely important, and it often describes the external personality better than the Sun or the Moon. When reading a horoscope, one of the first things you look at is the sign of the Ascendant.

Princess Diana's Ascendant is Sagittarius. Perhaps you can check this for yourself, using our method for finding the Ascendant in Chapter Fourteen.

She was born at 7.45 p.m. on 1 July 1961, in Sandringham, Southern England. When looking up her Ascendant, remember to take off one hour for summer time. Look at Ascendant table 26, for Southern England, then line up 1 July with 6.45 p.m., and you'll find Sagittarius.

Chapter Fourteen tells you about the meaning of the Ascendant through the signs. Remember, it tells us about the mask, the image that we are presenting to the world. We describe a Sagittarius Ascendant in the following way: 'Sagittarius rising is characterized by an open and optimistic approach to life. People with this Ascendant like to speak their mind and as a result have a certain (justified?) reputation for tactlessness.

Travel is very important and they love the thrill of visiting new, exciting and even dangerous places. A breadth of vision and adventurousness makes Sagittarius rising a fascinating person to have as a friend. However, they hate it when their freedom of action is interfered with, and will avoid making commitments at all costs. There are some people who find these aspects of Sagittarius rising rather hard to handle.'

So with her Sagittarius Ascendant, Diana wants to show the world that she is full of activity and capable of doing many different things. It may also be that sport and travel are very important to her. She may be constantly looking for action, which can help put the spark back into her life.

Step Five: The Ruling Planet

Chapter Fourteen includes a section on the ruling planet, where we told you how to find it and what it means. In the case of Diana, her Ascendant is Sagittarius, and Jupiter rules Sagittarius, so her ruling planet is Jupiter.

The ruling planet describes the way people express themselves and it is a particularly good indicator of the things which people like doing most. You should take a careful look at the ruling planet. Check out the meaning of its *sign* placement (the meaning of the Moon in Aries, for example, or Venus in Capricorn, etc.) in Section Two, then turn to Chapter Seventeen to get an insight into the meaning of its *house* placing.

We have already looked at Diana's ruling planet and the role it has in her life. We observed that Jupiter is an optimistic planet, which gives her the faith to overcome the obstacles which are put in her path. Her Jupiter is in Aquarius and if you look at Chapter Ten you can read the following description for this sign placement:

Jupiter in Aquarius: Jupiter in Aquarius people are idealists. They believe that the world can be turned into a better place, if only people can learn to trust each other. It is very important for them to feel part of a wider group of people and as a result they are constantly looking for ways of improving their social life. Unfortunately, they are often let down. Their friends don't always live up to their high expectations and, at times, their good nature is taken advantage of. However, this needn't be a problem, if only they could be a little more choosy in whom they trust and confide.

So we get a clear impression that Diana is idealistic and humanitarian, and feels a great need to do something which is of lasting benefit to society.

The house position of the ruling planet can give revealing information about a person's potential. Diana's Jupiter is in the third house. In Chapter Seventeen we wrote the following about this placement:

Jupiter in the Third House: Third house Jupiter people often have a great interest in the arts. They enjoy going to the theatre and to the opera, and are very knowledgeable about paintings and the history of art. Jupiter in the third house usually indicates better than average writing abilities and these people should at least make an effort to write a few short stories.

Diana is certainly well-known for her love of theatre, the arts and particularly opera. However, what about writing? Well, she would be quite capable of writing, if she gave herself a chance. Perhaps she could write a few racey novels about dark intrigues behind the palace doors.

Step Six: First House Planets

Astrologers regard the first house as being the most important house. Any planet in this house is going to be very important in terms of an individual's life, and is going to be an integral part of the personality. Planets in the first house will always be in the same sign as the Ascendant, or rising sign. This is why astrologers sometimes call these planets 'rising planets'.

If someone has planets in the first house, turn to Chapter Seventeen and check their meanings out. You will see that these planets are particularly good at describing the way that people interact with the world.

So, for example, if someone has Venus in the first house, you would read as follows:

Venus in the First House: Venus in the first house is charming and attractive. These people make those around them feel at ease, and Venus in this position tends to be very popular. This house placement bestows a natural understanding of how to behave in social situations, so they hardly ever embarrass themselves (or anybody else, for that matter!). When it comes to finding a love partner, the only problem is being spoilt for choice.

Not everyone has planets in the first house, so you won't always be able to apply Step Six to their horoscopes. As you can see, Diana has no planets in her first house. However, later in the chapter you will be able to look at Madonna's first house, which contains the Moon, Mercury and Pluto.

Step Seven: The Superstar Aspect

In Chapter Eighteen, we told you how to find the superstar aspect. You will remember that this is the aspect in the horoscope which has the highest star rating. As you know, some people can have more than one superstar aspect. The superstar aspect tells us about the strongest energy in someone's life, and you should always pay great attention to it.

Diana has both the Moon and Jupiter in the sign of Aquarius. These planets are, therefore, in conjunction. If you look in Chapter Nineteen, you will notice that Moon conjunct Jupiter has a five-star rating. She has no other five-star aspects, so Moon conjunct Jupiter is her superstar aspect.

Now read what we say about this aspect:

The Moon Conjunct Jupiter: The Moon's conjunction with Jupiter is a really nice aspect. It brings both luck and generosity, as well as an optimistic and carefree nature. Usually, these people are very popular and have no trouble making friends. At the same time, they love children, and women with this aspect will want to have as many as possible. Men with this configuration are attracted to extrovert women with a wild sense of humour.

Star rating: *****

We can immediately tell that Diana is a generous person, who is optimistic and popular. As far as children are concerned, she only has two. However, it is very likely that in her heart of hearts she wants more.

Step Eight: Putting It All Together

By the time you have been through the first seven steps, you will have assembled a considerable amount of information about the person you are dealing with. It is now simply a question of putting it all together. This is made easier if you take notes as you go through the steps.

Below, we give an example of how we might assemble a brief description of Diana's character. In brackets, you will find the astrological reasoning behind our statements. When you get to put a horoscope together yourself, try to follow this method.

A Brief Description of Princess Diana's Character: Princess Diana is a warm and caring person, who does her best to help other people (Sun in Cancer, Moon conjunct Jupiter). Her family is very important to her and she is very protective towards her children (Sun in Cancer).

Diana is a very good mother (Sun in Cancer), who knows how to look after her children's practical needs (Earth the strongest element). Not only that, but she knows how to keep them amused (the Moon conjunct Jupiter).

However, it would be wrong to think that Diana is a stay-at-home sort of person. She enjoys plenty of activity and variety in her life (Sagittarius Ascendant), and quickly feels trapped if she is forced to stay in one place for too long.

Although it is important for her to be in an exciting environment, it is sometimes difficult for her to find her inner spark (no planets in Fire signs). As a result, she needs to be supported and encouraged by people who share her optimism (Moon conjunct Jupiter) and her love of action (Sagittarius Ascendant).

As far as Diana's emotions are concerned, it is possible that she has a moody streak (Sun in Cancer). One reason why she may get moody is that her role as a public figure may prevent her from leading an independent life (Moon in Aquarius).

Having independence and being free to do what she likes, when she likes, is indeed very important to Diana's happiness (Moon in Aquarius). Fortunately, she will find it easier to do her own thing as she grows older (Moon in Aquarius). This may mean that she has more time to pursue her interests in the arts, and perhaps to do a bit of creative writing (Moon conjunct Jupiter).

INTERPRETING MADONNA'S HOROSCOPE IN EIGHT STEPS

You now know about the eight steps to successful horoscope interpretation, and you have seen them applied to Princess Diana. To get you used to this method, we think it might be a good idea for us to go through another horoscope. Yes, you guessed it, it's none other than the horoscope of our favourite pop star, Madonna. For reference, look back to diagram xvi, p. 298.

Princess Diana at the opera.

Step One: The Elements

Madonna's elements are as follows:

Fire:	Sun (Leo), Venus (Leo), Saturn (Sagittarius)
Earth:	Moon (Virgo), Mercury (Virgo), Mars (Taurus)
Air:	Jupiter (Libra)
Water:	–

So she has 3 planets in Fire, 3 planets in Earth, 1 planet in Air and no planets in Water. This means that Fire and Earth are strong in her horoscope. The Fire gives her plenty of energy, as well as a certain measure of luck. The Earth, on the other hand, makes her something of a 'material girl', who knows how to look after her own financial and professional interests. Madonna has only got 1 planet in Air, and this may suggest that she doesn't spend ages analysing the pros and cons of a particular action. Instead, she just does it.

When it comes to the element of Water, there is a complete blank. This needs to be taken seriously. When someone has no planets in Water signs (remember that we are not counting her Neptune in Scorpio) it usually means that there is some difficulty when it comes to expressing emotion. The person may find it difficult to express emotion in a natural way. And when he or she does express emotion, it can seem a bit forced and over-sentimental. Madonna's lack of Water suggests that she might be uncomfortable with many of her feelings. When it comes to her music and art, she may find it difficult to connect love with genuine emotion. Instead, she may dwell on the physical and sexual aspects of love.

Step Two: The Sun Sign

Madonna's Sun is in Leo. This means that she is a proud person who likes to have her own way. She enjoys having attention and appreciation, and hates being ignored. As far as her career is concerned, Leo is a sign which likes everything to be larger than life, and this may be reflected in her extraordinary success.

Madonna's Sun in Leo must also contribute to her talents as a musician and a dancer. After all, Leos know how to perform, particularly when they're centre-stage. An example of another great Leo performer is the almost immortal Mick Jagger.

Step Three: The Moon Sign

Madonna has her Moon in the sign of Virgo.

The Moon in Virgo: The Moon in Virgo is very conscious of the physical environment. People with this Moon position quickly pick up on small details and are disturbed when they see things which are out of place or out of order. Their bodies really do matter and people with Moon in Virgo are careful to ensure that their diet is balanced and healthy. They don't have to be told how important it is to eat plenty of fresh fruit and vegetables. However, at times they may underestimate how sensitive they are to the chemical additives so often found in today's food.

With the Moon in Virgo, Madonna is quick to notice details, both in the environment and in other people. She instinctively knows when things aren't absolutely right and, as a result, she is an incredible perfectionist. Virgo is a sign which is connected with the body and with health and, by all accounts, fitness and exercise are very important to her.

As we discussed when we looked at Princess Diana's horoscope, in a woman's chart the Moon sign tends to become stronger as she grows older. So we would expect Madonna to become increasingly Virgoan as the years pass. Perhaps when she started out in her career, it was the Sun in Leo that was the most important influence on her. She wanted attention and she may have been a little vulnerable to flattery. However, as

Madonna progressed through her twenties, she may have become more of a perfectionist and more concerned about detail. She may also have become more materialistic – after all, Virgo is an Earth sign.

Step Four: The Sign of the Ascendant

Madonna's Ascendant is Virgo. This means that she has a double dose of Virgo, because her Moon is in this sign as well. In Chapter Fourteen we described the characteristics of a Virgo Ascendant:

Virgo Ascendant: A highly resourceful placement, which also gives a good eye for detail. Virgo rising signifies a person who is efficient, practical and eager to help others. This makes for a person in much demand. However, people with Virgo rising need to guard against some of their more negative attributes. These include a narrow outlook on life and a tendency to get bogged down in details. When dealing with other people, they should avoid being overly critical and make sure that they focus on other people's good points as well as their bad ones. Health and hygiene matter a great deal and there is usually an insistence that food, clothes and living conditions are spotlessly clean.

As you can see, much of this description echoes what was said about the Moon. However, it should be borne in mind that the Ascendant has a strong connection with the external environment and with other people.

So we might expect Madonna to be concerned about external details, and physical appearance. She may be very aware of what she looks like and it may be that she puts a lot of effort into choosing the right clothes and the right style. At the same time, the physical appearance and physical attributes of other people may also be very important to her.

Step Five: The Ruling Planet

Madonna has a Virgo Ascendant. Mercury rules Virgo, so her Mercury in Virgo in the first house is her ruling planet. By looking at the ruling planet, we can find out about how Madonna expresses herself, and we can perhaps get insights into her real talents.

To start off with, we look at the ruling planet itself, which is Mercury. Mercury is the planet of communication, so we would expect Madonna to be something of a communicator. Mercury's sign position is Virgo, so we turn to Chapter Seven, where we can check out what this means:

Mercury in Virgo: This is a brilliant position for Mercury. Mercury in Virgo has a good head for detail and usually finds it easy to deal with money and other material matters. Very clear ideas about the true value of things is a natural talent, and this means that Mercury in Virgo is a skilled financial negotiator. These people are excellent interior designers: they know what looks right and have good colour sense. If you are planning on redecorating your home, make sure that you invite one of them round to give you the benefit of their good taste.

So we get an idea here that Madonna is a great organizer. She is also very good at negotiating favourable business deals for herself. Unfortunately, we haven't a clue whether or not she's a natural interior designer, but we are sure that she could be if she wanted.

Mercury is in her first house. This is a very powerful place for Mercury to be, and it will guarantee that her communication skills are extremely good. As you can see, from the description in Chapter Seventeen:

Mercury in the First House: This is an extremely communicative place for Mercury to be in. These people find it easy to get the message across, and often make excellent salesmen or politicians. The only possible problem with Mercury in the first house is that they talk too much. Once they have put their message across, they should make a real effort to shut up. That way, their audience won't get bored with them.

Perhaps this description is a little unfair on Madonna. After all, it seems that her audiences never get bored with her!

Step Six: First House Planets

Madonna has three planets in the first house: namely the Moon, Mercury and Pluto. Those who have many planets in this house are good at projecting their personality, and tend to leave lasting impressions on other people.

However, the particular nature of each planet in the first house will affect the way a person comes across. We have already seen, in the previous section, how Mercury has influenced Madonna. Its position in the first house has made it easy for her to get her message across, and may also have helped her negotiate favourable business deals.

The other two planets in the first house are also going to be important. Let's have a look at what Chapter Seventeen says about the Moon in this position:

The Moon in the First House: People with the Moon in the first house often have a sensitive streak. They are quick to pick up on other people's feelings and their moods can change quickly. The Moon in this house can also result in rapid weight changes. A few days of overeating can lead to a few burst seams, although, on the plus side, first house Moon is very responsive to crash diets.

This gives us a rather different picture of Madonna. We don't know whether or not she has a tendency to put on weight. If she did, it wouldn't matter, because she takes so much exercise. She may well be sensitive to other people's moods. Indeed, this may be the secret of her success. When dealing with other people and negotiating with them, she may be able to pick up on their inner feelings and this may give her the edge.

More importantly, Madonna may use her sensitivity to tune into the mood of the public. This means that she is instinctively able to make records which they want to buy.

As far as Pluto in the first house is concerned, Chapter Seventeen says the following:

Pluto in the First House: This is a fairly defensive house position. These people are wary of the outside world and are careful to reveal as little about themselves as possible. At the same time, Pluto in the first house people have a powerful charisma and usually get what they want out of others. This placement is also very unforgiving and will go to great lengths to settle old scores.

Madonna certainly has a powerful personality, and is able to get what she wants out of people. We can't comment on whether or not she is unforgiving, or goes to great lengths to settle old scores. If she is, we'll hear about it soon enough.

Step Seven: The Superstar Aspect

Madonna has only one aspect which has a five-star rating: the Moon conjunct Mercury. This is, therefore, her superstar aspect. This is how we describe this aspect in Chapter Nineteen:

The Moon Conjunct Mercury: The conjunction between the Moon and Mercury gives excellent communication skills and a good intellect. These people are able to express their desires and feelings without having to think. There is frequently a connection with writing. In the horoscope of a man, it can mean that he is looking for a partner who is not only intelligent and witty, but who can also hold her own in an argument.

The same old theme is emphasized: Madonna really can communicate! It also shows her spontaneity and her ability to express herself without having to think too much.

Step Eight: Putting It All Together

It is now time to put the previous seven steps together and describe Madonna's personality.

A Brief Description of Madonna's Character: Madonna is a proud woman who believes in herself and her talents (Sun in Leo). She has plenty of energy (Fire strongly emphasized), and in many ways she is a natural performer (Sun in Leo).

She is also a great perfectionist (Moon in Virgo), and when she is working on something, she is never satisfied until she has got it absolutely right.

Madonna is sensitive to physical details (Moon and Ascendant in Virgo, so the element of Earth is strongly emphasized) and she is very aware of other people's looks and appearance (Virgo Ascendant). Some would say that she over-emphasizes physical factors and that when dealing with other people there is a possibility that she finds it difficult on an emotional level (no planets in Water). So perhaps she needs to make a greater effort to get in touch with her inner feelings.

There can be little doubt that Madonna is an exceptional business woman (lots of Earth and Mercury in Virgo) and that she knows exactly how to safeguard her professional and financial interests.

She is a skilled negotiator (Mercury in Virgo), who is able to strike a hard bargain. One reason for her negotiating success might be her ability to tune into the inner motives of the people she is dealing with (Moon in the first house).

However, it should also be borne in mind that she is extremely charismatic and that, in the end, she always gets what she wants (Pluto in the first house).

Now that we have done the hard work in interpreting Princess Diana and Madonna's horoscopes, it's your turn. Take out your own horoscope, or the horoscope of someone you know, and analyse it, using our eight-step method. When you have done that, you can then move on to the next four chapters, where you will discover how to find love, family, career, children and money in the stars.

....

WHAT IT ALL MEANS: FIRST STEPS TO BECOMING AN ASTROLOGER

23. LOVE, FAMILY AND CAREER

In the last chapter you learnt about our eight steps to successful horoscope interpretation. We showed you exactly what to look for in the horoscope, and illustrated our method, using Princess Diana and Madonna. You saw how we were able to give broad descriptions of their characters, their public life and their emotional make-up.

You can now draw up the horoscopes of your friends and loved ones, and impress them with your amazing astrological insight. If you are really ambitious, you might want to advertise your services as an astrologer and charge people money. Seeing clients is certainly a very rewarding thing for an astrologer to do, particularly if you can help them to solve their problems. However, clients can be very demanding. They can bombard you with all kinds of questions, which they expect you to answer instantly. No two questions are going to be exactly the same, and you will have to tailor your answers to suit the needs of each individual client.

That's the bad news. The good news is that 90 per cent of

the questions that astrologers are asked fall into three broad categories: love, family and career. These areas cover many topics, as you can see from the following lists:

Love	Family	Career
Relationships	The home	Career choice
Marriage	Childhood	One's job
Sex	Children	Career change
Sex-drive	Moving home	Money
Attractiveness	Father	Other people's money
Secret affairs	Mother	Promotion
Emotions	Relations	Demotion
Falling in love	Pets	Getting the sack
Splitting up	Family holidays	Self-employment
Courting	Christmas	Tax

We could have listed money and career as separate topics, and we could have given children a heading of their own. However, we don't want to confuse things by creating endless lists of special categories. By sticking to love, family and career, we can keep things nice and simple.

The next three chapters are devoted to love, the family and career. In each chapter we will tell you exactly what to look for when answering clients' questions. By the time you reach the end of these chapters, you should find that you are able to deal with practically every client that comes your way.

24. FINDING OUT ABOUT LOVE

Astrologers are asked about love more than any other topic. It is, therefore, vital that you know how to deal with matters of the heart. This is not just a question of astrological knowledge. You also need tact and discretion. You must never betray a client's confidence, and you must never make throwaway remarks, like 'your love life is a never-ending disaster which can only end in breakdown and despair'.

Everyone has the capacity to relate, and everyone has the capacity to find a fulfilling relationship. There are, nonetheless, differences in the way people relate to each other, which are reflected in the horoscope.

The horoscope describes a person's unique capacity for finding romantic happiness, and it also describes the perfect partner. At the same time, the horoscope tells us about the obstacles which threaten to frustrate a person's love life. The best way to analyse a person's love life is to follow our usual step by step approach. This will ensure that you are able to build up an accurate and meaningful love profile.

Step One: The Sign and House Position of Venus

Venus is the planet of love, so it is not surprising that it has a crucial influence on romantic matters. The sign position of Venus gives you an idea of how people respond within a relationship, and it can also describe the things they want from their love life.

To take an example: people with Venus in Cancer want a warm and emotional relationship, and they expect their partner to provide plenty of love and sympathy. This contrasts with Venus in Aquarius. Those with this sign position don't want their loved ones clinging to them at every turn, and in relationships they demand a high degree of freedom.

The house position of Venus can give more precise details about someone's relationships. It can even describe the environment where a person will meet his or her eventual partner. If someone has Venus in the ninth house, he or she may find lasting love while on holiday. If Venus is in the tenth house, this may suggest a more career-based relationship.

In a man's horoscope, the sign position of Venus has a special importance. It not only describes his ability to relate to other people, but also the kind of women that he is attracted to. So, if you want a description of his ideal partner, you should first turn to Chapter Eight, where you will find descriptions of Venus through the signs. For example, Mick Jagger has Venus in Virgo. We say the following about this sign position:

Venus in Virgo: Virgo is not one of Venus's better sign placements. Venus in Virgo people are very concerned about details, and will be quick to home in on a partner's every fault. Venus finds it difficult to enjoy love for its own sake. This may be because love is seen as something which has a price tag. At worst, Venus in Virgo will weigh up the material pros and cons of a relationship before deciding whether to pursue the matter further. The sexual aspects of any relationship are important, however, often to the exclusion of everything, except money.

This suggests that Mick often finds himself involved with women who have a keen eye for detail. At times they may be a little too materialistic for his liking.

Step Two: Aspects to Venus

Aspects involving Venus can give us further information about love and romance. You need to look at your completed horoscope form and then look up all of Venus's aspects in Chapters Nineteen to Twenty-one.

The aspects with a four- or five-star rating will be particularly important. You could also look at three-star aspects, but don't put too much emphasis on them, unless Venus has no four- or five-star aspects. Venus's one- and two-star aspects are probably not worth looking at, unless you are planning on giving your client a really detailed love profile.

In the case of Princess Diana, she has the following aspects to Venus. The star ratings for each are in brackets:

> Venus opposition Neptune (★★)
> Venus trine Mars (★★★★)
> Venus trine Saturn (★★★★)
> Venus trine Pluto (★★)

Venus opposition Neptune and Venus trine Pluto only have two stars, so we don't have to pay much attention to them. However, she has two four-star aspects involving Venus, namely Venus trine Mars and Venus trine Saturn. Have a look at what we say about these two aspects in Chapter Twenty-one:

Venus Trine Mars: The trine is an attractive aspect, which other people find irresistible. As a result, these people tend to be followed around by a crowd of admirers. This is fine, provided that their flirtatious temperament doesn't make their partner jealous. They are not afraid of using their charm to get ahead in their careers, and their employers often find it difficult to refuse their gentle requests for pay rises and promotion.

Venus Trine Saturn: People with this aspect keep control over their emotions, and rarely allow passion to interfere with their ambitions. In most cases, they only fall in love with someone after they have made a cost-benefit analysis of the situation. This often involves prior meetings with accountants and image consultants. From a creative point of view, these people are able to control their bodies as well as their emotions. As a result, they make excellent dancers.

Diana's Venus trine Mars makes her very attractive, so much so that she has hundreds of admirers. When it comes to relationships, it is possible that her partner may become jealous of all the attention she receives. This aspect is a very good one to have, and anyone who has this aspect is going to find it easy to find a relationship. Perhaps too easy!

Our description of Venus trine Saturn may be a little extreme, but it at least emphasizes the point that Diana has some capacity to control her emotions. However important love is, she won't allow it to destroy her life.

Step Three: The Sign Position of Mars

Mars is not as important as Venus when looking at relationships. However, it still needs to be considered, particularly in the horoscope of a woman. Mars is a male planet and by looking at its sign position in a woman's horoscope you may get information about the kind of lovers she is attracted to. To illustrate this point, let's look at the description of Madonna's Mars in Taurus, which we have taken from Chapter Nine:

Mars in Taurus: Mars is a fast, energetic planet and wants quick results. Mars, therefore, doesn't work very well when placed in slow-moving Taurus. A person with Mars in Taurus often finds that it is difficult to make things happen, particularly when it comes to career and finance. As a result, Mars in Taurus often has a hidden anger and impatience, which can erupt in wild displays of temper. Mars in Taurus needs to be a little more relaxed and shouldn't worry if things take longer than expected. This sign position is also very stubborn, and once these people have made up their minds on something, they will not budge.

★

Madonna seems to handle this Mars position very well. While she may be stubborn and inflexible, it seems that she is able to make things happen quickly. This description of Mars in Taurus may also describe the men in her life. If it does, we would expect her to be attracted to men who share her possible inflexibility. Perhaps they can erupt in wild displays of temper.

Step Four: The Sun and the Moon

In a *female* horoscope it is important to have a careful look at the Sun. In a *male* horoscope, attention must be paid to the Moon.

The Sun in a female horoscope can tell you about the kind of man that a woman is looking for, so look at the Sun's sign position. If the Sun is in conjunction aspect with any planets, then you should look up the meanings of these conjunctions in Chapter Nineteen, because these will give added information about the character of her man.

To continue with the example of Madonna; she has the Sun in Leo, which may mean that she tends to get involved with men who have big egos, and who need plenty of attention. Her Sun is also conjunct Uranus. In Chapter Nineteen we describe this configuration as follows:

Sun Conjunct Uranus: The Sun conjunct Uranus finds it very difficult to relax and quickly gets bored. As a result, behaviour can be erratic and unpredictable. A woman with this configuration often finds herself drawn towards men who are unusual and who have strange ideas. There is nothing wrong with this, provided that she doesn't find herself hitched up to Rasputin.

Madonna would be strongly advised to avoid mad Russian monks with hypnotic eyes – unless she can use them in her act.

The sign position of the Moon gives details about the kind

of woman that a man wants to share his life with. You can get added information about his perfect woman's character if the Moon is in conjunction aspect with any planet. In the case of Mick Jagger, he has the Moon in Taurus.

The Moon in Taurus: This is a wonderful sign for the Moon to be in. The Moon in Taurus is very down-to-earth and has a natural appreciation of physical beauty. The senses are very important and these people have a refined sense of touch. People with this Moon position are generally at their best in the countryside, where they can see, smell and touch the beauty of nature. When relating to other people, body contact is very important, even if it is only the shake of a hand or a gentle kiss. It is through such contact that the Moon in Taurus tunes into someone's real personality.

This suggests that he likes his women to be attractive and sensual, although he may also appreciate a practical streak. This description can be compared with the description given of his Venus in Virgo, in Step One.

Step Five: Putting Together a Description of the Partner

In the last four steps, you were drawing together information about the love life. As you can see, Venus plays a particularly important role. The only thing you may be worried about is conflicting descriptions.

You learned that, in a *woman's* horoscope, both the Sun and Mars represent the men in her life, while in a *man's* horoscope, the Moon and Venus represent the women in his life.

In Mick Jagger's case, it is quite easy to blend together his Moon in Taurus with his Venus in Virgo. Taurus and Virgo are both Earth signs, so it is a fairly safe bet that he is looking for sensual women who enjoy the physical aspects of a relationship. They are also likely to be fairly practical and even materialistic.

However, what would you do if the two planets were very different? For example, what about a woman who has both the Sun in Aries and Mars in Virgo in her horoscope? The Sun in Aries suggests that she wants a man who is dynamic and who is always able to take the initiative. Mars in Virgo gives a different description – we get a picture of a person who is obsessed by detail and finds it difficult to do anything unless it has been carefully planned.

So, let's pretend that a female client has come to see you. She is single and looking for love. She asks you, as an astrologer, to describe the man who she will eventually marry. This woman has the Sun in Aries and Mars in Virgo. What do you tell her?

Well, there are three possible things you can do. We advise you to go for the first possibility, but you might like to try the other two:

1. Try to blend the meanings together. Imagine a man who has the traits of both the Sun in Aries and Mars in Virgo. He might be someone who is always trying to take the initiative, but who tends to get bogged down in details.

2. Tell her that there are two different kinds of men that she is looking for: one who is dynamic and assertive, and the other who is cautious and over-concerned with detail. You could describe the advantages and disadvantages of both kinds of men, and then tell her that it is up to her which one she should go for. If she wants security, then your client should go for a Mars in Virgo type and if she wants adventure she should go for the Sun in Aries. Alternatively, you could tell her to marry Mars in Virgo for security and to get her excitement by having a simultaneous affair with the Sun in Aries!

3. The final choice is to use an astrological rule which is thousands of years old. We can't tell you the reason behind this rule, or why it might work, because its history is lost in the sands of time. So you'll just have to take it or leave

it. The rule is as follows: If a woman is born in the hours of daylight, the Sun represents her future husband. If she is born at night, it is Mars. If a man is born in the day-time, Venus describes his wife. If he is born at night, it is the Moon.

On that note, we'll leave love and move on to Chapter Twenty-five, which tells you all about the family.

25. FINDING OUT ABOUT THE FAMILY AND CHILDREN

Astrologers are frequently asked about family matters, so you must be prepared to give clients a profile of their family situation. When describing the family, be positive and up-beat. Don't say negative things about your client's domestic life.

When it comes to creating a family profile, it is simply a question of going through the various areas of family life, step by step. The first steps will describe the overall domestic situation; having done that, you will be able to focus on children.

Step One: Family Life in General

When building up a family profile, the first thing you need to do is get a general picture of family life. We do this by looking at the fourth house of the horoscope.

In our descriptions of the twelve houses in Chapter Sixteen, we said that the fourth house was particularly associated with the home and family. So by focusing on the sign of the fourth house, we can get valuable insights about a person's family life.

You should be able to find the sign of your fourth house by glancing quickly at your horoscope. However, if you want to make it really easy for yourself, look at the table on p. 390. The left-hand column lists the sign of the Ascendant, and the right-hand column lists the corresponding signs of the fourth house.

Madonna has a Virgo Ascendant. We can then read off from the table that this Ascendant has a Sagittarius fourth house. Diana, who has a Sagittarius Ascendant, has a Pisces fourth house. Now look for your own Ascendant, and then work out your own family house or fourth house.

Ascendant	Fourth House Sign
Aries	Cancer
Taurus	Leo
Gemini	Virgo
Cancer	Libra
Leo	Scorpio
Virgo	Sagittarius
Libra	Capricorn
Scorpio	Aquarius
Sagittarius	Pisces
Capricorn	Aries
Aquarius	Taurus
Pisces	Gemini

To make things even easier for you, we are now going to list each Ascendant, with its fourth house sign, and give you a description of what kind of home life can be expected. Check your Ascendant against our descriptions and see what we have to say about your home life. Remember, our descriptions are based on the meaning of the fourth house sign, rather than on the Ascending sign.

Aries Ascendant: Cancer Fourth House: The domestic environment will be secure and loving. Those with this placement are often very protective of their home and family and usually have very sophisticated burglar alarms.

Taurus Ascendant: Leo Fourth House: These people are very proud of their homes, and will spend a lot of money on making them look like palaces. However, they need to be careful that their over-expenditure doesn't make the neighbours jealous.

Gemini Ascendant: Virgo Fourth House: If you have Virgo in the fourth house, you are likely to be very fussy about your home. These people like everything to be spotlessly clean, and if anyone spills red wine on their snow-white carpets they tend to go berserk.

Cancer Ascendant: Libra Fourth House: These people want a harmonious and relaxing home life. They don't want to argue with other members of their family, and will do anything to keep the peace.

Leo Ascendant: Scorpio Fourth House: When it comes to domestic matters, these people are extremely secretive. They don't like other people to know about their family, and they hate it when visitors arrive uninvited.

Virgo Ascendant: Sagittarius Fourth House: Somewhat surprisingly, the home life of these people is extremely exciting. There is always something going on and they often excel at throwing good parties.

Libra Ascendant: Capricorn Fourth House: People with this combination hate being ostentatious and, as a result, they will decorate their homes in a way which is simple and practical. If possible, these people like to run businesses from home.

Scorpio Ascendant: Aquarius Fourth House: These people are often very idealistic about running their homes. They don't like telling their families what to do and they encourage them to be as creative as possible.

Sagittarius Ascendant: Pisces Fourth House: This is an indication of people who have families that are chaotic and out of control. They never know what the members of their families are doing and routine events like meals and bedtimes are impossible to organize.

Capricorn Ascendant: Aries Fourth House: When it comes to domestic matters, these people think they know best. They tell their family what to do, and anyone that opposes them tends to get shouted down.

Aquarius Ascendant: Taurus Fourth House: This sort of combination makes people regard their house as the centre of the universe. They want it to be as comfortable as possible, and they are particularly keen on having a big garden.

Pisces Ascendant: Gemini Fourth House: These people don't like spending too much time at home, because they get bored easily. They are happiest when they are able to move from place to place, so perhaps they should live in a mobile home.

Step Two: Planets in the Fourth House

Planets in the fourth house can provide further details about a person's family life. However, you do have to be careful when you find Mars, Saturn or Pluto placed here. These planets warn you that you may be dealing with a defensive person, who doesn't like discussing domestic issues.

Madonna has Saturn in her fourth house. We hope she doesn't mind us discussing this placement. In Chapter Seventeen we wrote about Saturn in the fourth as follows:

Saturn in the Fourth House: The fourth house can be a fairly difficult placement for Saturn. These people may often feel that family life is a burden from which they cannot escape. At the same time, they may not find it easy to discuss their inner feelings. To discover real peace of mind, it is important that Saturn in the fourth house people create a special place for themselves, where they can be free from interruption and disturbance.

So, in one sense, Madonna may not be happy with the idea of a normal family life. It may cramp her style and prevent her from finding peace of mind. However, Saturn is a strange planet, and its house placement describes those things which we both fear and desire. Perhaps she is yearning for a family, but a family which respects her needs and which allows her to be free from interruption and disturbance.

Step Three: Children and the Fifth House

The fifth house rules children. By looking at this house you

392

can gain an enormous amount of information about a person's children. You can not only find out about the character of the children, but also about a person's attitude towards them.

In order to do this, you must first look at the sign of the fifth house in a person's horoscope. Finding this sign is very easy. You just look up the sign of the Ascendant in the following table and then read off the sign of the fifth house.

If we take the example of Princess Diana: she has a Sagittarius Ascendant, therefore the sign of her fifth house is Aries.

Ascendant	*Fifth House Sign*
Aries	Leo
Taurus	Virgo
Gemini	Libra
Cancer	Scorpio
Leo	Sagittarius
Virgo	Capricorn
Libra	Aquarius
Scorpio	Pisces
Sagittarius	Aries
Capricorn	Taurus
Aquarius	Gemini
Pisces	Cancer

We are now going to go through the twelve Ascending signs and describe the role of children. Our descriptions are based on the characteristics of each Ascendant's fifth house sign.

Aries Ascendant: Leo Fifth House: These people are tremendously proud of their children and like showing them off to their friends. They have good reason to be proud, because their children tend to have powerful creative abilities.

Taurus Ascendant: Virgo Fifth House: People with this combination make careful parents, who always look after their children's needs. However, there are times when they worry too much. This is particularly the case when their children go off on school trips.

Gemini Ascendant: Libra Fifth House: The children of these people usually have very good manners and know exactly how they are expected to behave. At the same time, they are friendly and well-adjusted.

Cancer Ascendant: Scorpio Fifth House: Those with a Cancer Ascendant and a Scorpio fifth house tend to have powerful children who are good at manipulating their parents. As these children almost always get their way, there is little point in arguing with them.

Leo Ascendant: Sagittarius Fifth House: The children of these people are usually very active, and find it difficult to keep still for a moment. At times, their behaviour can be a bit uncontrollable, so the sooner they take up sports the better.

Virgo Ascendant: Capricorn Fifth House: These people often have children who are serious-minded. These children are capable of working hard at school and from a young age they understand the importance of money and qualifications.

Libra Ascendant: Aquarius Fifth House: Libra Ascendant people usually respect their children, and feel very unhappy about telling them what to do. As a result, these people can be friends to their children, as well as parents.

Scorpio Ascendant: Pisces Fifth House: These people are extremely sensitive to their children's feelings, and know exactly what makes them happy and unhappy. As a result, they make sympathetic and caring parents.

Sagittarius Ascendant: Aries Fifth House: The offspring of these people are usually impulsive, and act first and think later. If these children can be taught a bit of responsibility and self-discipline, they can develop qualities of true leadership.

Capricorn Ascendant: Taurus Fifth House: These people are good parents who try very hard to make the right choices for their children. However, they should avoid coming to decisions about their future without first consulting them.

Aquarius Ascendant: Gemini Fifth House: Those with Aquarius Ascendant and Gemini fifth house tend to have children who are intelligent and versatile. It is, therefore, important that these children are intellectually challenged, both at home and at school.

Pisces Ascendant: Cancer Fifth House: These people know how to create a warm and loving environment. As a result, their children are comfortable with their feelings, and able to give their friends and family plenty of emotional support.

Step Four: Planets in the Fifth House

To get further information about children, it is always worth looking at planets in the fifth house. Whenever you see a person with planets placed here, it is a sure indicator that children are in some way important to this person. By looking at the precise nature of the planet, you will get an idea of why they might be important. At the same time, the planet may help describe the characters of a person's children.

For example, let's say we had someone with Uranus in the fifth house. Chapter Seventeen gives the following description:

Uranus in the Fifth House: These people think that they are totally different from the rest of humanity. They usually realize this in the first years of life and from then on do their best to develop unique skills and unusual beliefs. Very often, Uranus in the fifth people have children who are even more independent-minded than they are, so they probably won't have to lecture their children on how to rebel.

Uranus is an erratic and independent-minded planet, so when it is in the fifth house you would naturally expect a person to have erratic and independent-minded children. If you see a client with this placement in his horoscope, you should advise him not to interfere with his children's freedom of expression, because otherwise they will rebel.

26. FINDING OUT ABOUT CAREER AND MONEY

As astrologers, we often have to deal with career and money matters. Here are some of the questions we have been asked over the last few years:

★ 'Will I keep my job?'
★ 'Will I ever be a millionaire?'
★ 'Will I pay the electricity bill on time?'
★ 'What is my true calling in life?'
★ 'Should I train to be a teacher?'
★ 'Can I ever make a decent living out of reading crystal balls?'

To help answer these questions, we need to be able to build up a career and money profile. This is not a difficult task, and if you follow our step by step method you should find that you too are able to dispense deep and meaningful advice.

Step One: The Tenth House and Career

In astrology, the tenth house rules career matters, and if you look at the sign of this house, you can find out about a person's career and the way they respond to their working environment. In order to find this sign, simply look at the horoscope and check which sign covers the tenth house. Alternatively, you can look at the table below. Find your Ascendant, then read off the sign of the tenth house. For example, Madonna has a Virgo Ascendant and a Gemini tenth house.

Ascendant	Tenth House Sign
Aries	Capricorn
Taurus	Aquarius
Gemini	Pisces
Cancer	Aries
Leo	Taurus
Virgo	Gemini
Libra	Cancer
Scorpio	Leo
Sagittarius	Virgo
Capricorn	Libra
Aquarius	Scorpio
Pisces	Sagittarius

If you want to know about your career, just look down the following list until you find your Ascendant. Then read our description, which will be based on your tenth house sign.

Aries Ascendant: Capricorn Tenth House: Those with Aries Ascendants are extremely ambitious and they will do practically anything to succeed. However, they are prepared to take their time, and they often plan their career moves years in advance.

Taurus Ascendant: Aquarius Tenth House: People with a Taurus Ascendant and Aquarius tenth house are adventurous in their career choices. They want to do something unusual which makes them stand out from the crowd. For example, we both have this combination and we are both astrologers.

Gemini Ascendant: Pisces Tenth House: People with this combination are often very cultured and seek careers as actors, actresses and artists. You may be interested to know that Robert, the cartoonist for this book, has a Gemini Ascendant.

Cancer Ascendant: Aries Tenth House: These people usually want careers where they are free to take their own initiative, without having to worry about other people interfering. As a result, they should avoid employment in large organizations.

Leo Ascendant: Taurus Tenth House: These people tend to choose careers which pay well, and are particularly attracted to banking and stockbroking. However, from the point of view of job satisfaction, they should consider farming or real estate.

Virgo Ascendant: Gemini Tenth House: Those with Gemini in the tenth house have a great need to communicate, and often do well in the areas of writing, publishing and journalism. At the same time, they often feel the need to do two different jobs simultaneously.

Libra Ascendant: Cancer Tenth House: These people are well-suited to careers which involve looking after others. As a result, they do very well as nurses, social workers and bodyguards.

Scorpio Ascendant: Leo Tenth House: Whatever they say on the surface, these people feel a great need to be appreciated in their work. If they are not given such appreciation, they soon start to sulk.

Sagittarius Ascendant: Virgo Tenth House: Those with Virgo in the tenth house are good at jobs which require precise attention to detail: they, therefore, make excellent watchmakers and fingerprint experts.

Capricorn Ascendant: Libra Tenth House: In their working lives, these people are natural diplomats. They know how to resolve office arguments, and when it comes to business deals, they are masters of negotiation.

Aquarius Ascendant: Scorpio Tenth House: These people are extremely intuitive, and always know what is going on in their working environment. So don't try to outmanoeuvre them, because they'll rumble your plans very quickly.

Pisces Ascendant: Sagittarius Tenth House: Sagittarius tenth house people need a job which is full of variety. They find it

398

difficult to work in one place for too long and, as a result, they prefer jobs which involve plenty of travel.

Step Two: Planets in the Tenth House

Planets in the tenth house can give you important clues about someone's career: a person with Mercury in the tenth house may do well at jobs which involve communication; Venus placed here could indicate a career in beauty or fashion.

When considering career questions, planets in the tenth house will have a greater influence than the sign of the tenth house. Neither Madonna nor Princess Diana have planets in the tenth house, so we'll look at the example of Mick Jagger, who has Mars in the tenth house. In Chapter Seventeen we say about this position:

Mars in the Tenth House: These people are extremely ambitious and will do practically anything to succeed. They are able to throw everything they've got at their career and very often get to the top. Mars in the tenth house could guarantee success, if only these people were a little more sensitive. Sometimes they are so keen for results that they forget about the needs of their colleagues, and this in turn leads to bad feeling.

Although Mars can be a rather difficult planet, it can be well placed in the tenth house. As you can see, it makes Mick very ambitious, and has no doubt helped him get to the top. However, it may be that, in order to be successful, he had to learn to be more sensitive to the feelings of his colleagues.

Step Three: Money and the Second House

Money is dear to everyone's heart and as astrologers we are always having to deal with financial questions. However, it is often difficult to separate money and career. After all, if a person's career is going well, this usually translates into a healthy bank balance.

In astrology, the second house is connected with money. By looking at the second house, we can get important details about someone's overall financial situation, as well as their attitude to money and the way they make their money.

The first thing we need to do is explore the sign of the second house. To find the sign of your second house, all you have to do is refer to the table below. Look down until you find your Ascendant, then read off your second house sign. To give you an example of how this works, Princess Diana has a Sagittarius Ascendant. The sign of her second house is therefore Capricorn.

Ascendant	Second House Sign
Aries	Taurus
Taurus	Gemini
Gemini	Cancer
Cancer	Leo
Leo	Virgo
Virgo	Libra
Libra	Scorpio
Scorpio	Sagittarius
Sagittarius	Capricorn
Capricorn	Aquarius
Aquarius	Pisces
Pisces	Aries

We will now go through all the Ascendants, describing the role of money in their lives. Look down the list until you find your Ascendant, then read what we have to say about finances:

Aries Ascendant: Taurus Second House: Money is very important to those with a Taurus second house. They like having as much of it as possible, and they are always careful in their choice of savings schemes and pension plans.

Taurus Ascendant: Gemini Second House: These people are good at making money. They are quick to spot financial opportunities, and their income often derives from several different sources.

Gemini Ascendant: Cancer Second House: Those with this combination have a natural understanding of property and property prices. As a result, they should consider investing their money in property – economic conditions permitting.

Cancer Ascendant: Leo Second House: These people like splashing their money out on friends and family, and often buy their loved ones expensive presents. However, they should make sure that they are not being taken advantage of.

Leo Ascendant: Virgo Second House: People with this combination seem to be quite easy about money – on the surface. In actual fact, they watch every penny they spend, and hardly ever buy things which they can't afford.

Virgo Ascendant: Libra Second House: These people want to look their very best and, as a result, they spend a lot of money on clothes. At the same time, they often find that relationships are a considerable drain on their financial resources.

Libra Ascendant: Scorpio Second House: The Libra Ascendant combined with the Scorpio second house makes people extremely intuitive when it comes to finances. They invest their money in successful and profitable schemes, and they can spot a financial disaster area a mile off.

Scorpio Ascendant: Sagittarius Second House: These people are optimistic about their financial prospects, and often get excited about get-rich-quick schemes. However, to avoid disaster it is important that they think before they invest.

Sagittarius Ascendant: Capricorn Second House: People with Capricorn in the second house are surprisingly careful with their money. Although they want to be big spenders, they know that they have to live within their means.

Capricorn Ascendant: Aquarius Second House: These people

regard money as important – not because they want expensive cars and houses, but because they understand that money is the only thing which can buy freedom.

Aquarius Ascendant: Pisces Second House: These people find it difficult to keep in touch with their finances. They lose track of their expenditure and are often put into a state of shock by their bank statements and credit card bills.

Pisces Ascendant: Aries Second House: Those with this combination like spending money and often overestimate their income and their savings. When they buy things, they tend to look at the price tag only *after* they've handed over the money.

Step Four: Planets in the Second House

When you are looking at someone's horoscope, always check to see if there are any planets in the second house. These planets will often give you valuable information about a person's finances. Not only that, but they indicate the easiest way for a person to make money.

Let's take the example of a person with Uranus in the second house. He is desperate to be rich and you have to give him advice. What do you tell him? Well, if you look at Chapter Seventeen, this is what we say about Uranus in the second:

Uranus in the Second House: These people are always having new ideas for making money. A few of these ideas are worth pursuing, but most of them are no-hopers. If there is a way for them to become rich, it may be through the sale of communications equipment and computers. Sometimes Uranus in the second may be prepared to throw all scruples to the wind, in which case they can make a killing out of the arms trade.

Astrologers often connect Uranus with computers, so, with Uranus in the second, this person may be able to make a lot of money out of them. As far as the arms trade is concerned, you must never advise your clients to break the law. If your client wants to export 20 tons of anti-personnel mines to Central America, he should make sure that he gets hold of the required import and export licences first.

To take a real life example, Madonna has Jupiter in the second house. We describe this placement as follows:

Jupiter in the Second House: Jupiter in this house can be a two-edged sword. On one hand, these people have definite money-making abilities. They are quick to spot good deals and their hunches usually pay off. On the other hand, people with Jupiter in this house need a lot of money, to be able to afford their desire for champagne, fast cars, boats, holidays in the Caribbean and any other extravagance you care to mention.

We don't think this needs much explanation. Jupiter in the second house is an extremely lucky combination which enables people to make a lot of money. However, they often have high overheads.

So, that's career and money covered. You are now ready to move to the final section of the book, where you will discover how to make predictions.

FINAL STEPS TO BECOMING AN ASTROLOGER

27. FIRST STEPS TO FORECASTING

We are now going to introduce you to astrology's final secret: the secret of prediction. If you want to be a successful astrologer, you will have to know about this, because clients regularly ask questions about their future. We don't want to get into an argument as to whether or not it is right to predict people's future. As astrologers, it is part of our work, and we have never known anyone to be harmed by a prediction. Indeed, as far as we are concerned, predictions help people.

To give an example, if we tell a client that he is going to have financial problems over the next few years, he can take appropriate steps to protect himself – like saving his money, rather than spending it on expensive holidays to the Seychelles. This means that he will have cash in reserve to tide him through a difficult patch.

In Chapter Two, we showed you how to make very basic predictions. These predictions were based on people's personalities, so if someone was a Gemini, you could safely predict that next week he would be indecisive. You could also predict that next month he would be indecisive, and that next century he would be indecisive. These kinds of prediction can be great fun. However, they are of limited practical use, because they cannot be used to specify a particular time when something will happen.

In the case of our Gemini person, it is impossible to look at his Sun sign, or anything else in his horoscope, and tell him straight away that he will be unusually indecisive at the end of the year. If we want to give him specific predictions, we have to use a special system, which we will explain in this chapter and in the following one.

In this chapter we are going to introduce to you a simple method for making predictions using the twelve houses. It is very easy and we don't expect you to have any problems with it. It will enable you to make general forecasts up to the year 2010. Once you have learnt this method, you can move to Chapter Twenty-eight, where we will show you how to make more detailed predictions.

However, before we tell you how to make predictions, we must explain the difference between horoscope planets and moving planets.

HOROSCOPE PLANETS AND MOVING PLANETS

Don't you dare skip this section! It's really important and if you miss any of it, we take no responsibility for the consequences. So, now that we have your full attention, we can proceed.

Before we tell you how to make predictions, we would like you to think about the planets. The planets are always moving through the signs. They never stop moving, not even for a second. They started moving when the solar system was created, about 6,000,000,000 years ago and they will stop moving only when our Sun explodes, which will happen in many millions of years' time. Fortunately, none of us will witness this event.

There are two planets in particular which we want you to concentrate on, namely Jupiter and Saturn. Like the other planets, they are always on the move. When you worked out their sign positions in the horoscope, in Chapters Ten and Eleven, you looked through tables which showed their movement thoughout the twentieth century. What you had to do was find the particular signs they were in at the date of your birth. In the case of Madonna, we found that on 16 August 1958 Jupiter was in Libra and Saturn was in Sagittarius. Just to confirm that, let's have a look at a section of the Jupiter table surrounding Madonna's birth year (table 16).

Table 16 **Jupiter Table**

13 Dec 1956–19 Feb 1957	Lib
20 Feb 1957– 6 Aug 1957	Vir
7 Aug 1957–13 Jan 1958	Lib
14 Jan 1958–20 Mar 1958	Sco
21 Mar 1958– 6 Sep 1958	Lib
7 Sep 1958–10 Feb 1959	Sco
11 Feb 1959–24 Apr 1959	Sag
25 Apr 1959– 5 Oct 1959	Sco
6 Oct 1959– 1 Mar 1960	Sag

You can see that at the top of the table, from 13 December 1956 – 19 February 1957, Jupiter was in Libra. It then moved on until, by early 1958, it was in Scorpio. Then it went back into Libra, from 21 March 1958 – 6 September 1958. This was the time during which Madonna was born. We freeze this position in Libra, and say that she has Jupiter in Libra in her horoscope.

However, time goes on, and by the end of 1958 Jupiter was in Scorpio. A year later, it was in Sagittarius. It then carried on moving, changing sign every year, and will continue to do so until the Sun finally explodes.

The point we are trying to make is that there are two ways of looking at planets. First, there are planets which are frozen in time, in the horoscope; they don't move; the Jupiter in

Madonna's horoscope will always be in Libra, and her Saturn will always be in Sagittarius. These are the positions of these planets at the time of her birth, and astrologers regard them as being extremely important. However, after Madonna's birth, or anyone else's birth, the planets move on. This is the second way of looking at the planets – that is as bodies which are in constant movement.

Now you can see that there is an important difference between horoscope planets and moving planets.

Let's have another look at Madonna's horoscope, so that we can make absolutely sure that we have got this point clear (diagram xxi). You can see her usual horoscope circle, which contains her horoscope planets, which never move. Outside the horoscope circle you can see moving Saturn. We show its sign positions from 1988 through to 1999. You can see that from 1988–1991 it was in Capricorn. From 1991–1994 it was in Aquarius, and then it moved into Pisces, where it stays until 1996. These positions are taken from the Saturn tables in

Diagram xxi

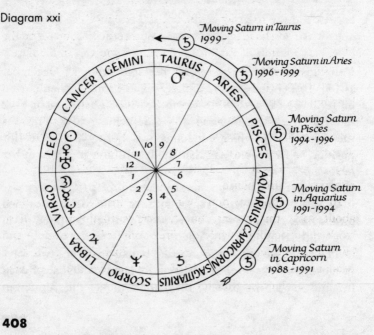

Moving Saturn in Taurus
1999–

Moving Saturn in Aries
1996–1999

Moving Saturn
in Pisces
1994–1996

Moving Saturn
in Aquarius
1991–1994

Moving Saturn
in Capricorn
1988–1991

Chapter Eleven, but for the purposes of this diagram, we have simplified Saturn's movement. We have left out times when it briefly went in and out of a sign (for example, its entry into Pisces in May and June 1993).

THE HOUSES AND PREDICTION

You now understand that a person's horoscope remains fixed for ever. The Ascendant remains the same, the houses remain the same and the horoscope planets remain the same.

You won't need to worry about the horoscope planets for the rest of this chapter. All that need concern you is a person's Ascendant and houses. As you learnt in Chapter Fifteen, each house has a sign attached to it. Madonna has a Virgo first house, a Libra second house and a Scorpio third house.

If you look at our house tables on p. 410 (table 17), you will see that on the left-hand column we list the twelve ascending signs. On the top row of the top table, we list the first six houses. On the top row of the bottom table we list the last six houses. All you have to do is find the sign of the Ascendant on the left-hand column of each table and then you can immediately read off the signs which cover each of your twelve houses.

The twelve houses provide a gateway through which the moving planets can influence our destiny. When a moving planet is in a particular sign, it affects the house that is covered by that sign. For example, if you look at Madonna's horoscope, you can see that Capricorn covers her fifth house. From 1988–1991, Saturn was in Capricorn, so from 1988 Saturn was affecting her fifth house.

In this section we don't want to go into too much detail about what this means, but Saturn is the planet of hard work and discipline, while the fifth house rules creativity and enjoyment. Therefore, we might say that from 1988–1991 Madonna had to work very hard to be creative, and there may not have been much time for pleasure.

Table 17 **House Tables**

| | | HOUSES | | | | | |
		1st	2nd	3rd	4th	5th	6th
Ascendants	Ari	Ari	Tau	Gem	Can	Leo	Vir
	Tau	Tau	Gem	Can	Leo	Vir	Lib
	Gem	Gem	Can	Leo	Vir	Lib	Sco
	Can	Can	Leo	Vir	Lib	Sco	Sag
	Leo	Leo	Vir	Lib	Sco	Sag	Cap
	Vir	Vir	Lib	Sco	Sag	Cap	Aqu
	Lib	Lib	Sco	Sag	Cap	Aqu	Pis
	Sco	Sco	Sag	Cap	Aqu	Pis	Ari
	Sag	Sag	Cap	Aqu	Pis	Ari	Tau
	Cap	Cap	Aqu	Pis	Ari	Tau	Gem
	Aqu	Aqu	Pis	Ari	Tau	Gem	Can
	Pis	Pis	Ari	Tau	Gem	Can	Leo

| | | HOUSES | | | | | |
		7th	8th	9th	10th	11th	12th
Ascendants	Ari	Lib	Sco	Sag	Cap	Aqu	Pis
	Tau	Sco	Sag	Cap	Aqu	Pis	Ari
	Gem	Sag	Cap	Aqu	Pis	Ari	Tau
	Can	Cap	Aqu	Pis	Ari	Tau	Gem
	Leo	Aqu	Pis	Ari	Tau	Gem	Can
	Vir	Pis	Ari	Tau	Gem	Can	Leo
	Lib	Ari	Tau	Gem	Can	Leo	Vir
	Sco	Tau	Gem	Can	Leo	Vir	Lib
	Sag	Gem	Can	Leo	Vir	Lib	Sco
	Cap	Can	Leo	Vir	Lib	Sco	Sag
	Aqu	Leo	Vir	Lib	Sco	Sag	Cap
	Pis	Vir	Lib	Sco	Sag	Cap	Aqu

In our experience, the most important moving planets are Jupiter and Saturn, and in this chapter and the next, we will be looking at the way they influence our destiny. These two planets are known by astrologers as the great rulers of time, and they control the precise way in which the future unfolds. As they pass through the signs of the zodiac, they will influence different areas of life, which can be described by the twelve houses of the horoscope.

When describing the effects of moving Jupiter and Saturn, astrologers often say that they are *activating* the houses. When Saturn was in Capricorn, therefore, it was activating Madonna's fifth house. In other words, Saturn was exerting an important influence on her fifth house.

In the remaining sections of this chapter we will take a look at what happens when the houses of the horoscope are activated by Jupiter and Saturn. We will not only describe their predictive power, but we will tell you how to use this power in your astrological work. This means that by the end of this chapter you will be able to make simple, but effective, predictions.

MOVING JUPITER ACTIVATING THE HOUSES

Jupiter is the planet of good fortune. It tells us about the areas of our life in which we can be most successful, and where with Jupiter's help we can make the very most out of the opportunities which come our way. However, we must not take Jupiter's energy for granted. If, for example, we see that in the future Jupiter is going to bring financial gain, we shouldn't hang around, waiting for wads of money to come pouring out of the sky. Instead, we should do our best to put ourselves in a position where we can take advantage of the luck that is coming our way.

Each of the twelve houses represents a different area of life. For example, the second house rules money; the fourth house rules the home, and the tenth house rules career. When moving Jupiter activates one of these houses, a person will often do well in the corresponding area of life.

To show you how this works, let's take the case of Madonna. From 22 July to 30 November 1988, moving Jupiter was in Gemini. Gemini is the sign which covers Madonna's tenth house, so we can say that from 22 July to 30 November 1988 Jupiter was activating this house. The tenth house rules career, while Jupiter rules good luck. So we can say that from 22 July to 30 November, Madonna had good luck in her career.

When you are making predictions for your clients, it is essential that you are able to build up a profile of moving Jupiter's changing influence over their destinies. Building up this profile is extremely easy, if you follow our simple, step by step approach. We will use Madonna's horoscope as an example.

Step One: Choosing a Time Period

The first thing you need to do is to decide which years you want to look at. For example, a client comes to see you at the beginning of 1995 and wants to know about his future. You have to ask him how far into the future he wants to go. Our tables for Jupiter and Saturn go up as far as 2010, so you could look fifteen years ahead. However, in practice, we wouldn't recommend this. Instead you should stick to a maximum of five years, although three will usually be enough.

If Madonna came to see us at the beginning of 1995, we might decide to look at her future for the years up until 1998. We might also want to know what has been happening to her in the recent past, so we would look at 1994 as well. So the entire time period that we are interested in runs from the beginning of 1994, through to the end of 1998.

What about your destiny? Do you just want to know about your year ahead, or do you want to look years, even decades, into the future? It's entirely up to you. Once you have decided how far into your future you want to look, you can move on to Step Two.

Step Two: Tracking the Positions of Moving Jupiter

In Chapter Ten we included a table which showed the sign positions of Jupiter from 1900 through to 2010. These tables can be used both for finding the horoscope Jupiter, and for tracking the position of moving Jupiter.

What we have to do is copy down the section of this table which covers the time period we decided on in Step One. So, if we wanted to know about Madonna's future from 1994 to 1998, we would copy down every line in the table which covered these years. This would include Jupiter's positions in Scorpio, from 10 November 1993 to 8 December 1994, and its position in Pisces, from 4 February 1998 to 12 February 1999.

Look at the table we have drawn up for Madonna (table 18). Before you move on to Step Three, draw up a Jupiter table for yourself, including all the years you want to cover. This shouldn't take you too long. Make the table nice and big, so that it's easy to read.

Table 18 **Jupiter: Step Two**

10 Nov 1993– 8 Dec 1994	Sco
9 Dec 1994– 2 Jan 1996	Sag
3 Jan 1996–21 Jan 1997	Cap
22 Jan 1997– 3 Feb 1998	Aqu
4 Feb 1998–12 Feb 1999	Pis

Step Three: Completing the Jupiter House Activation Table

As moving Jupiter passes through the signs, it activates different people's houses in different people's horoscopes. In the section 'The Houses and Prediction' we showed you a house table. Once you knew someone's Ascendant, you were able to read off which sign covered each of their houses. If we know

413

what sign a moving planet is in, we can tell what house it is activating.

We can now complete the table which we started drawing up in Step Two. Astrologers call this table a Jupiter house activation table. You see that from 10 November 1993 to 8 December 1994, Jupiter was in Scorpio. Madonna has a Virgo Ascendant, so Scorpio covers her third house. We can then tell that between these dates, moving Jupiter was activating this house.

On 9 December 1994, Jupiter moves into Sagittarius, where it stays until 2 January 1996. Sagittarius covers Madonna's fourth house, so this is the house that Jupiter will be activating during this time.

And so we work through the table, filling in the houses that Jupiter activates as it passes through each sign (table 19). Once you have completed your own Jupiter house activation table, you can move on to Step Four, where we tell you how to interpret moving Jupiter's activation of the various houses.

Table 19 **Madonna's Jupiter House Activation Table**

10 Nov 1993– 8 Dec 1994	Sco	3rd
9 Dec 1994– 2 Jan 1996	Sag	4th
3 Jan 1996–21 Jan 1997	Cap	5th
22 Jan 1997– 3 Feb 1998	Aqu	6th
4 Feb 1998–12 Feb 1999	Pis	7th

Step Four: Interpreting Jupiter's House Activation

All you have to do now is find out *what it means* when moving Jupiter activates each house. Jupiter brings good luck to everything it touches, and as it activates each house, we can see the areas in which people are fortunate.

So, from 10 November 1993 to 8 December 1994, when Jupiter was activating Madonna's third house, we would expect her to be lucky when it comes to writing and communication. From 9 December 1994 to 2 January 1996, Jupiter is activating her fourth house. The fourth house rules property, so this is a brilliant time for her to find a home in which she will be really happy. From 3 January 1996 to 21 January 1997, her fifth house is activated. The fifth house rules children, so she might seriously consider having children at this time.

We now go through the twelve houses and tell you what it means when each one is activated by Jupiter. Have a look down this list and see what's going on in *your* life.

Jupiter Activating the First House: This should be a period of considerable optimism, when people feel that they can make a real impact on their environment. Life will be great fun and there will be new and exciting ways for them to enjoy themselves. There is also a strong possibility that their love life will take a turn for the better. However, they should be careful that they don't overdo things and make sure that they take plenty of exercise, because weight gain is likely.

Jupiter Activating the Second House: With Jupiter activating the house of money and possessions, money-making abilities should be on top form and there should be numerous opportunities for increasing income. Unexpected windfalls, bonuses or even legacies are possible. However, Jupiter will only be activating the second house for approximately one year, so it might be a good idea to put some of this extra cash aside. At the same time, people will want more possessions – cars, stereos, boats, holidays – so there is an above average chance of going over the top on expenditure.

Jupiter Activating the Third House: Jupiter will have the effect of broadening the horizons and bringing all sorts of new opportunities through other people, but most especially through brothers, sisters or neighbours. This is an excellent time to press forward with third house matters. People who are experiencing Jupiter in the third house will feel like writing more than usual – letters, poems, even a novel if they feel ambitious. Alternatively, they will be able to benefit from any kind of education. Evening classes, or part-time courses are particularly well-starred. Young children at school will find the classroom stimulating and enjoyable.

Jupiter Activating the Fourth House: The emphasis is very much on the domestic environment and home life. Relationships with family, spouses and loved ones will be especially harmonious and enjoyable. There is a lot that can be done to make the home more secure and enjoyable. Redecoration is one possibility, or perhaps a beneficial house-move. Jupiter will certainly help you to make the right choice as far as a new home is concerned. Since the fourth house rules the land, this is a great time to get into a spot of gardening. The garden can be turned into a veritable paradise.

Jupiter Activating the Fifth House: This should be a wonderful period, when people are going to enjoy themselves. They are extremely creative and should be concentrating on developing latent artistic skills. Alternatively, other talents might be explored – amateur dramatics, pottery, poetry, script writing or calligraphy. People with Jupiter in the fifth house often feel like taking a bit of a risk and should be careful. Gambling and speculating can sometimes work, but not often. For women, this is potentially a brilliant time to get pregnant, especially if Scorpio, Pisces or Cancer is the sign covering the fifth house.

Jupiter Activating the Sixth House: At this stage in Jupiter's cycle, people often feel that they can benefit from a certain degree of self-discipline. They will want to organize their lives and create a stable routine for themselves. Because of this high level of organization, their career and working life will also benefit, not to mention the financial side of things. Diet and exercise will be of interest, and this means that they should be able to make great improvements to their health. Pets too will be important, and there is a strong possibility of buying a new pet for the home.

Jupiter Activating the Seventh House: This is a very important time when other people really will matter. Singles will find that it is much easier than usual to find a partner, and one particular relationship may blossom. Those already in a relationship may find that it takes on a new significance. However, as Jupiter can be a bit excessive, there is a danger of getting involved with too many different people at the same time. The challenge here is to focus on that one special person. The seventh house is not just about romance: people in business or thinking about going into business might get involved in a profitable partnership under Jupiter's benevolent influence.

Jupiter Activating the Eighth House: As Jupiter moves into the eighth house, life could become rather interesting, if a bit weird. People will feel drawn towards the hidden and the mysterious. This might involve the occult, or else they might find themselves asking questions like 'is there life after death?' or 'do I believe in reincarnation?' From an emotional and sexual point of view, there is a lot they can do – perhaps it is a question of letting go and exploring feelings which they have previously been afraid to touch. And from a materialistic point of view, they may be able to make major financial gains through other people. This is great, provided thay are not tempted to behave in an immoral or even illegal manner.

Jupiter Activating the Ninth House: There is some connection between Jupiter activating the ninth and Jupiter activating the eighth, at least from a spiritual point of view. Questions about life, death and rebirth may continue. People with Jupiter in the ninth should be able to benefit from their spirituality. If they already follow a particular faith, they may find themselves getting completely immersed in it. If they had previously been a bit sceptical, they may find a higher spiritual truth to believe in. At the same time, they may want to do something concrete in order to expand their view of the world. This might mean going abroad, or else going to college or university.

Jupiter Activating the Tenth House: People can do extremely well in their career when Jupiter is activating the tenth house. This could be the time when their career really comes together. Alternatively, they might finally decide what career they wish to pursue. Fame and recognition are also likely when lucky Jupiter is in such a brilliant position. If people want to succeed, nothing can stop them and they shouldn't hesitate for a moment. If they have been planning a major move and previously hadn't had the confidence to put it into action, well, now is the time to *do it*! There will be no regrets.

Jupiter Activating the Eleventh House: Friends and colleagues are of great use when Jupiter is travelling through the eleventh house. They are supportive of a person's goals – goals which may have been developing since Jupiter was travelling through the tenth house – and success may now be about effective team-work. From a social point of view, things will really be swinging, though care must be taken not to overdo it. There may be so many people around that life becomes cluttered. However, any problems may not be obvious until Jupiter moves into the twelfth house.

Jupiter Activating the Twelfth House: Planets going through the twelfth house are never particularly sociable – Jupiter included. People who have Jupiter in the twelfth will want to make progress, but will realize that they can't do it while there are so many people around. They need to try to create a bit of space around them, so that they can recharge their batteries and decide on the next steps to be taken. There may well be an important project which they want to work on, but it may not come together unless they work on it alone.

MOVING SATURN'S ACTIVATION OF THE HOUSES

Saturn is the planet of discipline and hard work. It represents the lessons that we have to learn as we go through life, as well as the need to face reality. When moving Saturn activates one of the twelve houses, it forces us to take this area of life very seriously. We have to be more disciplined and responsible in this area, and we won't be able to take any chances with it.

For example, when the sixth house of health is activated, we need to be careful about our health. This doesn't mean that we will definitely have health problems; rather, it indicates our health might suffer if we continue with self-destructive activities, like smoking and drinking.

To give you another example of how moving Saturn might work in practice, let us look at Madonna's horoscope. From 29 January 1994 to 6 April 1996, moving Saturn is in the sign of Pisces. Pisces covers Madonna's seventh house, so during this time we can say that this house is being activated by Saturn.

The seventh house rules relationships, while Saturn is the planet of lessons, responsibility and reality. If we put this together into an interpretation, we can forecast that Madonna might have to take close relationships more seriously than she has done in the past. It may be that a couple of events which happen in her life force this change of attitude.

Making predictions with moving Saturn is very straightforward, because you use the same method that we used for Jupiter. However, to make sure that you get the hang of things as quickly as possible, we will give you step by step instructions, using Madonna's horoscope as an example.

Step One: Choosing a Time Period

When we looked at moving Jupiter, we said that it was important to decide what time period you were going to look at. Choose this time period and then check the positions of moving Jupiter and moving Saturn.

In the section on Jupiter, we decided to look at Madonna's future from 1994 to 1998. Now that we know what influence moving Jupiter is going to have on her during these years, we can turn to the influence of moving Saturn over this same time period.

Step Two: Tracking the Positions of Moving Saturn

In Chapter Eleven you found a table listing the positions of moving Saturn from 1900 to 2010. Copy out the positions of Saturn for the time period that you are interested in. If you are interested in the period from 1994 to 1998, you need to list five entries from the Chapter Eleven table, as shown below (table 20).

Table 20 **Saturn: Step Two**

30 Jun 1993–28 Jan 1994	Aqu
29 Jan 1994– 6 Apr 1996	Pis
7 Apr 1996– 8 Jun 1998	Ari
9 Jun 1998–25 Oct 1998	Tau
26 Oct 1998–28 Feb 1999	Ari

Step Three: Completing the Saturn House Activation Table

You can now fill in the rest of Madonna's house activation table. When Saturn is in Aquarius, it is travelling through her sixth house; when in Pisces, Saturn travels through her seventh house; when in Aries, through her eighth house, and when in Taurus, through her ninth. (See table 21.)

Table 21 **Madonna's Saturn House Activation Table**

30 Jun 1993–28 Jan 1994	Aqu	6th
29 Jan 1994– 6 Apr 1996	Pis	7th
7 Apr 1996– 8 Jun 1998	Ari	8th
9 Jun 1998–25 Oct 1998	Tau	9th
26 Oct 1998–28 Feb 1999	Ari	8th

Step Four: Interpreting Saturn's House Activation

Interpreting Saturn's house activation is very easy. We list each house, and describe how it is affected by moving

Saturn. In the case of Madonna, we have already seen that the area of relationships could be very important up until 1996.

You can see that from 7 April 1996 to 8 June 1998, Saturn will be activating her eighth house. This could be quite a heavy time, which may be emotionally draining. She should also be very careful in all her financial dealings, because the eighth house is often connected to other people's money.

From 9 June 1998 to 25 October 1998, Saturn moves out of Aries and into Taurus. This will mean that attention moves away from eighth house matters and starts focusing on the ninth house, because in Madonna's chart Taurus covers the ninth house. Perhaps she will have to face difficulties in her dealings with foreigners or foreign countries. If, for example, she went on an overseas tour, she would have to be particularly careful that her arrangements were all in order.

On 26 October 1998, moving Saturn goes back into Aries. Sometimes planets do go backwards for a short time. This means that Saturn stops activating her ninth house and starts re-activating her eighth house. So, old emotional issues which she had to face over the previous few years may rear up again.

Now that we have dealt with Madonna's destiny, draw up your own Saturn activation table. You can then check the list below, and see what Saturn has in store for you.

Moving Saturn Activating the Houses

There is always an area of our lives which is both difficult and challenging. Every few years this area changes. It might be money in 1994 and toxic waste in the back garden in 1998. This ever-changing trouble spot is called Saturn. The house it activates shows us where we're most vulnerable and where there is most room for improvement. By looking at Saturn's activation of the houses, we can save ourselves a lot of grief and perhaps save the local wildlife from being poisoned.

Saturn Activating the First House: This is a period when considerable changes can and should be made in the pattern of a person's life. Past events and past mistakes may have to be acknowledged and some people may experience a process of readjustment. Their friends may see them as being different - as being wiser, but more crumpled and world-weary. Whatever happens it is vital that those experiencing this activation accept that it is time to move on and face the future. This may mean saying goodbye to friends and acquaintances who are of no further use.

Saturn Activating the Second House: With Saturn in the second house, people are completely obsessed about their money. Perhaps they will feel that they don't have enough, or that they want more. This is good, because it will motivate them to make more money for themselves. Generally, however, much care is required when it comes to finances and they need to think very carefully before making any extravagant gestures. Saturn really is telling them to live within their means. If for one moment they forget this, they could get into major financial trouble.

Saturn Activating the Third House: This could be quite a useful period. People may suddenly come to the conclusion that they don't know enough, and this realization may force them to study something, which in the long-term could really improve their self-esteem. However, study will be hard work and they will have to take it very seriously. At this time, they might also have to reassess their relationship with brothers and sisters – points of friction may suddenly come to the surface, so they should be ready to deal with them.

Saturn Activating the Fourth House: During this time, people frequently have to make an extra effort to look after friends, family and loved ones. Security will not be given to them on a plate and they will have to work at it. However, if they are prepared to face these responsibilities, they should be able to create a stable framework for the future. On a material level, they must make sure that the home is in good order, because unexpected problems may crop up – like a leaking roof, or burst pipes. Nevertheless, these are problems which can be avoided, if care is taken.

Saturn Activating the Fifth House: This may not be a particularly enjoyable period. Life may be hard work, and people often have to struggle in order to make the most out of their talents. They might be tempted to avoid this problem – perhaps by being ridiculously indulgent. However, if they do this, they will be living a lie and Saturn will force them into line. If they have children, they must accept their full responsibilities towards them. It may be difficult, but sooner or later, they will realize how important it is.

Saturn Activating the Sixth House: As Saturn moves into the sixth house, people need to ask themselves certain questions about how they are organizing their lives. There may be many aspects of their routine which need to be improved on, particularly in the areas of work and health. Sloppiness won't be so easily forgiven as it has been in the past, so they really have to get their act together. However, it is likely that they will accept their responsibilities, and will eventually want to make the required changes. The emphasis should be on eating properly, giving up smoking, or getting more exercise. And people experiencing this activation may also appreciate why all those annoying little chores at home and at work are so important.

Saturn Activating the Seventh House: With Saturn in the seventh house, the emphasis swings to relationships. People see others for what they really are, and this may be quite a difficult experience. However, they can prepare for this if they recognize that no one is perfect and that everyone has faults. It may not be a good idea for them to give others their total trust, because they may get let down – particularly in a business partnership. Another side to Saturn in this house is the question of responsibility. They may – for the first time – be aware that there are people relying on them and that, as a result, they have to make a special effort to support them, either emotionally or financially.

Saturn Activating the Eighth House: People may well have to confront many of their fears while Saturn is going through this house. Perhaps they will realize that there are certain emotions which they are afraid of, which they don't want to know about. Many of these emotions might have something to do with other people – about real emotional commitment to someone else, which they are afraid might undermine their sense of self. On another level, they might have to be careful in all kinds of financial transactions, as the eighth house can rule other people's money. The signing of contracts should be undertaken carefully, with special attention to the small print.

Saturn Activating the Ninth House: At this stage, people often feel that they want a lot more out of life, and that the current situation is making them feel trapped. Their job might not have enough meaning, or the petty details in their immediate environment might feel suffocating. They might yearn to get away, perhaps to the other side of the world, or feel desperate to give their life a new spirituality. So what's stopping them? Probably their own fear of broadening their horizons. The moment they are able to summon up the courage to reach out for a more meaningful existence, they will find that everything improves and that they really can escape from their self-imposed prison.

Saturn Activating the Tenth House: This period in a person's life might turn out very well. Saturn can be quite a career-orientated planet and it can, therefore, work well while it is going through the house that rules career. If people are prepared to take their career seriously and work hard, then they could be extremely successful. Especially if their chosen career is right for them. However, if they are in the wrong job then there might be problems. They might feel restricted at work and may then start thinking about alternative careers. Saturn travelling through the tenth house will then motivate them to do something about this problem.

Saturn Activating the Eleventh House: Other people may present something of a problem to those who have Saturn travelling through their eleventh house. In group situations they may not be their normal selves, and may feel that the current social scene has lost its sparkle. Maybe it is time to meet new friends, who have a genuine understanding of the world and its problems. At this time there is often a keen interest in issues such as homelessness, unemployment, poverty and pollution. Indeed it's often the case that people start getting involved in either protest movements or political parties while Saturn is activating this house.

Saturn Activating the Twelfth House: There are certain similarities between Saturn going through the eighth house and Saturn going through the twelfth, in the sense that there will be quite a bit of emphasis on emotions, and certain hidden fears may come to the surface. Feelings may be adrift and people may not be quite sure where they are going. They will need to make an extra effort to get themselves back on the rails. At the same time, they do need to take their emotions seriously. Rather than wallow in them, however, they should find a way of using them constructively.

28. YOUR DESTINY REVEALED

You have now learnt how to make simple predictions based on the twelve houses of the horoscope. These predictions can give you valuable information about people's destiny and, in most cases, they will satisfy your clients' curiosity. However, there is a method of making more specific predictions, which we are going to tell you about now. This method is very similar to the one you encountered in the previous chapter. It is just as easy to learn and you should, therefore, have no trouble with it.

In the previous chapter, you learnt that there were two kinds of planets: the horoscope planets and the moving planets. The signs in which the horoscope planets are positioned never move, so if Jupiter was in Libra at the time of birth, it will stay that way. The moving planets, on the other hand, are by definition always moving. As they move through the signs, they activate different houses in the horoscope. This activation often causes real events in the outside world.

As we have already said, there are only two moving planets which are of any real importance, namely Jupiter and Saturn. The other moving planets have very little influence over our destinies, which is why we don't describe their specific influences. We told you that Jupiter and Saturn's activation of the twelve houses showed us the pattern of our unfolding destiny. So, during the years when moving Saturn is activating our seventh house, we are destined to learn about the importance of the seventh house (e.g. relationships, partnerships etc.).

In this chapter you will discover that moving Jupiter and moving Saturn do not just influence the *houses* of the horoscope. They also influence the *planets* of the horoscope. Therefore, moving Jupiter can activate the Sun, the Moon, or any other planet in the horoscope. This activation will cause events which are usually more specific than the events caused by the activation of the houses.

By making use of this new system of planetary activation, you should find that your reputation as an accurate astrologer reaches new heights.

PLANETARY ACTIVATIONS, MEETINGS AND OPPOSITIONS

We have just told you that moving Jupiter and Saturn can activate horoscope planets and, as a result, cause external events to happen. They activate horoscope planets in two ways. Either by *moving through the same sign* as a horoscope planet, or by *moving through an opposite sign*.

When a moving planet activates a horoscope planet by being in the same sign, we call this a *meeting*. When it is in the opposite sign, it is known as an *opposition*. Finding meetings and oppositions is very easy. We will show you exactly how to do it, and explain what meetings and oppositions mean. One thing you should bear in mind is that horoscope Uranus, horoscope Neptune and horoscope Pluto are discarded when looking at planetary activations. This is because the activation of these horoscope planets by moving planets is hardly noticeable in the real world.

Throughout this book we have emphasized the point that each planet in the horoscope represents a part of the personality. For example, Venus is our capacity to love, Mars is our capacity to be assertive and the Moon is our capacity to feel. When moving Jupiter and Saturn activate these horoscope planets, the corresponding part of the personality is affected. Their activation of horoscope Venus, for example, will affect both our relationships and our capacity to give and receive love.

FINDING MEETINGS BETWEEN MOVING PLANETS AND HOROSCOPE PLANETS

Let's use the example of Madonna. She has her planets in the following signs:

Sun:	Leo
Moon:	Virgo
Mercury:	Virgo
Venus:	Leo
Mars:	Taurus
Jupiter:	Libra
Saturn:	Sagittarius

Remember, when looking at planetary activations, we are not interested in Uranus, Neptune or Pluto, which is why their sign positions are not included.

A moving planet will meet one of Madonna's horoscope planets when it is in the same sign. So from 10 November 1993 to 8 December 1994, moving Jupiter was in Scorpio. Does moving Jupiter meet up with any of Madonna's horoscope planets? The answer is no, because she has no planets in Scorpio (except Neptune, which we don't count).

From 9 December 1994 to 2 January 1996, moving Jupiter is in Sagittarius. Any activations? Yes, because Madonna has her Saturn in Sagittarius. We can, therefore, say that from 9 December 1994 to 2 January 1996, moving Jupiter meets up with Madonna's horoscope Saturn.

Let's take another example: From 18 August 1990 to 11 September 1991, moving Jupiter was in Leo. Madonna has her Sun and Venus in Leo (as well as Uranus). So, during this time period, moving Jupiter was in the same sign as her horoscope Sun and Venus, and therefore moving Jupiter was meeting both these planets. If you look at our diagram, we portray moving Jupiter as an angelic figure meeting Madonna's happy horoscope Sun.

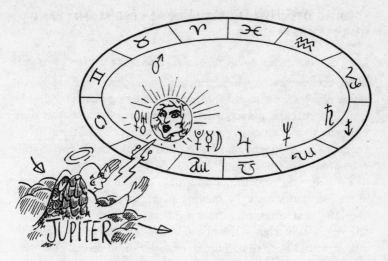

Moving Jupiter meets Madonna's happy horoscope Sun.

What Do Meetings Mean?

At the end of this chapter we include lists of all the possible planetary activations, giving detailed descriptions of each one. In a general sense, periods when horoscope planets are being met by moving planets are quite useful. They give people a lot of power and enable them to get things done.

Meetings involving moving Jupiter can be very beneficial. They bring good luck, and allow those people who are affected by them to make the most out of their potential. These activations are frequently happy and spontaneous, both at work and at play.

Saturn is a harsher planet. When moving Saturn meets a horoscope planet, it often makes people cold and unemotional. They become preoccupied with money and hard work, and find it difficult to enjoy themselves. However, at the end of the day their hard work is usually rewarded.

FINDING OPPOSITIONS BETWEEN MOVING PLANETS AND HOROSCOPE PLANETS

The second way in which moving planets can activate horo-scope planets is through oppositions. A moving planet is opposi-tion a horoscope planet when it is passing through the sign opposite to a horoscope planet. So, if someone has their horo-scope Sun in Virgo, moving Saturn would be opposite this Sun when it passes through Pisces.

To help you find the oppositions, consult the table below. Find the sign which the moving planet is passing through in the left-hand column. In the right-hand column you can see the opposition sign – that is, the sign in which a horoscope planet would have to be placed, in order to be activated by the moving planet.

Sign of Moving Planet	Opposition sign
Aries	Libra
Taurus	Scorpio
Gemini	Sagittarius
Cancer	Capricorn
Leo	Aquarius
Virgo	Pisces
Libra	Aries
Scorpio	Taurus
Sagittarius	Gemini
Capricorn	Cancer
Aquarius	Leo
Pisces	Virgo

In the case of Madonna, we notice that from 7 February 1991 to 20 May 1993, and from 30 June 1993 to 28 January 1994, moving Saturn was in Aquarius. You can see from the table that Leo is the sign opposite Aquarius. Madonna has the Sun and Venus in Leo. This means that during these time periods her horoscope Sun and Venus were opposed by moving Saturn.

If you look at the illustration, you can see what the opposition to the Sun might look like. An unpleasant figure, representing moving Saturn, is hovering around the sign of Aquarius, blowing a rather nasty wind at Madonna's horoscope Sun.

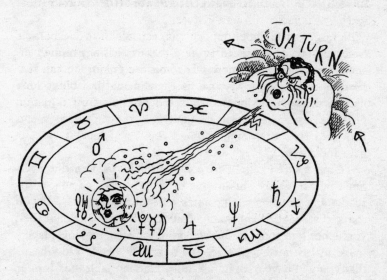

Moving Saturn blows a rather nasty wind at Madonna's horoscope Sun.

What Do Oppositions Mean?

Oppositions tend to be a bit difficult. When horoscope planets are opposed by moving planets, life can become more complicated. There are increased levels of friction and stress and arguments become more common.

When moving Jupiter makes oppositions, it often indicates excessive behaviour. People may find it difficult to control themselves and problems like over-eating and over-indulging are likely to occur. On the plus side, moving Jupiter tends to give plenty of energy and enthusiasm. Moving Saturn's oppositions are a more serious matter. Those who experience these oppositions often feel frustrated, and may find it impossible to take clear initiatives. They therefore need a great deal of patience.

DRAWING UP AND INTERPRETING PREDICTION TABLES

When someone comes to see you in order to have their horoscope read, you need to give them quick answers which show that you really know what you are talking about. If a client asks you about his love life, you should be able to look him in the eye and immediately tell him what his romantic prospects are for the year ahead. What you can't do is spend half your time thumbing through this book, looking for our help and advice.

To make sure that you are confident in giving a reading, you must be prepared. This means drawing up the client's horoscope, and perhaps taking notes on its main features. If you think that your client wants you to make predictions, then you'll need to look at the activations which moving planets make to his horoscope over the next few years. This means that you will have to draw up full prediction tables for Jupiter and Saturn.

In the previous chapter, we showed you how to draw up house activation tables for these planets. In this chapter, we are going to extend these tables to include planetary activations. This means that on the same table you will be able to see activations of both the houses and the planets.

We will now show you how to draw up and interpret these full prediction tables, first for Jupiter and then for Saturn. As usual, we will take an easy to follow, step by step approach, using Madonna's horoscope as an example. If you remember, in the previous chapter we were looking at her past, present and future, between the years 1994 and 1998. We will continue to use these years.

CREATING AND INTERPRETING JUPITER'S PREDICTION TABLES

Step One: Extending the Jupiter House Activation Table

In the previous chapter we showed you how to create a Jupiter house activation table. This house activation table is the foundation for the full prediction table, and the first thing we do is draw it up. However, this time round we include two columns, one for moving Jupiter's meetings and one for its oppositions. Below, we show Madonna's Jupiter house activation table, with the added columns (table 22).

Table 22 **Madonna's Jupiter House Activation Table**

		Meetings	Oppositions
10 Nov 1993– 8 Dec 1994	Sco 3rd		
9 Dec 1994– 2 Jan 1996	Sag 4th		
3 Jan 1996–21 Jan 1997	Cap 5th		
22 Jan 1997– 3 Feb 1998	Aqu 6th		
4 Feb 1998–12 Feb 1999	Pis 7th		

Step Two: Filling in Jupiter's Meetings

It is now time to fill in moving Jupiter's planetary activations, starting with the meetings.

From 10 November 1993 to 8 December 1994, Jupiter was in Scorpio. Madonna has no horoscope planets in Scorpio, so we put a dash in the meetings box. Then Jupiter moves into Sagittarius. She has horoscope Saturn in Sagittarius. We can, therefore, write 'horoscope Saturn' in the appropriate box, showing us that from 9 December 1994 to 2 January 1996, moving Jupiter meets horoscope Saturn.

Moving Jupiter makes no meetings when going through Capricorn, Aquarius or Pisces, because Madonna has no planets here. Now we can move on to Step Three.

Step Three: Filling in Jupiter's Oppositions

Now that we have filled in the meetings on the prediction table, we can focus on the oppositions (see table 23). In 1993 and 1994, Jupiter was in Scorpio. We notice from the opposition table given at the beginning of the chapter that Taurus is opposition Scorpio.

Table 23 **Madonna's Full Jupiter Prediction Table**

			Meetings	Oppositions
10 Nov 1993– 8 Dec 1994	Sco	3rd	——	Horoscope Mars
9 Dec 1994– 2 Jan 1996	Sag	4th	Horoscope Saturn	——
3 Jan 1996–21 Jan 1997	Cap	5th	——	
22 Jan 1997– 3 Feb 1998	Aqu	6th	——	Horoscope Sun
				Horoscope Venus
4 Feb 1998–12 Feb 1999	Pis	7th	——	Horoscope Moon
			——	Horoscope Mercury

Madonna's horoscope Mars is in Taurus, so, between 10 November 1993 and 8 December 1994, moving Jupiter was opposition Madonna's horoscope Mars. Moving Jupiter makes no oppositions while in Sagittarius and Capricorn, so we can put dashes in these boxes.

From 22 January 1997 to 3 February 1998, moving Jupiter is in Aquarius. Leo is opposition Aquarius, and Madonna has her horoscope Sun and Venus in Leo. We can, therefore, write in moving Jupiter's oppositions to these two planets. Finally, in 1998, moving Jupiter switches signs into Pisces, where it opposes Madonna's Moon and Mercury.

Step Four: Interpreting the Full Jupiter Prediction Table

The full Jupiter prediction table tells us about both the *horoscope houses* and the *horoscope planets* which Jupiter is activat-

434

ing. So we can see at a glance that from 9 December 1994 to 2 January 1996, moving Jupiter is activating Madonna's horoscope fourth house *and* that it is also meeting her horoscope Saturn.

In the previous chapter, we said that when Jupiter is activating the fourth house, it may be a good time to move house. Later in this section, we say that Jupiter's meeting with horoscope Saturn is a good time to confront long-standing obstacles and fears. Perhaps we can blend these predictions together and suggest that property moves at this time may force her to confront certain fears.

Once you have drawn up Jupiter's prediction table, you can consult our descriptions. For the descriptions of Jupiter's house activations, turn to the previous chapter. For the descriptions of the planetary activations, you will find the relevant entry in the following list:

Jupiter Meets the Sun: Jupiter's meeting with the Sun gives people the golden touch and, as a result, projects that they are involved in usually succeed. This applies not just to career, but also to creative endeavours. This would be an excellent time to direct a production for the local amateur dramatics society. Women with this contact often find that it coincides with a lucky career break for their husbands or boyfriends.

Jupiter Opposes the Sun: This is a time of great optimism, when people feel that they can change their lives for the better in every single way. They might simultaneously seek a better job, a better car, a better home, a better social life– even a better partner. In practice, it will be very difficult for them to achieve all their goals, and they would be advised to focus on a single ambition . . . like getting to work on time!

Jupiter Meets the Moon: This contact brings happiness and fulfilment. On an emotional level, things are smooth and easy, and close relationships will work out very well. If people are unattached at this time, there is a good chance that they will meet someone special. Those who are already in a relationship are likely to find that existing bonds are intensified. The reason for this may be marriage or childbirth.

Jupiter Opposes the Moon: Jupiter opposing the Moon is great fun. People's social life will pick up and there should be plenty of good parties for them to go to. To make things even better, they will have the opportunity to go off on fabulous foreign holidays which will be crammed with exotic nightlife. On the down-side, this contact is connected with overeating, over-drinking and being overweight.

Jupiter Meets Mercury: This is a wonderful time for all kinds of communication and negotiation. Interview skills are on great form, and people applying for jobs are certain to impress their prospective employers. Used car salesmen do particularly well during this period. They know exactly what to say to their customers, and can effortlessly explain away cracked wind-screens, clocked speedometers and missing steering wheels.

Jupiter Opposes Mercury: Jupiter's opposition to Mercury makes people talk too much. They go on and on and on, with the result that they bore their friends and family to death. On a more serious note, those experiencing this contact should avoid getting arrested. Otherwise, they will end up confessing all their many crimes to the nice, friendly police officer – including illegal parking, murder and assorted terrorist offences.

Jupiter Meets Venus: Those who are fortunate enough to be enjoying this contact are able to benefit from increased attrac-tiveness and charm. It is, therefore, easy for them to attract members of the opposite sex, and any romance which starts at this time is almost certain to blossom into a beautiful relation-ship. As an added bonus, Jupiter's meeting with Venus often brings unexpected financial gains.

Jupiter Opposes Venus: This is a time of high romantic expecta-tions, when people are very demanding of their loved ones, both emotionally and sexually. If they feel that their partners aren't satisfying all their needs, they may find it difficult to be faithful. When it comes to finances, great caution is required. This contact encourages over-expenditure, particularly on luxury items, like fine wines and illicit affairs.

Jupiter Meets Mars: Those who are influenced by the power of this meeting want to make the very most out of life and, as a result, they find it difficult to relax for more than a couple of seconds. At this time, they are capable of performing superhuman feats of endurance, particularly in their career. So if they are desperate to impress their bosses, they won't think twice about working a ninety-hour week.

Jupiter Opposes Mars: Jupiter's opposition with Mars can be tricky. People who are experiencing this contact frequently feel tense because they don't know what to do with all their pent-up energy. As a result of this tension, they may get involved in fights and arguments. If they want to avoid trouble, they are advised to channel their energy into a punishing exercise routine, which includes plenty of running and weight-lifting.

Jupiter Meets Jupiter: This is a very important contact, which allows people to discover their true vocation. However, in order to do this, they must spend a lot of time alone and, in particular, they must avoid listening to other people's advice. The one person they can safely turn to is you, because you're an astrologer! You can look at their horoscopes and tell them about their real talents. At least, we hope you can.

Jupiter Opposes Jupiter: Those who are affected by this contact have a high opinion of themselves, and often exaggerate their qualifications and their abilities. As a result, they may be tempted to apply for jobs in which they have no experience. In most jobs they can probably bluff their way through, but for everyone's sake they should avoid making fraudulent claims about their expertise in brain surgery and nuclear safety.

Jupiter Meets Saturn: Jupiter's meeting with Saturn can be extremely useful. It gives people the courage to confront long-standing obstacles which had previously been blocking their progress. For example, this might be a time when someone who is terrified of cars finally decides to take driving lessons. Alternatively, it may enable a timid husband to stand up to his tyrannical wife, and tell her to cut her own toenails!

Jupiter Opposes Saturn: These individuals are undergoing a transformation. They are about to abandon their Victorian taste in clothes and start wearing the latest in post-futuristic junk fashion. At the same time, they will soon have an insatiable desire to groove their nights away at the most talked about clubs in town. As far as their career is concerned, it is probably best that they prepare themselves for a dive into the unknown.

CREATING AND INTERPRETING SATURN'S PREDICTION TABLES

Step One: Extending the Saturn House Activation Table

As you can see (table 24), the Saturn house activation table we give below is the same one we used in the last chapter, for Madonna. The only difference is that we have added two extra columns.

Table 24 **Madonna's Saturn House Activation Table**

			Meetings	Oppositions
30 Jun 1993–28 Jan 1994	Aqu	6th		
29 Jan 1994– 6 Apr 1996	Pis	7th		
7 Apr 1996– 8 Jun 1998	Ari	8th		
9 Jun 1998–25 Oct 1998	Tau	9th		
26 Oct 1998–28 Feb 1999	Ari	8th		

Step Two: Filling in Saturn's Meetings

From 1994 to 1998 there is only one meeting. This is from 9

June 1998 to 25 October 1998, when moving Saturn is in Taurus. Madonna has her horoscope Mars in Taurus, so we can say that, during this time, moving Saturn is meeting her horoscope Mars.

Step Three: Filling in Saturn's Oppositions

As you can see, Madonna has quite a few oppositions from moving Saturn between 1994 and 1998 (see table 25). In 1993 and 1994, Saturn is in Aquarius and is, therefore, opposite her horoscope Sun and horoscope Venus. Then it moves into Pisces, where it is opposition her horoscope Moon and Mercury. When moving Saturn is in Aries, it is opposite her horoscope Jupiter. It is only when Saturn reaches Taurus that Madonna is free of these oppositions.

Table 25 **Madonna's Full Saturn Prediction Table**

			Meetings	Oppositions
30 Jun 1993–28 Jan 1994	Aqu	6th	——	Horoscope Sun Horoscope Venus
29 Jan 1994– 6 Apr 1996	Pis	7th	——	Horoscope Moon Horoscope Mercury
7 Apr 1996– 8 Jun 1998	Ari	8th	——	Horoscope Jupiter
9 Jun 1998–25 Oct 1998	Tau	9th	Horoscope Mars	——
26 Oct 1998–28 Feb 1999	Ari	8th	——	Horoscope Jupiter

Step Four: Interpreting the Full Saturn Prediction Table

When interpreting activations made by moving Saturn, care is required. As you will soon see, some of the descriptions we give for its planetary activations need careful thought. However, our aim is to give you an idea of the kind of things that moving Saturn can do. If you see that someone is experiencing a difficult moving Saturn opposition, there are constructive things you can do about it. You can advise them to focus their attention on self-development and positive thinking.

Now we've sorted all that out, you can discover what Saturn has in store for you.

Saturn Meets the Sun: During the period when Saturn meets the Sun, people find that they cannot achieve anything, unless they work extremely hard. The situation is made worse by the fact that no one is prepared to give them any support or encouragement. When they come to you for help, advise them to relax and not to take life so seriously. If they are showing signs of stress, instruct them to leave the rat-race and join a commune.

Saturn Opposes the Sun: Those experiencing this contact find that other people are interfering with their creative self-expression. They may, for example, be told to give up dancing school and do a management course instead. As an astrologer, you can tell these aspiring artistes that you have looked into the stars and discovered that in five years' time, unemployed managers will be far more common than unemployed dancers.

Saturn Meets the Moon: During this period, it is difficult for people to get in touch with their emotions and, as a result, their friends and family may regard them as being unusually cold. Politicians experiencing this contact often make cruel decisions. They might be lying in the bath one Sunday afternoon and suddenly decide to either close down a children's hospital or bulldoze a ten-lane motorway through an area of outstanding natural beauty.

Saturn Opposes the Moon: Saturn's opposition to the Moon is a heavy contact. Those labouring under its influence take life very seriously and often go around dressed in black. They are not interested in parties and other social events, and their idea of bliss is curling up in a coffin with a good horror novel.

Sometimes these people want to go further and turn fiction into reality. As a result, they start dabbling in black magic.

Saturn Meets Mercury: Individuals experiencing this contact will find that their brains are on brilliant form and that they can concentrate on a subject for long hours at a stretch – so this is a great time to study for exams. They will also find that they are unusually perceptive and good at understanding other people's motives and intentions. This may mean that they start seeing a loved one in a completely different light.

Saturn Opposes Mercury: During this period, people find the world boring and uninspiring. Their friends will have lost their sparkle, and their social and cultural life will be appallingly tedious. Under these circumstances, they need to make some changes. At the very least, they should make new friends who are exciting and up to date. However, if things are really bad, they should move to a different town, or even to a different country.

Saturn Meets Venus: This is a time when people are good at controlling their emotions. They realize that it is dangerous to fall in love and they will always find out about a person's character and bank balance before making lasting emotional commitments. Relationships that start while this contact is in operation sometimes lack warmth and compassion. They can nonetheless be long-lasting, provided that the money keeps flowing in.

Saturn Opposes Venus: Those who are experiencing this opposition are desperate for love and, as a result, they are not too fussy about who they go out with. This approach is not to be recommended, because it usually leads to disappointment. If these people are seriously looking for a fulfilling relationship with a partner whom they can love and trust, they are advised to put romance on hold until this rather difficult contact is over.

Saturn Meets Mars: Individuals experiencing this contact need to throw everything they've got into the achievement of their aims. It is particularly important that they don't worry about other people's feelings, and under no circumstances should they allow compassion or mercy to cloud their judgement. If they find that someone is deliberately upsetting their plans, they should take immediate steps to neutralize him or her.

Saturn Opposes Mars: This is a very difficult contact. It makes people feel terribly frustrated and they often find it impossible to take successful initiatives. There is some danger that they take out their anger on society. This is a bad idea, because it may all end in tears and bullets. If people want to get through this period unscathed, they are advised to tune into their spirituality and to get involved with a prayer group.

Saturn Meets Jupiter: Those who are experiencing Saturn's meeting with Jupiter need to be a little more disciplined. In the past, they have taken their creative abilities for granted and they haven't done enough to develop them. If they seriously want to do something special with their talents, it is now essential that they start working very hard on them. This most certainly means further study, perhaps at a college or university.

Saturn Opposes Jupiter: This is a time when people are forced to question their most fundamental beliefs. So, if they have been fascist bigots all their lives, they may suddenly find themselves losing arguments to easy-going liberals. After that, it is only a matter of time before their faith in Mussolini and Hitler is shattered. On a different note, this period can cause a spiritual crisis, which may lead to a change in their religious beliefs.

Saturn Meets Saturn: Saturn's meeting with Saturn is a crucial contact which astrologers call the 'Saturn Return'. It occurs every twenty-nine years. The first Saturn Return happens at around the age of twenty-nine, the second at the age of fifty-eight and the third at the age of eighty-eight. At these times, it is important to face reality and accept that some things in life are inevitable. Like hard work, retirement, death and rebirth.

Saturn Opposes Saturn: Those who experience this contact are forced to look back at their lives and ask themselves what they have and have not achieved. They then feel that they have to make up for lost time and, as a result, there can be a flurry of hard work. However, there are some individuals, usually in their mid-forties, who want to be young again during this period, and so they adopt teenage clothes, teenage language and sometimes teenage lovers.

ASCENDANT FINDERS

Table 26 Southern England, France, Germany and Southern Canada

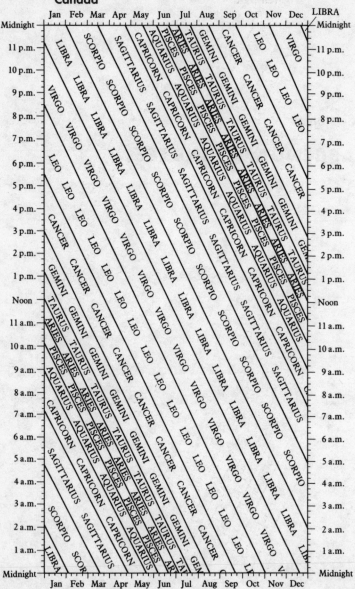

Table 27 **Northern England, Scotland and Southern Scandinavia**

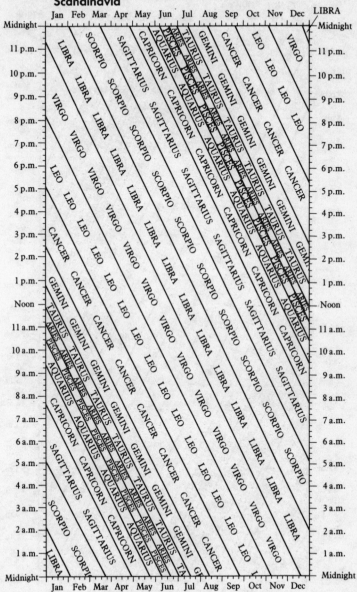

Table 28 **Southern Europe, Northern United States and the Great Lakes**

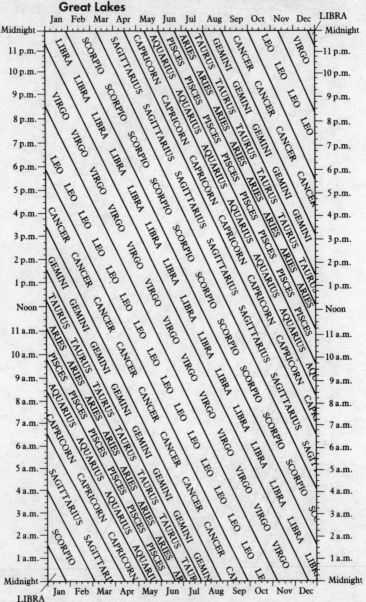

Table 29 **Southern United States**

Jan Feb Mar Apr May Jun Jul Aug Sep Oct Nov Dec LIBRA

Left axis	Right axis
Midnight	Midnight
11 p.m.	11 p.m.
10 p.m.	10 p.m.
9 p.m.	9 p.m.
8 p.m.	8 p.m.
7 p.m.	7 p.m.
6 p.m.	6 p.m.
5 p.m.	5 p.m.
4 p.m.	4 p.m.
3 p.m.	3 p.m.
2 p.m.	2 p.m.
1 p.m.	1 p.m.
Noon	Noon
11 a.m.	11 a.m.
10 a.m.	10 a.m.
9 a.m.	9 a.m.
8 a.m.	8 a.m.
7 a.m.	7 a.m.
6 a.m.	6 a.m.
5 a.m.	5 a.m.
4 a.m.	4 a.m.
3 a.m.	3 a.m.
2 a.m.	2 a.m.
1 a.m.	1 a.m.
Midnight	Midnight

Jan Feb Mar Apr May Jun Jul Aug Sep Oct Nov Dec

The chart contains diagonal bands labeled with the zodiac signs: LIBRA, SCORPIO, SAGITTARIUS, CAPRICORN, AQUARIUS, PISCES, ARIES, TAURUS, GEMINI, CANCER, LEO, VIRGO.

449

Table 30 **New Zealand, Southern Australia and Cape Province**

	Jan	Feb	Mar	Apr	May	Jun	Jul	Aug	Sep	Oct	Nov	Dec	LIBRA

Midnight — LIBRA / Midnight

Left axis (top to bottom): Midnight, 11 p.m., 10 p.m., 9 p.m., 8 p.m., 7 p.m., 6 p.m., 5 p.m., 4 p.m., 3 p.m., 2 p.m., 1 p.m., Noon, 11 a.m., 10 a.m., 9 a.m., 8 a.m., 7 a.m., 6 a.m., 5 a.m., 4 a.m., 3 a.m., 2 a.m., 1 a.m., Midnight

Right axis (top to bottom): Midnight, 11 p.m., 10 p.m., 9 p.m., 8 p.m., 7 p.m., 6 p.m., 5 p.m., 4 p.m., 3 p.m., 2 p.m., 1 p.m., Noon, 11 a.m., 10 a.m., 9 a.m., 8 a.m., 7 a.m., 6 a.m., 5 a.m., 4 a.m., 3 a.m., 2 a.m., 1 a.m., Midnight

Zodiac bands (diagonal): SCORPIO, SAGITTARIUS, CAPRICORN, AQUARIUS, PISCES, ARIES, TAURUS, GEMINI, CANCER, LEO, VIRGO, LIBRA

Midnight / LIBRA

	Jan	Feb	Mar	Apr	May	Jun	Jul	Aug	Sep	Oct	Nov	Dec

450

Table 31 **Northern Australia and South Africa**

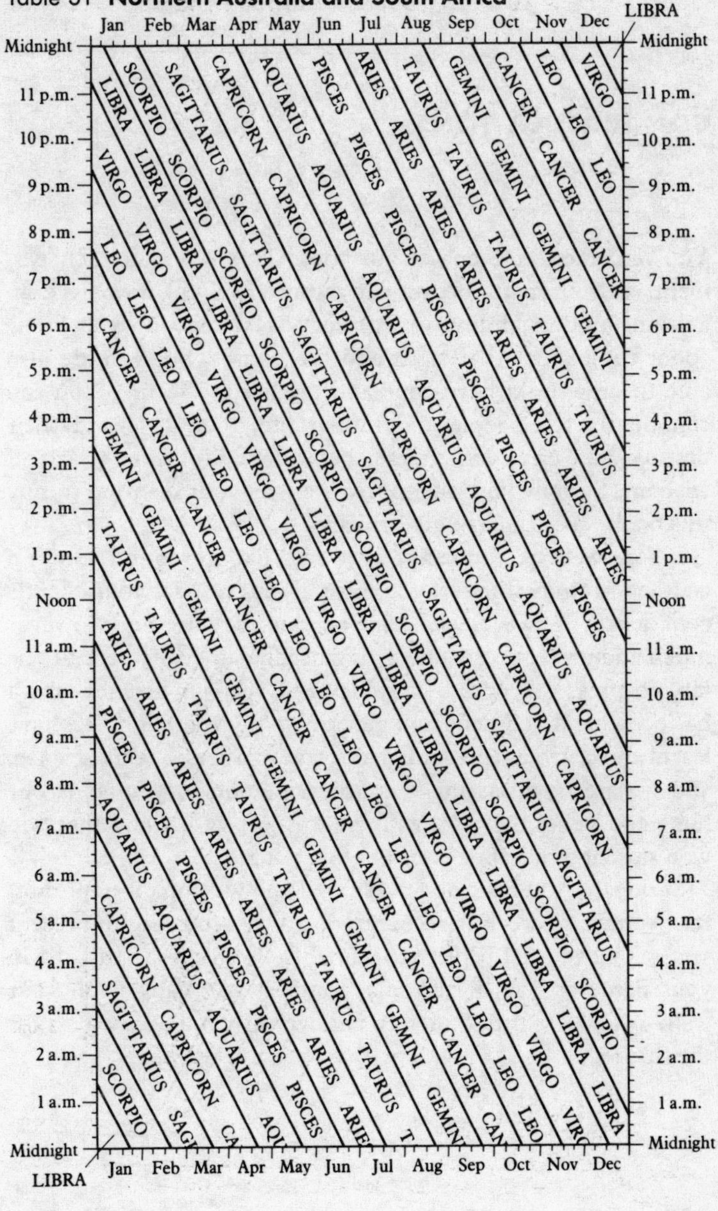

LIBRA
Jan Feb Mar Apr May Jun Jul Aug Sep Oct Nov Dec
Midnight
11 p.m.
10 p.m.
9 p.m.
8 p.m.
7 p.m.
6 p.m.
5 p.m.
4 p.m.
3 p.m.
2 p.m.
1 p.m.
Noon
11 a.m.
10 a.m.
9 a.m.
8 a.m.
7 a.m.
6 a.m.
5 a.m.
4 a.m.
3 a.m.
2 a.m.
1 a.m.
Midnight
Jan Feb Mar Apr May Jun Jul Aug Sep Oct Nov Dec
LIBRA

CONGRATULATIONS!

You've come to the end of our book. This is a major achievement on your part, because it means that you now have an amazing understanding of astrology. Not only do you know about the planets, the signs and the houses, but you are also able to draw up a horoscope and predict the future. You can confidently tell people about their life, their love and their destiny, and can even charge them money for your pearls of wisdom. So now you can appreciate why your decision to buy this book was so amazingly brilliant.

Before we part company, we would like to remind you of a couple of things. Firstly, you must always respect your client's confidences, however rich and famous they are and however much money you can make from selling their secrets to the tabloid press. Secondly, astrology is a very old science which has been handed down from generation to generation. We have learnt our astrological skills from true masters of this science, and we are now passing this knowledge on to you. It is our hope and belief that you will use this gift wisely and that you won't use it to get the better of other people.

Seriously, you have done very well and we think it important that your hard work is recognized. So we are going to present you with a special diploma, signed by both of us. Just fill in your name on the dotted line, frame it and hang it on your wall. Yes, we're proud of you, and we wish you all the best for the future.

Diploma

═══════

This is to certify that

....

has successfully completed a course in

the astrology of life, love and destiny

Barbara Dunn

Archie Dunlop

Signed Barbara Dunn & Archie Dunlop